The
Arbuthnot Lectures
1970-1979

⌘ The
Arbuthnot Lectures
1970-1979

Association for Library Service to Children
American Library Association

With a biographical sketch
of May Hill Arbuthnot
by Zena Sutherland, compiler

AMERICAN LIBRARY ASSOCIATION
Chicago • 1980

Library of Congress Cataloging in Publication Data
Main entry under title:

The Arbuthnot lectures, 1970-1979.

  CONTENTS: Fisher, M. Rights and wrongs.—Townsend, J. R.
Standards of criticism for children's literature. —Ørvig, M. One world
in children's books? [etc.]
  1. Children's literature—History and criticism—Addresses, essays,
lectures. I. Arbuthnot, May Hill, 1884-1969. II. Sutherland, Zena. III.
Association for Library Service to Children.
PN1009.A1A74   809'.89282   79-26095
ISBN 0-8389-3240-1

Printed in the United States of America

Contents

v

The May Hill Arbuthnot
Honor Lectureship

Scott, Foresman and Company, publishers of most of the many books written by May Hill Arbuthnot, proposed in 1968 to the Children's Services Division (now the Association for Library Service to Children, ALSC) of the American Library Association (ALA) that it be the administrator of an award, to be funded by Scott, Foresman, in honor of Mrs. Arbuthnot's long and outstanding contribution to children's literature. The division's counter-proposal, after long and careful deliberation, was that a lecture series be established. Officials at Scott, Foresman agreed with enthusiasm, and in 1969 plans were made for the first lecture to be given at Case Western Reserve University, where Mrs. Arbuthnot had taught for so many years.

The announcement of the lectureship was first made at the ALA Annual Conference in 1969. At that meeting, Mrs. Arbuthnot, eighty-five and in the last year of her life, spoke of her delight in the form of the honor: "[I am] a strong believer in the efficacy of direct speech, the spoken word, ... [This lectureship] means we shall be hearing new voices speak with new insight and new emphasis in this field of children's literature."

The hosts for the lectures, chosen from among those institutions which apply, and the speakers are selected by each year's Arbuthnot Committee of ALSC. Lectures have been given in April or May and published in the June issue of *Top of the News*. In this collection of the first ten Arbuthnot Honor Lectures, ALA is pleased to bring together some of those insights and emphases spoken of by Mrs. Arbuthnot.

May Hill Arbuthnot

May Hill Arbuthnot, born in Mason City, Iowa, in 1884, spent part of her childhood in Massachusetts and Illinois. She specialized in kindergarten and primary education, receiving her degree at the University of Chicago in 1922. There she met the eminent educator William Scott Gray, who was later to become her colleague in writing textbooks for children at Scott, Foresman. The books, the Curriculum Foundation Readers, became better known as the "Dick and Jane" series, and were more widely used than widely acclaimed. Perhaps because of this, *Children and Books,* Mrs. Arbuthnot's own textbook, was not universally welcomed when its first edition appeared in 1947. Some critics felt that the author, as an educator, placed too much emphasis on function and not enough on literary merit.

As time passed and subsequent editions appeared, however, Mrs. Arbuthnot's high standards of evaluation, her insistence on the prime importance of literary quality, and her concern for giving children the best in world literature won recognition, and the book, in its revised editions, is still the best-selling textbook on children's literature published in the United States. Her work was characterized by a sense of dedication, a joy in sharing the best in children's books, and a zeal tempered by her understanding of the practical problems in bringing children and books together.

Mrs. Arbuthnot received her master's degree from Columbia University in 1924. In 1927, joining the faculty at Western Reserve University in Cleveland, she helped establish the first nursery schools there. The kindergarten-primary training school of which she was the principal became the university's department of elementary education. At Western Reserve, now Case Western Reserve University, she met and married Charles Arbuthnot, a professor in the economics department. Mrs. Arbuthnot retired in 1949 and spent many quiet, busy years writing, reviewing, lecturing, and participating in several professional organizations. She died in a Cleveland nursing home on October 2, 1969.

Mrs. Arbuthnot served as the review editor of children's books for the magazines *Childhood Education* and *Elementary English* (now *Language Arts*). Among her major works, most of which appeared in several editions, were *The Arbuthnot Anthology of Children's Literature* and *Children's Reading in the Home,* published by Scott, Foresman (as was, and is, *Children and Books*) and *Children's Books Too Good to Miss,* published by Western Reserve University Press, and subsequently by the University Press Book Service, Indiana University.

Among the honors she received were election to Phi Beta Kappa, Pi Lambda Theta, and Delta Kappa Gamma. In 1959, she received the Constance Lindsay Skinner Medal, given by the Women's National Book Association for a distinguished contribution to the field of books. Western Reserve University awarded her the Doctor of Humane Letters degree in 1961. In 1964 the Catholic Library Association awarded her the Regina Medal for distinguished contributions to the field of children's literature.

A woman of warmth and compassion, of flexibility and humor, May Hill Arbuthnot was distinguished for that rare quality, a truly open mind. A wise and blithe spirit, she has made a permanent and significant contribution to children's literature.

ZENA SUTHERLAND

Margery Fisher

Margery Fisher is internationally known for *Growing Point,* her magazine reviewing children's books, and for several professional books: *Matters of Fact* (Crowell, 1972), which discusses nonfiction for children; *Intent Upon Reading* (Watts, 1962), an examination of children's fiction; and *Who's Who in Children's Books* (Holt, 1975), a mini-encyclopedia that describes major characters in children's books.

Mrs. Fisher, who lives in Northampton, England, has also edited stories for children and is the author of several scholarly monographs. Critic, teacher, author, television consultant, lecturer, and reviewer, she has been an active participant in international organizations in the field of children's literature, and in 1966 received the first Eleanor Farjeon Award from the Children's Book Circle in England. Her lecture, "Rights and Wrongs," was presented on April 10, 1970, in Cleveland, Ohio, at the School of Library Science, Case Western Reserve University.

Rights and Wrongs

O<small>N</small> J<small>UNE</small> 23, 1969, May Hill Arbuthnot wrote to the Children's Services Division of the American Library Association accepting the honour of an endowed lectureship bearing her name. The letter is a model of what a formal letter of acceptance can be when it is written from the heart. I am sure that many of you, when you heard the sad news of Mrs. Arbuthnot's death, remembered this letter and the lines she quoted from Yeats's *Sailing to Byzantium:*

> An aged man is but a paltry thing,
> a battered coat upon a stick, unless
> Soul clap its hands and sing and louder sing
> for every tatter in its mortal dress.

. . . "that is what I am going to do from now on," she wrote, " 'Sing and louder sing,' for with this honor lecture Scott, Foresman has lent dignity to the tatters and left the mortal dress with quite a jaunty air."[1]

[1] *Top of the News* 26:1. November 1969, p. 15.

3

I have to thank you very sincerely for allowing me the privilege of being the first speaker for this lectureship. It is a great pleasure to me to meet so many people here in Cleveland whom I already know by name and by achievement. You will guess how I felt when I knew that I was not after all to have the pleasure of meeting May Hill Arbuthnot herself on this occasion. I venture to think that we would have had a great deal in common; certainly there is much that I would have liked to discuss with her, since my work has been in the spheres of teaching, reviewing, and lecturing where she has established such a fine tradition. But most of all I would have wished to meet her as a confirmed, enthusiastic, lifelong reader. I would like it to be as a reader first and a critic afterwards that I offer you certain views on children's books, and work on children's books, in our own day.

Professional Amateurs?

In the world of sport nowadays the distinction in social terms between "amateur" and "professional" is becoming steadily more blurred, so that we are almost coming back to the original meaning of the word "amateur"—a lover, whether of cricket or of books. We in this room are, technically, professionals. One way or another we are employed in the administration, the classifying, the scrutiny of literature written for children. But we can never do our job properly unless we are amateurs first—lovers of children, maybe, but before that, and far more than that, lovers of books.

The men and women of May Hill Arbuthnot's generation may sometimes have envied their successors—librarians, teachers, critics—for more effective machinery, more ordered systems of training, opportunities more readily available. But there is much that *we* can envy in *their* working lives. In particular there is a note of leisure, a quality of reflectiveness in the way they write about children's books which gives their opinions a special authority. It seems to me that Mrs. Arbuthnot, like others of her generation, used time more wisely than we do. To communicate such a cultivated, close relationship with the books she talked about, she must have approached each one as a separate entity and a separate adventure. With a judgement broadened by the years of reading, she chose as an adult—with children in mind but with her own personal response coming first. It may seem an impertinence for me to speak so confidently of someone I have met only through the printed word but I feel sure that the literary opinions May Arbuthnot communicated to other people came from the hours when she was *alone with the books.*

It is this quietness, this leisure to digest and reflect and feel, that I believe we are in danger of losing. We may have devised many ways of saving time but what do we do with the time we save? Is it used to read more and more books more and more quickly? I am very much afraid of the onset of "instant criticism," of computerised lists and encapsulated stories and set forms of literary assessment. We have made time go very fast in the past few years. In terms of the world of children's books I think we have reached a point when we need to slow it down.

Slowing Down

We can do this partly by thinking of ourselves as amateurs first and professionals afterwards. This is far from easy. Children's books do need specialised treatment and children do need to be helped to find books and to get the best out of them. Every reader has his prescriptive rights. He is entitled to expect certain things from a book and he knows how to complain when they are missing. But a child can only lose when he does not get what he deserves from a book. He has no redress except with our help and it is our responsibility to exercise his rights for him, to compensate for his lack of reading experience. How far does this responsibility go?

It is customary in many spheres of life to take stock at the end of a decade and although there is no essential difference between 1970 and 1969, it is tempting to look back over the '60's in regard to children's books. I believe that those years do show an increasing tendency to put the child first and the book second; to use books as an educational tool instead of accepting them as creations in their own right. This is the debit side of the increased attention paid nowadays to children and their reading. It is only a step from discovering what they read to deciding what they should read and only one more step to putting pressure on authors to provide what we believe children need at a certain age or stage. Children's fiction is more often than not reviewed and analysed for its content and not for the sum of its parts, so that a book of limited literary value, perhaps weak in character-drawing or insipid in vocabulary, can be recommended because it delivers a strong message on an important question. This approach to books for the young must eventually dilute their quality as mainstream literature. As a creative artist the writer is more susceptible to pressure of this kind from his public than musicians or artists are. We have yet to find a way of manipulating a chord so that it directly teaches; we accept that music must make its point more subtly. At present at least we do not expect painters to illustrate problems in their pictures—though it is not so long since we did. But while we can smile at the lugubrious moralizing of books like *Ministering Children* or *Jessica's First Prayer* (incidentally overlooking many excellences of dialogue and scene-painting) we hardly notice that we are tending to demand from authors a moral just as overt, if less lugubrious, than the moral of a Victorian story for the young.

New Moralizing

I do not mean to suggest that it is the *moral* that is wrong. Any writer is at liberty to use a story to air a current problem or to state a principle of living; if he does this from a strong personal conviction and with literary tact his theme will be accepted as an integral part of his story. But we should not *expect* children's stories to be sermons or judicial arguments or sociological pamphlets. As independent works of art they must be allowed to appeal to the imagination, the mind, and the heart on their own terms.

Perhaps it is not altogether fair to quote as an extreme example of purposive analysis Dr. Jesse Gordon's attack on Robert Closkey's *Make Way for Ducklings* in 1967—which attack, you will recall, was very adequately countered in *Top of the News*. You will remember that this tender and comical picture-story book was condemned as "juvenile situation-comedy" which "sidesteps the opportunity" offered by the theme of danger.[2] "The safety of the duck family," wrote Dr. Gordon, "is assured by the essentially benign and personal forces of the seemingly overwhelming and dangerous world, and mama duck need not change her ways, make any decision, solve any problems, to survive." The book, the author concluded, was therefore not "literature." Here is a hammer to crush a butterfly. Yet the point was seriously made and is still being made. A great many people still feel that children should be improved by the books they read. To be lifted by laughter, to be transported to exotic or magic worlds, to feel the shiver of a fine phrase or the shock of an encounter with a genuine eccentric—this is not enough, they feel; there must be a message stated in unmistakable terms.

Surely the writer must be free to make his own decision on this point. It is not in his interest to yield to pressure and tack a message on to his story. In an adventure story recently published, *Kavik the Wolf Dog*, Walt Morey described a gruelling journey made by a dog seeking his first and best-loved master and showed how Kavik, whose nerve had been badly shaken by an accident, gradually learnt to be brave again—which, in dog terms, meant facing a rival and beating him in fair fight. Children are always ready to see animals in human terms and I imagine they find no difficulty in relating the point of Kavik's trial in adversity to their own experience. The author trusted them to do this, in fact, by integrating the message properly in his story and letting it *appear* without strain. Then, perhaps feeling that he had not

[2] Jesse Gordon. *TON.* 23:4. June 1967, p. 55.

satisfied the current demand for something more explicit, he rather hastily, at the end of the story, drew a parallel in the life of the boy hero's father, who had sunk into gloom and idleness after difficulties with his fishing business but who was now inspired by the dog's example to pull himself together and make a fresh start. This parallel is made so suddenly and with such inadequate motivation that it stands out as an excrescence on an otherwise good story. This is of course my personal opinion, as any opinion of a book must be. I believe it is a fair example of the way the balance of a book can be spoiled because of prevailing fashion in criticism.

Inverted Snobbery

In England at the present time a natural reaction against the dominance, in the past, of the middle-class adventure story has been carried far enough to create a kind of inverted snobbery in which stories with urban settings and working-class backgrounds start with a built-in advantage. As a writer of children's stories once said to me, "If you set your story in a Liverpool back street you're in. Too bad if you don't want to."

The dangerous ground of class-conscious fiction has been trodden by some writers whose choice has been dictated primarily by fashion. Industrious collecting of domestic detail will hardly on its own bring a novel about a working-class family to life. John Rowe Townsend, who was among the first to explore new streets of fiction, approached city life in our North Country from an interest in people, not in class distinctions. Not for him a set scene with an aspidistra or a plaster Alsatian as centre-piece. Each detail in his books is selected for its part in the narrative. The children in *Gumble's Yard,* his first story, are involved in adventures *because* of their background, the home where they are barely looked after by their shiftless father and his blowsy mistress, and because the very uncertainties of their life have made them resourceful and bold enough to enter upon adventure at all. A paragraph like this is not merely background description:

Saturday tea time was usually the high point of the week at 40 Orchid Grove. Walter generally went to the match too—though he never took me with him— and Doris went to see a friend, and they both used to come home for a hot tea before going round to the George to spend the evening. It would be a good tea with sausages or beans or tomatoes, and there'd be a big fire, and if United had won Walter would be in a happy mood. He'd even been known to hand out sixpences and shillings (which we spent at once in case he tried to take them back next day) .[3]

Atmosphere, character, and plot are all forwarded here. The flexibility of passages like this are evidence that the author has written what he

[3] John Rowe Townsend: *Gumble's Yard*. London, Hutchinson, 1961, p. 14.

wanted to write, for the responsible reasons of a novelist. He is telling
a story about certain people in a certain environment and to some extent his story has dictated his choice of a setting; certainly fashion or
sociology have had no part in the decision. And here I should perhaps apologise for choosing an illustration so conspicuously English
in its elements. This is, of course, the strength of *Gumble's Yard*. And
although I may guess at the nuances of class which bedevil your novels
or expand them (according to the writer), I should be rash indeed to
try to identify them.

Artistic Choice

In whatever idiom or language an author writes, he must make his
own choice. We have no right to suggest that he should come down on
one side of the social fence or the other—more broadly, if we make him
feel he is under any obligation to conform to rules other than literary
rules. Let us suppose, then, that he has chosen to treat a contemporary
problem in a contemporary setting. Even then he is subject to pressures—above all to that demand for a happy ending which is not solely
the province of elderly ladies in circulating libraries. A good deal of
fiction is being written nowadays, consciously and often conscientious-
ly, for that blurred age-range of twelve to sixteen when many boys and
girls are still in training, as it were, for adult fiction, and only too ready
to decide that children's books are for kids. It is harmless enough to
woo them as "young adults." Is it as harmless to woo writers by creating a demand for books tailor-made for these "young adults"? Should
we suggest to writers—and this seems inevitably the next step—that
they should write to certain specifications of length and style, that they
should beware of convention, that they should deal with problems (it
may be of sexual deviation or race hostility or drug addiction) in terms
that are basically optimistic and unshocking?

Seventeen years ago Margaret Scoggin wrote in the *Horn Book:*

. . . though I am the first to admit that teen-agers do have complex problems, I
am not convinced that complex matters can be successfully handled in what is
really a superficial story.[4]

And she suggested that authors had the task of bringing the junior
novel "closer to the good adult novel in style, characterization, and
human understanding." We can still count on our fingers—perhaps
only on the fingers of one hand—the junior novels which have come
anywhere near this last prescription, and it could be argued that books
like *The Owl Service* and *The Endless Steppe,* and I would include a
recent story from Russia, Vadim Frolov's *What It's All About,* are only

4 *TON* 25:1. November 1968, p. 75.

partially and incidentally for the young. This indefinable section of the reading public is more often fobbed off with books that are sketches, blue-prints, not novels, books which promise to be realistic (whatever we mean by this) but hardly fulfil their promise. To take one of the latest examples, Paul Zindel's *My Darling, My Hamburger* seems to me as evasive about sexual matters as any novel of the last century, and for less valid reasons. I have to judge this picture of American high school life from reading rather than from observation but I would not expect it to provoke more than an impatient if reminiscent smile from young readers. As for passion, for commitment to a theme, for the sincere exploration of the dilemma of a pregnant schoolgirl—Paul Zindel's book seems to me utterly cold. His story is enlivened by literary gimmicks; notes passed between Liz and her friend Maggie in school hours, official notices of activities, even a short story written for an assignment, break up the orthodox parts of the narrative and are set in various appropriate types. These tricks may rouse a sleepy reader to attention. They are meant to work on a less superficial level, of course—to enhance feeling as well as to forward the plot. In fact these interpolations make further inroads on the space that is already inadequate for anyone less subtle than Paula Fox to draw living people and inspire conclusions about them. Liz and Maggie and their boyfriends remain pieces on a chess-board; the author places them in one situation after another—situations that really need exploring properly. When Maggie, sitting in the school hall on graduation day, lets her thoughts play on what has happened, we are offered just one more bald statement:

It was always there in one form or another, the past—always lurking, smiling, no matter how you painted over it. You could yell at it and insist it didn't exist. You could fight it and say it was gone. But it was still inside of you all along, Maggie knew.[5]

Unfortunately, the author never gets inside Maggie. Without passion, individuality, the compulsion of properly imagined characters, the case-history of these young people would have been more use on a practical level in the form of a magazine article or a pamphlet. Meanwhile to be valid emotionally the situation really needs the freedom of an adult novel. I would mind less if books like *My Darling, My Hamburger* or the somewhat similar story by Joan Tate about young people in England, *Sam and Me,* were offered frankly as light reading; but they are thrown into the lucky dip of junior novels and for junior readers the package hardly seems worth the price.

[5] Paul Zindel: *My Darling, My Hamburger* (New York: Harper and Row, 1969) London: Bodley Head, 1970, p. 166.

Compromises

If a writer cannot say what he really feels, if he cannot be serious in developing a theme relevant to life today, if he has in any way to minimise, then he should surely not cast his material in the mould of a story for adolescents. Robert Lipsyte's story, *The Contender*, seems applicable here. With modern problems and a modern setting—drugs and violence in Harlem—the book is potentially what many advisers to young people are looking for; but does it really tackle the subject? As I read the book I felt that the author was holding back, simplifying the issue and avoiding a truly searching analysis of the effect of evil associations on character. I felt he was manipulating his characters so as to provide a reassuring ending to the story and that the characters had, as it were, stiffened into stereotypes as a result.

By contrast Ivan Southall's latest book, *Finn's Folly*, carries realism to extremes. An outline of the plot suggests nothing less than nightmare—a terrible road accident in which two people are killed and another fatally hurt; a lorry-load of cyanide scattered over the hill road where two children are desperately looking for the place of the accident, fearing their parents may be involved, and also looking for their little brother, a mentally defective child who has run away in the confusion; in addition, a selfish and self-centered husband and wife whose moral cowardice is shown up by the nervous, exhausted courage of the children.

Writing Down

It is in bare terms like these that David Holbrook has described what he considers to be a "repulsive" book. It is arguable that Southall has crowded so much into his plot that it is hard to follow, and that he may have made his point about human nature more effectively in a far simpler story, *The Fox Hole*. But we have to approach his books as squarely as he has approached disaster through the eyes of a child. He has said that he will not write down to children; he tries to be honest with his characters and with his readers. He described an earlier book, *Ash Road*, as a "raising up, not a writing down" and said that he intended it as an "appreciation of the vivid colour of childhood, of its heightened reality, of the tensions, impressions, perceptions, toughness, and anxieties that the adult forgets and dismisses as ultimately unimportant." At certain points in *Finn's Folly* I believe he had done this—especially in dialogue, in the halting exchanges between brother and sister on the hillside, in the searchingly innocent talk between Max and Alison as he tries to free her from the wrecked lorry. I believe that in this book he has touched truth about young feeling which could not have been expressed in weaker terms. When we look at the waste and confusion that exist at the end of the story we should look also at the way the macabre meeting between boy and girl has given them both a personal security, a strengthening against the demands of the future.

Not all children will like *Finn's Folly* but I do not feel that for this reason they should be protected from it. "As soon as you can read," Edward Blishen has said, "you are at risk." Children are at risk every day when they open the newspaper but not when they read of disaster and death explored by a writer whose theme really matters to him. They are at risk when they read stories which offer an easy way out of what purports to be real trouble. "Nine out of ten novelists," Storm Jameson once said, "deserve to be prosecuted under an Adulterated Emotions Act." Young people have a right to the truth and we have a right to demand from writers on their behalf a passionate honesty, a real commitment to their themes and their characters.

Search versus Hope

There is a feeling in the air nowadays that a writer must guarantee his readers the security of a happy ending, no matter whether this suits his fiction or not. It is easy to confuse a desire for *security* in a story with a desire for *hope*. *The Day of the Bomb* by Karl Bruckner, one of the saddest books ever written for the young, never promises security but it does offer hope; the writer's obvious belief in sheer goodness lights up his story without destroying its integrity. There have been many books for children written in the aftermath of the second world war, books which in various ways explore the whole question of man's search for freedom in the context of persecution, imprisonment, destruction. The questions young people ask—Who am I? What is expected of me? What is my responsibility to other people, and theirs to me?—these questions become more searching and intense in the setting of war. Those who look to junior novels for an answer to their questions may find incomplete answers but they must not be cheated by false ones.

Last autumn a book was published in England whose author had come to terms with some of the limitations of writing for the young. *Fireweed* by Jill Paton Walsh is a reconstruction of the London blitz of 1940 from the point of view of a boy of fifteen and a girl a year or two younger. The circumstances that throw Bill and Julie together are stated almost baldly in the opening paragraph of the book:

Remember? I can still smell it. I met her in the Aldwych Underground Station, at half past six in the morning, when people were busily rolling up their bedding, and climbing out to see how much of the street was left standing. There were no lavatories down there, and with houses going down like ninepins every night there was a shortage of baths in London just then, and the stench of the Underground was appalling. I noticed, as I lurked around, trying to keep inconspicuous, that there was someone else doing the same. I was lurking because I wanted to stay in the warm for as long as possible, without being one of the very last out, in case any busybody asked me tricky questions. And there was this girl, as clearly as anything, lurking too.[6]

Bill is a boy from a working-class district who has run away from the Welsh farm where he was evacuated. His father is in the army somewhere in France, he is not fond of his aunt, his house has been bombed; he is happy to be on his own even in this time of strange confusion. Julie, who hides her real name (Julia Vernon-Greene), was torpedoed on the way to Canada and ran away from the hostel where she was waiting for another ship; her escape is from the emotional poverty of her upper-class family. She is genuinely afraid of committing her parents to another leave-taking. At first sight the book looks like another Robinsonnade—one of innumerable holiday adventures in which boys and girls borrow the role of adult householders. But this is no holiday adventure. Avoiding the temptation to be sensational, the author has described danger—falling houses, dirt and disease, hunger —as they seem to Bill and Julie. For them survival is a matter of pride and freedom is intoxicating even with bombs falling. But they can't play at housekeeping forever. The basement where they have set up house is bombed while Bill is out foraging; he stands by while a rescue team excavates and when Julie is brought out he believes she is dead:

They uncovered her shoulders, part of her body. Her attitude was stiff; statuesque, she stood rigid, with one hand extended in front of her. She had been turned to stone. She looked like one of those angels of death which stand on tombstones, slowly crumbling with weather and time. I watched a stream of tiny particles of dust flow down her cheek from the laden strands of her hair.[7]

In the stress of the moment the casual tone of his first-person narrative (he tells his story after an interval of some years) is deliberately broken by the author into an inflated, almost hysterical speech in which he snatches at images outside himself to help him bear his recollections.

Then, for a moment, we suspect the author of contriving a happy ending, for Bill is told the girl is alive and he traces her to a hospital. But this is a relationship doomed to be temporary, tied as surely to its moment of crisis as the drawing together of Max and Alison in *Finn's Folly*. Children cannot order their lives, though in less honest stories they often do. Bill is a working-class boy: Julia's family is well-bred. In 1940 this matters a great deal. The accomplished distantly sympathetic gratitude of Julia's mother is far colder than the derelict home the children had innocently shared and they are too young to keep alive the warmth of the love that has grown between them. A happy ending would have spoilt the story. It is about an impossible freedom and everything about the book—its mode of expression, its sadly reminiscent note, the choice of detail—everything warns of the conclusion.

[6] Jill Paton Walsh: *Fireweed*. London, Macmillan, 1969, p. 7.
[7] Jill Paton Walsh: *Fireweed*. London, Macmillan, 1969, p. 124.

Search versus Symbolism

Freedom is the theme of *I Am David* by Anne Holm, a theme expressed in a wider context and with an almost symbolic, anonymous
atmosphere behind the precision of domestic and geographical fact.
Here, as in *Fireweed,* a young person, a boy, is looking for freedom and
beyond that, for an identity. When David is helped to escape from a
concentration camp somewhere in Eastern Europe he does not know
who he is or where he came from. He has only a name, a small bundle
(containing a bottle, a compass, a box of matches, a loaf of bread, and
a pocket-knife) and a few very general directions for the route he
must take to a country called Denmark "where there is a King." In the
course of his difficult journey through Italy and Switzerland David
learns a good deal about how life—everyday life—is conducted; he learns
something of the way human beings are involved with one another
(his relations with the little Italian girl Maria seem entirely true to
the nature of a boy whose affections have had little to exercise them).
An escape into life—this is the kind of expandable theme that we need
to help children to grow emotionally through the books they read.
Two things disappoint me in *I Am David,* all the same. The first is the
happy ending, its particular form; the coincidence by which David
finds his mother hits one almost like a blow. I feel that emotionally
and from a literary point of view as well the story demands a more
stringent, more exacting, even a sadder ending to match its spare, mysterious, strong beginning. And then I find David too passive, too
much a recipient, perhaps too much of a symbol to be convincing as a
person. In this search for an identity, we should expect more than the
discovery of a name and a home; but David does not develop as a
character, he does not find a *self,* and so the deeper claim of the book
is hardly satisfied. Perhaps the author's use of her material brings
this about. By giving David anonymity she has made him in a sense
representative. At many moments—most of all in his meeting with the
Danish artist—the actuality of his search seems to clash with its underlying symbolism.

What happens when an author uses symbol directly and consistent-
ly? Julia Cunningham's *Dorp Dead* was not written specifically about
war but its theme of tyranny, imprisonment, the fight for personal
freedom is likely to be interpreted by young and old alike in the light
of a cold war and a precarious world. Gilly Grand is an individual—
aged eleven, perverse, brilliant, self-absorbed, lonely; he is placed in a
world with the anonymity, the figurative decoration of fairy tale. Good
and Evil as he meets them—or Tyranny and Liberty—are represented
by the Hunter and the Carpenter (the latter's single name, Kobalt, is
significantly un-human too). We would usually demand a name and a

face to support a fictitious character; these two figures win reality with few orthodox attributes. Here is the Hunter, in Gilly's words:

I pause to find out if he has anything to ask me, but there is no sound in the tower except the tiny ruffles of wind that lick gently at the crumbled edges of the entryway. There is no awkwardness in or around him and not the slightest stir in his body. He is planted and peaceful, enthroned there on my chair, and the tower seems his instead of mine but somehow I do not resent it. I am the one who is restless. I remember my loaf of bread and three carrots. The thought strikes me as a little crazy but I wish I had a plate to put them on and a knife, both silver, before I say, 'Would you like some lunch?'[8]

In the same way the concrete details of the story—the descriptions of furniture, landscape, buildings—are carefully restrained and generalised, from the fifteen saws in Kobalt's workshop, "their teeth wiped utterly free of sawdust, their handles undulled by fingerprints or dried sweat" to the fifteen clocks with their "nine conceived strokes, all of them with voices no more strenuous than a titmouse's cheep." This leaves each and every reader free to interpret the story for himself, to go beyond the immediate suggestions of war in our time to the suggestion of youth emerging from the chrysalis of custom and control. Meanwhile the author, freed from orthodox scene-setting, can strike right to the heart of her meaning through the overtones of her story. In the march of her strong, simple sentences there is an extraordinary force of feeling, that necessary passion in which the young may find an echo of their own fears and perplexities. Gilly is "real" to each reader because the author has used her literary skill to find a form in which she can satisfy each personal response. *She* offers a symbolic tale: *we* turn it into actual terms by the way we read it. Here again an author has found a new, exciting, and valid form within the range of feeling in the young but again a form which does not inhibit her full meaning.

The Human Condition

Finally, imprisonment and escape in the form of a fantasy-adventure. Lucy Boston's fourth book for the young, *A Stranger at Green Knowe,* is a sharply personal, partisan, unique piece of literature. It concerns a small boy and a gorilla, brought together first at the London Zoo and then in the depths of the English county of Huntingdon. The two places where these lives touch are enormously important. The ancient house and garden called Green Knowe form in every sense the centre of this, as of all but one of Lucy Boston's stories. The bamboo thicket which bounds the garden on one side reminds the child

---

[8] Julia Cuningham: *Dorp Dead* (New York: 1965) London: Heinemann, Pyramid Books 1967, p. 14.

Ping of the Burmese jungle from which he was taken to "a life on concrete" in the portentously styled International Relief Society's Intermediate Hostel for Displaced Children; and it makes him imagine the forests where the gorilla Hanno had lived until he came to the Zoo where "there was neither sunrise nor sunset, mist or dew or the smell of changing seasons."[9] The story works through the setting as much as it does through events or through the thoughts and exclamations and wonderings of Ping. The author has something to say about freedom and she says it, strongly and with passionate conviction, through each and every element in her story. You do not learn her message in your mind; you experience it as you read. It is because of the passion and the beauty and the subtle and personal undercurrent of humour in the book that you accept the fantastic element in it—the gorilla's escape, his arrival at the very place where Ping, who had admired and sympathised with him in his cage, is on a visit to Mrs. Oldknow.

Lucy Boston has approached the delicate matter of writing about the "feelings" of an animal in her own way. The superb and scientific description of a gorilla family in the wild which opens the book states its theme and establishes Hanno *as an animal*. The author never plays tricks about this; nothing Hanno does is really outside the possibilities of animal behaviour. Yet cross-references make it possible to believe in the friendship—or the adoptive familial relationship—that develops between gorilla and boy; it is always through Ping that we guess the gorilla's reactions to events. When Ping offers Hanno his picnic-basket, this is how he sees his rather alarming companion in the Thicket:

He looked like a very important gentleman taking a picnic in a quiet spot, having shaken off even his secretary. Ping admired again his appearance of being superbly well dressed—black bearskin sleeves, silver-grey shirt and opossum trousers, worn with style and pride as if he were fully conscious that he was turned out to strike the fear of God into lesser beings. But now he was off duty, enjoying himself in privacy.[10]

Ultimately Lucy Boston's value for the young is that she is not afraid of emotion. It may be expressed in the delightfully casual, affectionate chat between Mrs. Oldknow and Ping. It may be expressed in heightened prose which transcends any limitations of "writing for children":

Hanno stood resting his arm against the door post, his great head searching the room. He dwarfed the opening. He loomed like a natural force of the first order, causing the same thrill of recognition that a bather gives to an immense wave that has pulled up out of the ocean and suddenly towers hissing over him. It was impossible to see Hanno without taking in at the same time the dominance of the equatorial sun, the frier of the earth. The weight of silence in a thousand miles of forest, the ruthless interchange of life and death, are a millenium without time.

All this precipitated itself into the room, taking, on all fours, a more familiar form of wildness.[11]

A Stranger at Green Knowe is not explicitly or obviously a book about the human condition in our own time; yet a boy or girl in the 'teens could travel far towards an understanding of self and world by reading it.

Fairies at the Bottom of the Garden

Nobody would question in a broad sense the right of an author to bring his own adult preoccupations and ideas to a story for children, of whatever age. How could we? Think of the difference between *The Snow Queen* and the kind of story beloved by magazines in my childhood (and still finding its way to publishers' desks) in which the Fairy Queen sips nectar from acorn cups and waves a star-tipped wand. The fairies were guided to the bottom of the garden by writers who felt it was necessary to establish a special level for their readers with a poor idea of what that level might be. To his story Hans Andersen brought himself—the child he was, the man he had become, the child he continued to be; so he made that story ageless as well as timeless. The layers of meaning in fairy tale or fantasy not only remove it from the restrictions of age-grouping but also offer a positive challenge to readers of any age at all. Ted Hughes has successfully hidden himself in his fantasy, *The Iron Man*. Quite young readers have enjoyed the book as a neo-fairy tale. Many have wanted to read it as an expression of hope for peace. The poet's own interpretation reaches down to the core of being and the beginning of myth-making. If few of us could put his deepest meaning into words at a first or even at a sixth reading, the emotional force of the story forces us to *feel;* and we get further by divining a meaning than by analysing it. Do we really know exactly what C. S. Lewis meant by the Narnia adventures or what secret wishes and fears went into Mary Norton's tales of the Borrowers or what degrees of meaning lie under the seemingly artless tales by Helen Cresswell—*The Piemakers, The Signposters, The Night-Watchmen* and *The Outlanders*—tales which are linked not by plot, only partially by setting, but most of all by the emphasis on the creative mind which strengthens each story. Helen Cresswell writes on many levels, to entertain, to provoke, to open our eyes to the world of everyday. In *The Piemakers* (the first, the simplest, and still, I think, the best of the four books) it is as a housewife that she enjoys the humour of transferring a domestic fact (the competition for the biggest pie in an En-

[11] L. M. Boston: *A Stranger at Green Knowe* London: Faber and Faber 1961, p. 148.

glish village) to a nursery-rhyme world where Arthy Roller wins the King's Prize with a pie for two thousand people. She is remembering a child's love of circumstantial detail when she works out how the meat was cooked (in three large washing-coppers), how the seasonings were calculated (with the help of the village school-mistress) and how the pie-dish, large enough to be taken for a barge, was floated down river to the secret bakehouse. She satisfies a child's sense of wonder when she sends her ten-year-old heroine down river in the pie-dish, where she feels like "a goldfish in a bowl." All through this and the associated stories she keeps—in Edward Blishen's phrase—"a child's eye at the centre." And all through the story we are aware of that fresh, sharp, new look at everyday that is the hallmark of fantasy. In a talk with the uncompromising title "On not writing for children" Pamela Travers asserted once more that literature for children must be thought of as any other form of writing. "If it is literature at all," she wrote, "it can't help being all one river and you put into it, according to age, a small foot or a large one." I suppose the foot Helen Cresswell dips into the river in her books is a small one but it is an important one none the less.

Heartsease

In fantasy that is properly grounded in a larger myth, a larger feeling, a child and author can meet on the same wave-length. The disparity in their experience of life is less important in the atmosphere of a fable; the depth of feeling can exist without the sometimes distracting presence of contemporary detail. The author may still express indirectly the preoccupations of his own times. A child is free to treat as fantastic adventure books like *The Sleepers* by Jane Louise Curry, in which King Arthur wakes to the present, or Peter Dickinson's two stories, *Heartsease* and *The Weather-Monger,* which depict an England reverted to the Middle Ages and governed by a superstitious horror of machines. The child may guess at the fear of regimentation which is at least one motive behind the stories; he will respond at a deeper and more general level to the plea for the freedom of the individual which is integral to them.

The theme of *Heartsease* is stated first in a definite, external way. An American who has come to investigate the Changes that have come about in England in the early 1970's is smelled out as a "witch" by old Mr. Gordon, the bigoted tyrant of a Cotswold village. The fate of a witch is to be stoned to death but Otto is saved by children who have secretly resisted the Changes:

No single stone seemed to make the cairn any smaller, but soon they had

cleared the body up to the waist. Tim had stopped his bubbling and was working with increasing urgency now that he could see enough of the witch's body
to know what it was; he cooed once or twice, a noise which Margaret hadn't
heard him make before. The witch had sheltered his head behind crooked arms,
but these were now stuck to the mess of clotted blood and clothing and hair
round his face; when Margaret tried to move an arm to get at a stone which
had lodged in the bend of the elbow he groaned with a new, sharp note.[12]

The tenseness here comes from more than physical suffering. The adventure, moving swiftly and with continual fluctuation, still allows
room for the author to explore his young characters so that we understand eventually why and how each one has escaped the fog of
Puritanism that envelops their elders; it allows room for a broader
interpretation to grow through the story so that at the end an intelligent reader will realise he has read something more than the tale of
good people escaping from bad. The impact of the author's style counts
towards his conclusion. This meaning is hidden in the kinds of
words he uses (unsophisticated words supremely well chosen), the
hints he offers in the conversations between people, the tempo and balance of his narrative. He does not tell the reader what to think; he asks
him to find out, through attentive reading.

Labeling by Age

However conscious a writer is that he is addressing himself to the
young, he will give himself more scope and will more nearly approach his concept if he chooses a universal theme that does not tie
him to an age-group or put too obvious a date-stamp on his story.
Though we are only too often asked to label books for a certain kind
of reader, we are surely thankful to find books which can be put into
every column right across the page. I think in particular of Philippa
Pearce's *A Dog so Small*—on the face of it the story of a boy, a dog and
a dream, but in depth a study in disappointment which each one will
read by the light of his own experience. I think of William Mayne's village comedy *A Parcel of Trees,* on the face of it the story of a girl of
fourteen, obliged to share a bedroom with a silently devilish younger
sister, who sets out to find a place of her own, but in depth a study in
the need for privacy which always reminds me of Virginia Woolf's
To the Lighthouse.

The theme of *A Parcel of Trees* is universal, and so is the humour
that underlines and decorates and makes real every one of its scenes.
From time to time a reviewer will remark that such and such a book is
"more for adults than for children." In relation to humour this indicates that the writer is indulging himself in a joke that children can-

[12] Peter Dickinson: *Heartsease* London: Victor Gollancz 1969, pp. 12-13.

not appreciate. The author may well be right and the reviewer wrong. Obviously children will enjoy the slapstick, banana-skin humour of *The Magic Pudding* but we might also trust them to see something of the shrewdness of the character-drawing. I would be sorry to deny them the pleasure of reading *The Christmas Bower*, Polly Redford's hilarious frolic in a New York store, because they might be too young to appreciate fully the quick caricatures of bird-watching types. I should be sorry for them to miss the fun of Will Nickless's tales of an animal village in *Owlglass* and its sequels because they might be puzzled by the whimsicality of seeing animals as clubmen of a vanished era. I should be sorry for them to miss a recent tall story by Paul Ries Collin, *Parcel for Henry*, because while they could easily see the joke of the English Channel wrapped up in a parcel, they might not appreciate fully the sophisticated satire on bureaucracy. It is a pity that a book should be deemed "unsuitable" for children because the author has put out the skill and experience of maturity to entertain them. We may expect him to provide for his young reader by giving him a special place in the story, a character he can identify with and a point of view he can understand, but not so as to sacrifice his own impress on the story. He must be free to communicate with children as an artist and also as a one-time child.

Librarians and the Reading Child

All of us have, very evidently, a duty to the reading child. Equally, we have a duty to meet writers with an open mind and to accept what they write as what they themselves mean and intend. A book is a man's own creation and can only be read as such. It is our business to introduce him to his readers or his readers to him in such a way that we do not interfere with either party. It is surely not for any abstract idea of "improvement" that we want children to read books of depth and discernment and humour, but because we want them to share our enthusiasm—I would even say we want them to learn how to *feel* enthusiasm for books. And here I would distinguish between enthusiasm and pleasure. A child can feel pleasure in reading a comic or a trivial adventure. By enthusiasm I understand a more positive, active engagement with a book and, through the book, with its author. Enthusiasm is an active, intelligent response which comes when children meet the challenge of books written perhaps "for" them but also for the author himself.

It is only too easy to be over-protective towards children and to deny them the right to make their own mistakes and their own discoveries in the world of fiction. Not long ago a New Zealand bookseller, considering the effect of mass media on books, made the following confident statement:

As long as human curiosity maintains its present extreme individual variations, so long will books be demanded and enjoyed, each at the reader's own rate of assimilation and reference back.[13]

Human curiosity, in young and old, is as uncontrollable as a kite in a high wind. Efforts at censorship in the children's book world are as misguided as they are useless. Recently there has been a move in certain children's libraries in England to ban Frank Richards's tales of Greyfriars because they encourage children to laugh at obesity through Billy Bunter; but to a child Billy Bunter is as fantastic as Worzel Gummidge. Nowadays we are abnormally sensitive about minorities but we must not lose our sense of proportion. If obvious caricatures like Bunter or Bumpo Prince of Jolliginki are to be snatched from children for fear of giving offence, it would be equally logical to excise from story-books all comic Frenchmen and coy parsons, all absent-minded professors and bad-tempered janitors and cantankerous or old-fashioned school teachers—everything exaggerated crude, in questionable taste. Interfere with the crude, then with the violent, then with the bizarre and the prejudiced, and it is questionable how much will be left for the child's curiosity to feed on. We all have to learn that there is no such thing as an average person and yet we are on the way to insisting that children's stories should concern themselves with carefully selected "average" heroes, crooks, and kids.

Librarians as Middlemen

Gordon Tait's comment on "human curiosity" and books ended, you may remember, in the phrase, "the reader's own rate of assimilation and reference back." We owe it to children to value their capacities correctly. As a writer said a hundred and twenty-five years ago, while reviewing books for the young, "Children seem to possess an inherent conviction that when the hole is big enough for the cat, no smaller one at the side is needed for the kitten."[14] The words "assimilation" and "reference back" also imply time and privacy. The child needs time and privacy just as we do. Nothing that we do, as middlemen in the business of children's books, is really final. It is conditional, introductory, intermediate. The final moment comes when the child meets the author in his book. Let us give such advice as seems appropriate, but let us found this advice first of all on our individual opinion of a book as an amateur, and only secondly on professional considerations. And then let us shut the door and leave child and author together. This is their right.

---

[13] Gordon Tate: quoted in *The Bookseller*, London, Saturday, January 1, 1970, no. 3345, p. 323.

[14] London, *Quarterly Review*, vol. LXXIV, June 1944, pp. 15-16.

John Rowe Townsend

John Rowe Townsend, until 1978 the children's
book editor of the *Guardian* (formerly the
Manchester Guardian), is a distinguished English
author as well as a critic. His professional writing
includes a study of English children's literature,
Written for Children (Lothrop, Lee & Shepard, 1965),
and a collection of essays on contemporary
children's authors, *A Sense of Story* (Lippincott, 1971;
reissued in a revised edition in 1979 as *A Sounding
of Storytellers*). Of his many books for children and
young people, several have been selected for
inclusion on ALA Notable Children's Books list,
including *Trouble in the Jungle* (originally *Grumble's
Yard;* Lippincott, 1969); *Pirate's Island* (Lippincott,
1968); *Goodbye to the Jungle* (Lippincott, 1967); and
The Intruder (Lippincott, 1970). Among his recent
books are *Noah's Castle* (Lippincott, 1976) and *The
Visitors* (Lippincott, 1977).

Mr. Townsend, who lives in Cambridge, England,
has taught at several universities in the United
States. His lecture, "Standards of Criticism for
Children's Literature," was presented on April 23,
1971, in Atlanta, Georgia, and was jointly sponsored
by the School of Library Service, Atlanta University,
and the Division of Librarianship, Emory University.

Standards of Criticism
for Children's Literature

To give the May Hill Arbuthnot Honor Lecture is the greatest privilege that can fall to a commentator on books for children. It is with some idea of matching my response to the size of the honor that I have decided at last to attempt the largest and most difficult subject I know in this field: namely, the question of standards by which children's literature is to be judged. This is not only the most difficult, it is the most important question; indeed, it is so basic that none of us who are professionally concerned with children and books ought really to be functioning at all unless we have thought it out to our own satisfaction and are prepared to rethink it from time to time. But, as in many other areas of life, we tend to be so busy doing what we have to do that we never have time to stop and consider the validity of the assumptions on which we act and the methods which we employ. True, Mrs. Arbuthnot herself had a good deal to say on this subject; but she would not have claimed to say the last word.

A Climate of Confusion

It seems to me that the assessment of children's books takes place in an atmosphere of unparalleled intellectual confusion. There are two

23

reasons for this. One is a very familiar one which I need not elaborate on. It was neatly expressed by Brian Alderson in an article in *Children's Book News* of London for January/February 1969, when he said that "everyone in the children's book business subsists in a slightly unreal world, where time, brains and energy are expended on behalf of a vast and largely non-participating audience." It has been pointed out time and time again that children's books are written by adults, published by adults, reviewed by adults, and, in the main, bought by adults. The whole process is carried out at one, two, three, or more removes from the ultimate consumer.

This situation is inescapable, but it is an uneasy one. Most of us think we know what is good for ourselves, but the more sensitive we are, the more seriously we take our obligations, the less we feel sure we know what is good for others.

The second cause of confusion is that children's literature is a part of the field, or adjoins the field, of many different specialists; yet it is the *major* concern of relatively few, and those not the most highly placed in the professional or academic pecking-order. Furthermore, the few to whom children's literature is central cannot expect, within one working lifetime, to master sufficient knowledge of the related fields to meet the experts on their own ground and at their own level. And yet, while the children's literature person obviously cannot operate at a professional level in all these various fields, the people operating in the various fields can and quite properly do take an interest in children's reading as it affects their own specialities, and are able to quite frequently pronounce upon it. But, understandably, such people are often unaware of or have not thought deeply about the aspects of children's literature that do *not* impinge upon their own field. The subject is one on which people are notoriously willing to pronounce with great confidence but rather little knowledge. Consequently, we have a flow of apparently authoritative comment by people who are undoubtedly experts but who are not actually experts on *this*.

I am not here to quarrel with those who see children's literature in terms of social or psychological adjustment, advancement of deprived or minority groups, development of reading skills, or anything else. I have said in the foreword to my new book, *A Sense of Story,* to be published by Lippincott this year, that "most disputes over standards are fruitless because the antagonists suppose their criteria to be mutually exclusive; if one is right the other must be wrong. This is not necessarily so. Different kinds of assessment are valid for different purposes." I would only remark that the viewpoints of psychologists, sociologists, and educationists of various descriptions have rather little in common with each other or with those whose approach is mainly literary.

Clearing the Jungle

We face, in fact, a jungle of preoccupations, ideas, and attitudes. I should like to begin my discussion today by clearing, if I can, some small piece of common ground which will accommodate most of us who care about children and books without placing too much pressure on us to resolve our legitimate differences of approach.

Let me borrow a phrase used by Edgar Z. Friedenberg in a book entitled *Coming of Age in America,* published in 1965. I do not agree with all that is said in the book, but I think the phrase I have my eye on is admirable. Friedenberg used it to describe the true function of the schools; I would use it to describe the duty of all of us, either as parents or, in a broad sense, as guardians. This aim, he said, was "the respectful and affectionate nurture of the young, and the cultivation in them of a disciplined and informed mind and heart."

Extending this formulation to cover the special interest which has brought us here today, I should like to suggest that we believe in "the respectful and affectionate nurture of the young, and the cultivation in them of a disciplined and informed mind and heart; and that in furtherance of these ends we would wish every child to experience to his or her full capacity the enjoyment, and the broadening of horizons, which can be derived from literature." I apologize to Friedenberg for adopting and adapting his definition; and if anyone suggests that what I have added is redundant, then I can only turn the other cheek. I do not claim to have improved upon the definition; I have merely tried to make it more specific in the direction with which we are at present concerned.

Diffidently I invite my hearers, and my readers, if any, to subscribe to this modest and unprovocative creed. What it asks is the acceptance of literary experience as having value in itself for the general enrichment of life, over and above any virtue that may be claimed for it as a means to a nonliterary end. Anyone who cannot accept the proposition is of course fully entitled to stand aloof; but I cannot think of anything to say to such a person, because if literature is *solely* a means to an end, then the best literature is the literature which best serves that end, and the only matters worth arguing about are whether the end is a good one and how effectively it is served. Furthermore, those points cannot be argued in general terms, but only in relation to a particular cause and a particular book.

Literature—from Many Angles

I wonder if from the tiny clearing we have made we can begin to find a way through the tangle that surrounds us. Let us try to consider what literature is, what it offers, and what is children's literature. I do not want to spend a lot of time on questions which, although they may present theoretical difficulties, are not really perplexing in practice. I am going to define literature, without appeal to authority, as consisting of all works of imagination which are transmitted primarily by means of the written word or spoken narrative—that is, in the main, novels, stories, and poetry—with the addition of those works of nonfiction which by their qualities of style or insight may be said to offer experience of a literary nature. This is a rather loose definition and may be open to objection on semantic grounds: for instance, can literature really be said to include the spoken word? Perhaps I have bent the borders so as to make sure I do not exclude storytelling. But in practical terms I think the definition will do, and no one will seriously quarrel with it. Literature is mostly fiction, poetry, and such nonfiction as does more than merely impart information.

What does literature offer? I have more than hinted already at my answer to this in previous statements, since one cannot define one's terms without assuming a preexistent definition of the terms in which one is defining them. Summarizing ruthlessly, I will say that what is offered by literature as such is, above all, enjoyment: enjoyment not only in the shallow sense of easy pleasure, but enjoyment of a profounder kind; enjoyment of the shaping by art of the raw material of life, and enjoyment, too, of the skill with which that shaping is performed; enjoyment in the stretching of one's imagination, the deepening of one's experience, and the heightening of one's awareness; an enjoyment which may be intense even if the material of the literary work is sad or painful. (A rough-and-ready definition, but my own, and perhaps over the years I shall be able to improve on it.) I should add that obviously not all literature can offer such a range of enjoyments; that no work of literature outside such short forms as the lyric poem can offer these enjoyments throughout; and that the deliberate restriction of aim is often necessary in children's literature as in much else.

What in particular is children's literature? That is quite a difficult one. There is a sense in which we don't need to define it because we know what it is. Children's literature is *Robinson Crusoe* and *Alice* and *Little Women* and *Tom Sawyer* and *Treasure Island* and *The Wind in the Willows* and *Winnie the Pooh* and *The Hobbit* and *Charlotte's Web*. That's simple; but it won't quite do. Surely *Robinson Crusoe* was not written for children, and do not the *Alice* books appeal at least as much to grownups?; if *Tom Sawyer* is children's literature, what about *Huckleberry Finn*?; if the *Jungle Books* are children's literature, what about *Kim* or *Stalky*?; and if *The Wind in the Willows* is children's literature, what about *The Golden Age?*; and so on.

Since any line-drawing must be arbitrary, one is tempted to abandon the attempt and say that there is no such thing as children's literature, there is just literature. And that, I believe, is true. Children are not a separate form of life from people; no more than children's books are a separate form of literature from just books. Children are part of mankind; children's literature is part of literature. While all this is true, it doesn't get you anywhere, because the fact that children are part of mankind doesn't save you from having to separate them from adults for certain essential purposes; nor does the fact that children's literature is part of literature save you from having to separate it for practical purposes (in the libraries and bookshops, for instance). I pondered this question for some time while working on *A Sense of Story,* and came to the conclusion that in the long run children's literature could only be regarded as consisting of those books which by a consensus of adults and children were assigned to the children's shelves—a wholly pragmatic definition. In dealing with current output, I came to the conclusion that, absurd as it might seem, the only workable definition of a children's book was "a book that appeared on the children's list of a publisher." This is not merely pragmatic, it is a definition that seems to hold itself up by its own bootstraps. Yet in the short run it does appear that, for better or worse, the publisher decides. If he puts a book on the children's list, it will be reviewed as a children's book and will be read by children (or young people), if it is read at all. If he puts it on the adult list, it will not— or at least not immediately.

Let us assume that we have found, in broad terms, a common aim; that we know roughly what literature is and the nature of the experience it offers; that we have a working definition of children's literature, even if it is more pragmatic than we would wish. Can we now make some sense out of the question of differing standards? So far today I have tried to examine what exists rather than to project a theoretical system out of my own head; this, I think, is a sound procedure which will give us the answers we need. We all know how often the application of a new mind to an old problem will fail because the new thinking is insufficiently grounded in what has been thought and done before; indeed, it often overestimates its own originality.

When we look for individual assessments of actual books (as distinct from general articles on children's literature and reading) we find that most of what is written comes under the headings of (a) overwhelmingly, reviews, (b) aids to book selection, and (c) general surveys. There is little writing that I think could be dignified with the name of criticism, a point to which I will return later. While examining reviews, selection aids, and surveys, in both the United States and Britain and in relation to imaginative literature, I asked myself not whether they were sound and perceptive or whether I agreed with them, but what they were actually doing and what their standards appeared to be. I was aware that similar inquiries had been carried out by others, and more thoroughly; but I was aware, too, that my findings would be matters of judgment which were not of simple fact, and that the scheme of my overall study required that the judgments should be my own. The hand must fit the glove. I cannot wear a glove, however fine its quality, which was made by and for another hand. At least I will spare you the raw material of my investigation and will keep my conclusions brief. I found, naturally, some differences between reviews in general and specialist publications, but from my point of view they were not crucial.

What the reviewers and selectors were largely concerned with, more often than not, it seemed to me, was telling you what the story was about: a necessary activity, but not an evaluative one. I came to the conclusion that where they offered judgments the writers always concerned themselves with one or more of four attributes, which I do not place in order of importance or frequency. These were (1) suitability, (2) popularity, or potential popularity, (3) relevance, and (4) merit. "Suitability" is rather a blanket term, under which I include appropriateness to the supposed readership or reading age or purpose, and also attempts by the reviewer or selector to assign books to particular age groups or types of child. "Popularity" needs no explanation. By "relevance" I mean the power, or possible power, of theme or subject matter to make the child more aware of current social or personal problems, or to suggest solutions to him; where a story appears to convey a message I include under "relevance" the assessment of the message. Finally, by "merit" I mean on the whole, literary merit, although often one finds that what might be called undifferentiated merit is discerned in a book.

Of the four attributes I have mentioned (please remember that my classifications are arbitrary and that there is some overlap) it may well have occurred to you that the first three are child-centered: suitability to the child, popularity with the child, relevance for the child. The fourth is book-centered: merit of the book. This is an important distinction; failure to perceive it has given us a great deal of trouble in the past, preventing us from understanding each other and understanding what we are about. In an article in *Wilson Library Bulletin* for December 1968 I rashly coined a phrase about "book people" and "child people." "Book people," I said, were those primarily concerned with books: authors, publishers, a great many reviewers, and public librarians. "Child people," I said, were those primarily concerned with children: parents, teachers, and (in England at any rate) most school librarians. This division was useful in a way, because it helped to account for two diametrically opposed views of the state of English children's literature: that it was in a very healthy state, with so many good books being published; and that it was in a very unhealthy state, because so many children didn't find pleasure in reading. "Book people," I thought, tended to take the former view; "child people" to take the latter. Incidentally, it was reflection on the fact that such totally opposite views could be held that led me to feel we needed an examination of standards, and in part, led me to offer my present hesitant contribution to that formidable task.

However, I did not and do not intend to set any group against any other group, and I must say at once that all children's "book people" I know are also "child people" in that they care about the child; and all the "child people" I know who are interested in books are on that account "book people." And I will repeat here what I said earlier in another context: that different kinds of assessment are valid for different purposes. Not only that, but different standards can coexist within the mind of the same person at the same time. That is why we get mixed up. Our judgments are rarely made with a single, simple purpose in mind, and we do not stop to separate our purposes any more than we normally stop to analyze our own processes of thought. Because we are both "book people" and "child people" and because we care about both books and children, book-centered and child-centered views are all jumbled together in our heads. Is it a good book, will children like it, will it have a beneficial effect on them? We ask ourselves all these questions at once, and expect to come up with a single answer.

It is easy for mental sideslips to occur, even when we are writing for publication. A simple instance (one of many that could be cited) is in the London *Times Literary Supplement* of 16 April 1970, where the anonymous reviewer of a book of verse by Alan Brownjohn discusses the book with much intelligence in the language of literary criticism, and finishes by saying that "this is a book all children will most definitely enjoy." The statement is unrelated to the rest of what is said, and unfortunately, cannot be true. Nobody has yet found a book that "all" children enjoy, and if there were such a book I do not think it would be a book of poems. The reviewer cannot have *thought* before writing that; he or she has made a remark either as a general expression of approval or as an unrealistic inference: "It is good, so they will all enjoy it."

There are people—Brian Alderson in an article provocatively entitled "The Irrelevance of Children to the Children's Book Reviewer"; Paul Heins, if I understand him correctly, in two articles in the *Horn*

Book called "Out on a Limb with the Critics" and "Coming to Terms with Criticism," in June and August 1970, respectively—who maintain that reviewing should be strictly critical. Alderson says: "It may be objected that to assess children's books without reference to children is to erect some absolute critical standard relating neither to the author's purpose nor the reader's enjoyment. To do much less, however, is to follow a road that leads to a morass of contradictions and subjective responses."

I do not wish to prolong my discussion of a subject already so much discussed as reviewing. On the whole I agree with Heins and Alderson, whose positions, I think, can fairly be described as purist. I would prefer the reviewer to address himself sensitively to the book which is there in front of him, rather than to use his space for inevitably crude assessments of suitability for some broad notional category of child, or speculations that the book will or will not sit long on the shelf, or that it will or will not help its readers to adjust to reality or understand how the other half of the world lives. Readers can use their intelligence and make these assessments or pursue these speculations for themselves. I suspect that library systems can manage the practical task of book selection without undue dependence on the individual reviewer. What they need to know from him, if they need to know anything from him (and if it isn't too late anyway by the time the review appears) is, does the book have literary merit?

Suitability, popularity, relevance—are these not questions for the buyer, and perhaps above all for those who are closest to the ultimate consumer? "Will this be suitable for *my* child, will this be popular with *my* class, will this be relevant for children in the area served by *my* library?" Surely only the parent, teacher, or librarian there on the spot can find the answer. He will find it in his own judgment and experience. And he will soon learn whether he was right.

The Critical Approach

I hope I have cleared the ground sufficiently to allow myself to move on to a discussion of critical principles in relation to children's literature. I am not sure whether I have sufficiently indicated the *usefulness* of the critical approach. If I have not, then I ought to do so; for although some of us would no doubt practice it quite happily for its own sake, if it is not useful, we cannot reasonably expect others to give their time and attention, their paper and print, to the result of our endeavors. So I will suggest first that a standard of literary merit is required, and indeed in practice is accepted, as the *leading edge,* so to speak, of book assessment since nonliterary standards relate so largely to specific aims and situations, times, places, and audiences. Literary standards are not fixed forever, but they are comparatively stable; that is part of their essence. Without this leading edge, this backbone if you prefer it, there can only be a jumble of criteria, a haphazard mixture of personal responses. And I have found in my own numerous discussions with people concerned with various aspects of books for children, that even those who most strongly condemn what they consider to be an excessively literary approach do in fact take it for granted that there is some independent standard of quality other than what children like or what is good for them or what brings them face to face with contemporary issues. "Wonderful stuff, but not for *my* kids" is a frequent comment.

I would suggest, too, and have suggested in the introduction to *A Sense of Story*, that a critical approach is desirable not only for its own sake but also as a stimulus and discipline for author and publisher, and, in the long run, for the improvement of the breed. Donnarae MacCann, introducing a series of articles in the *Wilson Library Bulletin* for December 1969, made this point and quoted from Henry S. Canby's *Definitions* (second series, 1967):

Unless there is somewhere an intelligent critical attitude against which the writer can measure himself . . . one of the chief requirements for good literature is wanting. . . . The author degenerates.

Donnarae MacCann goes on to say that "there is no body of critical writing to turn to, even for those books which have been awarded the highest literary prizes in children's literature in Britain and America." That seems to me to indicate a serious lack, and to suggest a further use for the literary criticism of children's books: to help them to achieve their proper status. There is a parallel between the standing of children's literature now and that of the novel a hundred years or so ago. Listen to Henry James in *The Art of Fiction* (1884):

Only a short time ago it might have been supposed that the English novel was not what the French call "discutable" . . . there was a comfortable, good-humoured feeling abroad that a novel is a novel as a pudding is a pudding, and that our only business with it could be to swallow it. . . . Art lives upon discussion, upon experiment, upon curiosity, upon variety of attempt, upon the exchange of views and the comparison of standpoints. . . . [The novel] must take itself seriously for the public to take it so.

We can apply Henry James's statements to children's literature today. As yet, it is barely discussible at a respectable intellectual level. But if we are to move onward from kiddy lit and all that the use of that squirmy term implies, then children's books must be taken seriously *as literature,* and this means they must be considered with critical strictness. Vague approval, praise for the work of established writers because they are established, and above all, sentimental gush will get us nowhere.

... and the Critics

I have suggested, diffidently, what I consider to be literature and what I believe in broad terms to be the nature of literary experience. From the latter it would be possible to derive, in equally broad terms, an elementary criterion for the assessment of literary merit. But we need something more detailed and sophisticated, which could hardly be drawn by legitimate processes of deduction from my simple premises; and I feel even more diffident when I think of the amount of distinguished American and British literary criticism in print. Is this even a case where the construction and application of abstract rules are proper? Perhaps we ought to see what some of the critics say.

We find in fact that the literary critics, both modern and not-so-modern, are rather reluctant to pin themselves down to theoretical statements. In the introduction to *Determinations* (1934), F. R. Leavis expresses the belief that "the way to forward true appreciation of art and literature and art is to examine and discuss it"; and again, "out of agreement or disagreement with particular judgments of value a sense of relative value in the concrete will define itself, and, without this, no amount of talk about values in the abstract is worth anything." The late T. S. Eliot was elusive about critical standards, and when he did make a firm statement it could be startlingly down-to-earth. He said, in *The Use of Poetry and the Use of Criticism* (1933):

The rudiment of criticism is the ability to select a good poem and reject a bad poem; and its most severe test is of its ability to select a good *new* poem, to respond properly to a new situation.

I should mention that Eliot, like many other critics, sometimes used the word "poem" as shorthand for any work of imaginative literature. Whether he was doing so here I am not sure, but his statement is a statement about criticism, not about poetry, and if for "poem" you substituted "novel," "painting," or "piece of music" it would be neither more nor less true.

In the same book, Eliot remarked that "if you had no faith in the critic's ability to tell a good poem from a bad one, you would put little reliance on the value of his theories." I do not recall that Eliot ever explained by what standard you were to judge whether the critic could tell a good poem, but obviously, it was some standard other than the man's own theory, and in fact, I am fairly sure that it was the consensus of informed opinion over a period of time. And that comes originally from Dr. Johnson, who said in the *Preface to Shakespeare* that the only test that could be applied to works of literature was "length of duration and continuance of esteem"; and also, in the *Life of Gray*, that "it is by the common sense of readers uncorrupted by literary prejudice that all claim to literary honours is finally decided."

Matthew Arnold in *The Study of Poetry* (1880) proposed, as aids to distinguishing work of the highest class, not rules but touchstones, examples from the great masters. Arnold says:

> Critics give themselves great labour to draw out what in the abstract constitutes the character of a high quality of poetry. It is much better simply to have recourse to concrete examples;—to take specimens of poetry of high, the very highest quality, and to say: The characters of a high quality of poetry are what is expressed *there*. They are far better recognised by being felt in the verse of the master than by being perused in the prose of the critic. . . . If we are asked to define this mark and accent (of 'high beauty, worth and power') in the abstract, our answer must be: No, for we should thereby be darkening the question, not clearing it.

Here Arnold was undoubtedly talking about poetry and not using the word as shorthand. His touchstone principle could be extended to prose, although it strikes me as not entirely satisfactory anyway since it would not help you to judge really original work. The main point is, however, that Johnson, Arnold, Eliot, Leavis, and Henry James, too, if I correctly interpret his critical writings (he is useful because he was concerned specifically with the novel)—are reluctant to prescribe an abstract framework against which a work of literature can be measured. They see the danger. "People are always ready," T. S. Eliot said, "to grasp at any guide which will help them to recognize the best poetry without having to depend upon their own sensibility and taste." Once establish a formula (this is myself speaking, not Eliot) and you open the door to bad and pedantic criticism by people who rely on rules instead of perceptions. Not only that but you risk creating a structure within which writers can be imprisoned. Writers should never be given the idea that there is one approved way of doing things. Far better to keep an open critical mind and encourage them with the words of Kipling:

> There are nine and sixty ways of constructing tribal lays, And—every—single—one—of—them—is—right!

The Critic and the Criteria

Am I, you may ask, suggesting that there should be no formal standards at all? Well, not quite that. It depends on the critic. Some find formal principles helpful in organizing their thought. Mrs. Arbuthnot did; and I am sure the "criteria for stories" which she sets out on pages 17–19 of *Children and Books* have been valuable to a great many people, especially those who are feeling their way into the subject. Mrs.

Arbuthnot suggests looking at stories with an eye to theme, plot, characters, and style, and that is excellent; it gives you somewhere to start; it gets you moving. The guidelines for the award in England of the Carnegie Medal are almost identical and are laid down with staccato brevity; they are not expanded and explained, as Mrs. Arbuthnot expanded and explained hers. But I believe that Mrs. Arbuthnot's standards are less valuable than her example, as seen in the perceptive, practical literary criticism and, I might add, art criticism all through her book. It may well be that the English Library Association realized that what mattered for the Carnegie were not a few bald words about plot, style, and characterization, but the knowledge and judgment of the people who were appointed to apply them. The terms of the *Guardian* award for children's fiction, with which I am associated, say only that it is to go to an outstanding work; everything else is left to the judges, and I see nothing wrong with that. A good critic will indeed be aware of theme, plot, style, characterization, and many other considerations, some of them not previously spelled out but arising directly from the work; he will be sensitive; he will have a sense of balance and rightness; he will respond. Being only human he cannot possibly know all that it would be desirable for him to know; but he will have a wide knowledge of literature in general as well as of children and their literature, and probably a respectable acquaintance with cinema, theatre, television, and current affairs. That is asking a lot of him, but not too much. The critic (this is the heart of the matter) counts more than the criteria.

He will have his standards, but they will have become part of himself; he will hardly be conscious of them. Certainly he will not cart them around with him like a set of tools ready for any job. He will, I think, if I may now quote myself again from *A Sense of Story*, approach a book with an open mind and respond to it as freshly and honestly as he is able; then he will go away, let his thoughts and feelings about it mature, turn them over from time to time, consider the book in relation to others by the same author and by the author's predecessors and contemporaries. (I hope to goodness all this is not for a review with a forty-eight-hour deadline!) If the book is for children, he should not let his mind be dominated by the fact, but neither, I believe, should he attempt to ignore it. Just as I feel the author must write for himself yet with awareness of an audience of children, so I feel the critic must write for himself with an awareness that the books he discusses are children's books.

A Book and Its Readers

This last point gives me my cue to return very briefly to an issue which I touched on but put aside at its logical place in my discussion, because I wanted to keep some edges clear and I feared it might blur them. I think I can now safely go back to it. When I indicated that a critical approach was book-centered rather than child-centered, when I said I agreed on the whole with the purists, I did not, emphatically not, mean to imply that the book exists in some kind of splendid isolation, and that whether it actually speaks to the child does not matter. Rather, I think that purists can go too far in their apparent disregard for popularity. There is a sense in which the importance, the value even, of a work, is linked with its capacity to appeal to the multitude. To take some exalted examples: does not common sense tell us that part of the greatness of a Beethoven, a Shakespeare, a Michelangelo lies in the breadth of their appeal, the fact that their works are rewarding not only to a few cognoscenti but to *anyone* in possession of the appropriate faculties? A book is a communication; if it doesn't communicate, does it not fail? True, it may speak to posterity, if it gets the chance; it may be ahead of its time. But if a children's book is not popular with children here and now, its lack of appeal may tell us something. It is at least a limitation, and it *may* be a sign of some vital deficiency which is very much the critic's concern.

Those of us with purist tendencies are also perhaps too much inclined to turn up our noses at the "book with a message." For the message may be of the essence of the work, as in the novels of D. H. Lawrence or George Orwell. The revelation of the possibilities of human nature for good or ill is a major concern of literary art, probably *the* major concern of literary art. If the writer engages himself with a contemporary problem, he may be engaging himself most valuably with the mind and feelings of the reader; and to demand that he be neutral on the issues raised is to demand his emasculation. Nevertheless, it needs to be said from time to time that a book can be good without being immensely popular and without solving anybody's problems.

You will have noticed that in this talk, now drawing to a close, I have refrained from discussing specific contemporary books for children. This has been a self-denying ordinance. We would all rather talk about books than principles. But to illustrate adequately—not just casually—the various general points I have made would require reference to many books and to many pieces of writing about them; it would be the task of a course of lectures, not of a single one. And so, having reluctantly maintained a somewhat abstract level throughout, I want to finish, as it were, on the theoretical summit of children's literature. T. S. Eliot, in the book already cited, remarks that:

In a play of Shakespeare you get several levels of significance. For the simplest auditors there is the plot, for the more thoughtful the character and conflict of character, for the more musically sensitive the rhythm, and for the auditors of greater sensitiveness and understanding a meaning which reveals itself gradually.

Now authors cannot all be Shakespeares, nor for that matter can critics all be Eliots. And even within our own limitations we cannot aim at the peaks of achievement all the time. But no one compels us to be modest in our ambitions; no one has compelled me to be modest in making claims on behalf of children's literature, nor have I any intention of being so. Let's all remember with pride and pleasure that children's books of the highest merit will work on several levels; they will work indeed on the same person at successive stages of development. The best children's books are infinitely rereadable; the child can come back to them at increasing ages and, even as a grownup, still find new sources of enjoyment. Some books, a few books, need never be grown away from; they can always be shared with children and with the child within. The writer for children need feel no lack of scope for high endeavor, for attempting the almost but not quite impossible. For of books that succeed in this comprehensive way, that bind the generations together, parents with children, past with present with future, we are never likely to have too many.

Mary Ørvig

Mary Ørvig is the director of the Swedish Institute of Children's Books; she has lectured in many countries and in several languages. A prolific writer of articles and monographs, she has also compiled a Swedish index of fairy tales; co-authored two Swedish texts on children's books, *Children and Books* and *Children's Literature in Sweden;* and co-edited, with Göte Klingberg and Stuart Amor, the proceedings of the Third Symposium of the International Research Society for Children's Literature, *Children's Books in Translation: The Situation and the Problems* (Almqvist & Wiksell International, 1978, an edition in English).

An active participant in many international organizations in the field of children's literature, Mrs. Ørvig has served as advisor to the International Youth Library in Munich and has taken many exhibits on tour throughout Europe. Her lecture, "One World in Children's Books?," was presented on April 14, 1972, in Chicago, Illinois, under the sponsorship of the Graduate Library School, University of Chicago.

One World in
Children's Books?

L ET ME AT THE VERY OUTSET say how honored I am by the invitation to
give this Third Arbuthnot Lecture. I visited this country for the first
time in 1946, soon after World War II, worked, and went to library
school here. There is probably no better foundation for an international
outlook than professional studies in a foreign country. To penetrate a
new language is only part of the matter, although vocabulary, grammar,
and linguistic structure require much time and effort on the part of the
foreign student. Apart from these things, a language enshrines so much
of the history and accumulated experience of a people and their country,
their way of life, values, climate of humor, and range of sensibility.
Things which can raise a laugh in Chicago or Stockholm may be of-
fensive or callous in Prague or Tokyo. The world is full of barriers:
national, political, ideological, social, economic, and linguistic. The linguistic barrier is perhaps the least difficult of them all, and a great deal
remains to be done in this respect for the sake of human communications
over the frontiers. Perhaps we should be more alive to what the apostle
Paul had to say to the Corinthians (I Cor. 14:10, 11): "There are, it
may be, many kinds of voices in the world, and none of them is without

signification. Therefore if I know not the meaning of the voice, I shall be unto him that speaketh a barba.ian, and he that speaketh shall be a barbarian unto me."

Barriers are raised, not only by our ideologies and national circumstances, but also by differences of human background as expressed in language. Deliberate linguistic planning at the international level, e.g., within the sphere of librarianship, would be an important investment. By this I mean something more than the current bi- or polylinguality which is traditionally incumbent on people in the small language areas of the world. This is a privilege that ought to be shared by the major language areas too. For words are difficult, all of us here today know that, words being part of our business, and words have never been more difficult or more dangerous than they are now. The younger generation must learn to defend themselves against the printed word and to build up their powers of resistance in the welter of ideas and ideologies that fills the world today. As Boris Pasternak has put it, we must "teach young people the habit of independent thought."

My two predecessors Mrs. Margery Fisher and Mr. John Rowe Townsend are both well-known authorities in the field of British children's books and come from a language area which has shown the way to the rest of the world in this particular field. Neither should it be forgotten that it was Britain and the United States who paved the way for the most important and democratic book instrument ever: the public library. It goes without saying that many stages have been passed and many countries have tried different roads and approaches especially within the field of library work for children and children's book methodology as a whole. There are many different worlds of children's books and many different approaches. It is about some of these I would like to speak today.

I come from a small language area. Sweden has just over eight million inhabitants. We have become known for a few things: an unbroken period of peace since 1812, during which it has been our good fortune to remain outside international conflicts. We have reached a high level of affluence which has facilitated social reforms: a welfare state costs a lot of money. We have become known for other things as well: steel, matches, furniture, sex, and sin. A number of our children's books have managed to break through the difficult barrier of language. Before World War II Selma Lagerlöf's *The Wonderful Adventures of Nils* was practically the only Swedish children's book to have been translated, apart from some of Elsa Beskow's picture story books. Our latest exports within the field of children's books are marked by their political awareness and social messages and have caused quite a stir abroad among those who love to report about events and pseudo-events in social-democratic Sweden. Yes, our exports indeed resemble our climate: les extrêmes se touchent. When we want to travel outside Scandinavia the Swedish language is not serviceable for very long: Dutch, Estonian, Finnish, German, Latvian, Lithuanian, Polish, and Russian are all spoken within a few miles of our national borders. This is quite a typical European language situation, a far cry from the linguistic uniformity of the North American continent. Despite the international attention it has gained since the last war, 50 percent or more of our children's literature is made up of translations. Many different streams flow together in our little corner of the world. The profile of children's literature in a small language area is a good starting point for anybody who sets out to study channels of distribution—one of the many Cinderellas of research in this field. The volume of publication in Sweden is unusually high in relation to the small number of people who understand the language: eight million. If one considers the number of titles published—8,484 in 1970 (637 of them books for children and young people), Swedish book publication per capita is more or less on a level with Great Britain, although England has the whole world for its reading public while Sweden's is less than the population of Greater London.

For many years my daily job was to bring books to children and children to books. Since 1966 I have, if I may say so, been trying to bring children's books to adults within the sphere of operations of the Swedish Institute for Children's Books. I was curious to see if working right in the adult camp, so to speak, would help me to understand why children's books were taken seriously by such a comparatively small number of groups and individuals and why children's literature, in spite of all assurances to the contrary, existed in a vacuum unrelated to literature as a whole. I found this indifference all the more incomprehensible in view of the educational ideal which has characterized children's literature through the ages and, whether we like it or not, continues to do so. But this seemed to me to be only part of a far greater complex of problems concerning the entire social situation of the child: not only children's culture but children themselves exist in a vacuum, almost entirely cut off from adult life. This lack of integration in the adult world is accentuated still further when children reach their teens. One Swedish research scholar in the field of children's books, Göte Klingberg, has among other things studied the social situation of children in earlier periods and analyzed the changing view of childhood. I quote:

It is adult views of childhood that make children what they are. This has always been so. We must not forget that children are not innocent, charming, natural or primitive by nature, any more than they are congenitally depraved. The child's age sets the limit for the possible. But these limits have indubitably shifted over the centuries at the behest of the adult generation.

Although, in most parts of the world children's books have not been made a natural component of the history of literature, few other genres have been so ruthlessly manipulated by the adult generation. It is their desires and expectations which have dominated the whole of children's literature in most countries and still do so today. At the same time we protest our disbelief in the adult domination of our children, we still expect the adults of tomorrow to develop into internationalists, patriots, pacifists, believers, unbelievers, democrats, republicans, or socialists according to our own convictions. More often than not our motives are quite impeccable: we want our children to make the world a better place than we have succeeded in making it ourselves.

It is a curious feat of intellectual gymnastics to believe that, with all these different aspirations, we can escape the realities of politics, ideologies, and economics in children's literature. It seems to me that our eyes have been closed quite long enough to some of these hard facts: we still work with too many romantic beliefs and sentimental slogans, both nationally and internationally. All the time decisions are being made at various levels about the reading of the young. Workers in the field of children's books can never ignore the educational system and its goals. In most countries, even the most democratic, education is the most important instrument that society needs and uses to attain its objectives. Other forces came into play in the course of time. It was during the nineteenth century that the children's book was found to be not only an excellent educational instrument but also a profitable consumer commodity and, judging by contemporary voices, the output of children's books on the continent of Europe must have seemed like a deluge. Plus ça change. . . . Every autumn season I reach down for a book by Friedrich Gedicke, who was headmaster of a high school in Berlin as long ago as 1787. This, translated into English, is one of the many things he has to say on the subject:

None of the consumer articles of today rides on the crest of such a wave as children's books, which are produced for all classes and ages. After every book fair in Leipzig they descend on us like a tidal wave. . . . We are engulfed by children's calendars, children's songs, children's novels, children's comedies, children's tragedies, there are books of logic for children, catechisms for children, morals for children, grammars for children, homilies for children and so on and so forth.[1]

Dr. Gedicke appears to adopt quite an original view of children's books for, at the same time he denigrates the dry-as-dust children's books of yesteryear, he finds those of his own time insufferably contrived or wishy-washy. It would have been interesting to hear his views on the enormous children's book explosion now occurring in the western world, when so many children in the third world are inexorably relegated to illiteracy with all the human degradation it implies.

[1] *Gesammelte Schulschriften* (Berlin: Johann Friedrich Unger, 1789) , v.1, p.422–66.

One looks in vain in the historical surveys of children's literature in different countries for the bulk of consumer literature for children: an important section of the primary material has simply been omitted. Practically all we find are the acknowledged children's books of the higher publishing trade stamped with what we consider literary merit. A few older popular titles may be let in now and then, for nostalgic reasons. Reading the different surveys of children's literature one wonders what the everyday reading of children has really been like for the past two hundred years. Which children and how many of them—even in countries with high educational standards—have had the reading ability and financial resources over these two centuries to choose the most educational or aesthetically appealing books, the books repeatedly mentioned in history after history of children's literature in different countries? Very few. The small percentage of children and young people who were literate obtained their reading material from the pedlar's pack and the stationer's, just as so many of the children and young people of today derive their daily cultural bread from the newsstand.

One looks in vain to the historical surveys of children's literature for facts instead of deprecating remarks on this tremendously widespread literary fare. Horst Kunze, the director of Deutsche Staatsbibliothek in Berlin, East Germany, and the founder of one of the first research institutions for children's books to be sponsored by a large national library, has said that we are all the time occupied with a small select distillation of earlier children's literature: not even in the major language areas, e.g., the German or Anglo-American, is there any fundamental presentation of material to be had. Nor is there any international comparative survey of children's literature which genuinely tries to trace and define the distribution routes and translation movements of children's literature. All that is done is to cull a little here and a little there, for instance, *Les Malheurs de Sophie* by Comtesse de Ségur from France, *Struwwelpeter* by Heinrich Hoffmann from Germany, *Pinocchio* by Collodi from Italy, *The Wonderful Adventures of Nils* by Selma Lagerlöf from Sweden, and last but not least *Orbis Sensualium Pictus* by Jan Komensky, as the Czechs themselves call him, from Bohemia. The picture of translation activities given in our histories of children's literature is woefully incomplete in every respect. The situation may improve now that sociologists, literary and otherwise, are devoting so much interest to children's books—especially the great volume of consumer literature. But the lack of documentation of this literature will give rise to innumerable difficulties. We should at least make sure that we play our part by documenting what exists today. A quotation from Robert Escarpit would not be altogether out of place in this connection:

It is not immaterial to the understanding of the people concerned that authorship is now an occupation . . . practised in the context of economic systems which have an undeniable influence on the creative process. It is not immaterial to the understanding of these people's works that books are products manufactured and distributed commercially and consequently subject to the law of supply and demand . . .[2]

So there is certainly not "one world of children's books" but many that we have failed to see both inside our own language and on the other side of the border. There are also many worlds of children's books that we have avoided seeing, not only because of linguistic inability but because of discrepancies with our way of thinking and our sets of values. As I see it children cannot and must not be shielded from social developments or world events. Reality should be interpreted in a way which children can understand and sustain. They need our honest and concrete help, not our adult disillusionment or cowardly euphemisms. What kind of truth do children obtain from their books and how do we interpret for them the realities of countries with political régimes and ideological frameworks which differ from our own? We respond with silence to the ideological struggle we see around us. But do we have the right to let the ideological worlds and realities of so many countries remain *terra incognita* to those who will one day grow up to succeed us?

In his novel *Cancer Ward,* published outside the USSR in 1968, Alexander Solzhenitsyn lets the exiled former literary historian Jelisaveta Antoljevna, now an eternally scrubbing hospital orderly, ask concerning her son:

. . . The trouble is, my boy's growing up, he's clever and asks about everything. How ought I to bring him up? Should I burden him with the whole truth? The truth's enough to sink a grown man, isn't it? It's enough to break your ribs. Or should I hide the truth and bring him to terms with life? Is that the right way? What would his father say? And would I succeed? After all, the boy's got eyes of his own, he can see.

Solzhenitsyn makes his alter ego Oleg Kostoglotov answer: "Burden him with the truth." Here in a few lines the Russian author has defined what is so often the burden of discussions concerning children's books: how large a portion of the truth should be served to the rising generation and in what way?

Early ideological and political criticism of established children's literature have been as sadly neglected by our national histories as the profile of children's books in eastern Europe or the prospect of a concrete exchange of children's books. If our standard surveys had told us about the ideological and political criticism which first developed, e.g., during the 1870s in the German Social Democratic movement, and which in due course was to receive its first practical field of work in the Soviet Union after the October Revolution, we would be in a better position to com-

[2] Robert Escarpit, *Sociologie de la Littérature* (1958) .

prehend present-day events, among other things. The first socialist children's books are now about 100 years old and ought by now to be innocuous enough for inclusion in the history of children's literature.

Apart from old and new national frontiers, the world is divided into clear ideological fields—political fields—which in no wise exclude the children's book. Far from it, the whole of our modern book industry is harnessed in the struggle for the souls of men—and the souls of children. There is nothing new in this of course: literature for both children and adults has long been made to serve a didactical purpose in society in a variety of ways. Even the French authoress Germaine de Staël von Holstein—Madame de Staël (1766–1817)—who was among other things banished from Paris and France by Napoleon, raised this important question in a work published in 1800: *De la Littérature Considerée dans ses Rapports avec les Institutions Sociales*. It was later published in England in 1812 under the title *The Influence of Literature upon Society*. In the introduction we read:

The object of the present work is to examine what influence religion, manners, and laws have upon literature and reciprocally how far literature may effect laws, manners, and religion.[3]

Unfortunately Mme. de Staël was not farsighted enough to draw on the children's books of her own time: probably they would have come as a profound shock to such a free thinking and cosmopolitan lady, though they would also have served her purpose admirably. The didactic children's books of the Enlightenment, i.e., Mme. de Staël's own period, catered for an affluent social class and were predominantly aimed at the defense of established authority and religion. Mme. de Staël did her countrymen a great service by acquainting them with other cultures and social systems in the midst of a turbulent Europe devastated by the interminable wars of Napoleon. Her cultural reportages from Germany paved the way for the French romantics. She certainly knew how to write controversially and as an agitator she overshadows more than a few, Marcuse and McLuhan among them. Her books disseminated ideas and knowledge of the new patterns of thought that were developing in the heart of Europe.

Children's books and politics have always been a delicate subject for western democracy and perhaps most of all for the people actually concerned with children's literature. Many people, both professionals and amateurs, would never dream of using books to exert any kind of political pressure on children. Here one stands to benefit from a perusal of earlier children's literature seen in a new perspective. In his preface to

---

[3] First ed. entitled: *A Treatise on Ancient and Modern Literature*. Illustrated by striking references to the principal events and characters that have distinguished the French Revolution (London, 1803) .

the first edition of his *Children's Books in England. Five Centuries of Social Life,* Harvey Darton writes that ". . . children's books were always the scene of a battle between instruction and amusement, between restraint and freedom, between hesitant morality and spontaneous happiness. That conflict is not confined to the nursery." Thus efforts have always been made to influence children religiously or politically, though perhaps with less divergent premises and less rigid ideological demarcations than at present. From its very inception the children's book was designed for the preservation of established society and catered first and foremost for the boys who would one day become the pillars of that society. In feudal Europe everybody was expected to know their station and, preferably, to remain there. Students of children's books commend Jean-Jacques Rousseau, among other things because he was one of the first to point out the intrinsic value of childhood, but we tend to forget that in his famous *Émile, ou de L'Éducation* from 1762 he too affirmed—in a good many pages—that girls did not need a literary education since their function in life was predominantly biological. Later on, as children's literature became sexually segregated, the roles and stations appointed for girls were meticulously dinned into them through their reading matter. But in many of these now so abhorrent girls' books one can discern an early protest against the current system of child education, against the so-called womanly virtues, against the lack of education and job opportunities. The many detractors of girls' books have been unduly monolithic in their approach and have shown too little interest in the background—the social status of girls, their educational, occupational, and economic opportunities. Behind the girl's book one can trace many features of the history and attitudes of the entire century, the background and activities of the first women writers, religious and social trends, economic conditions, the surplus of women, the women's emancipation movement and, what is perhaps most important of all, the ideal of womanly upbringing and education. Girls were deliberately excluded from the intellectual trends and social change of their times. But there were rebels among them, and many escapes were attempted.

There were of course many others who kept to the subjects of religion and suitable qualms of conscience, but these too are an important part of the picture. The glib repetitiveness of the serial books produced by the successful girls' writers should not be allowed to obscure the genuine environment and the psychological perception which this genre brought to children's literature. People nowadays are right in rejecting the idea of books for boys or girls only. But even then girls' books were popularly smiled at. Boys' books on the other hand were seldom viewed in the same critical light, which was unfortunate. If girls' books were prudish, boys' books were no less handicapped by their emotional sterility and their adulation of beefy biceps, not to mention their preoccupation with war, otherwise known as adventure.

During the romantic period, which among other things produced a series of nationalist revivals all over Europe, children's books became an important instrument of patriotism: in some countries they actually helped to consolidate opposition against political and foreign oppression. The collection of folktales and folk songs was part of these nationalist endeavors, but it also had a decisive influence on the literary languages of many small and in some cases nonindependent European countries, a fact which is often overlooked. This was the case, for instance, with the Norwegian folktales, which were collected at a time when there existed a great gulf between the written and spoken languages. Nor should we forget that in many countries, e.g., in central Europe, the right to use one's native language could not be taken for granted. This has contributed in no small measure to all sorts of nationalistic tub-thumping and the constantly recurring manifestations in book after book of the heroic past or the grandeur and beauty of the native tongue. It is a salutary exercise to stop and consider the implications of having to abandon one's own language in order to acquire education and be able to read and communicate in writing. Once again the third world comes to mind.

Romantic nationalism is perhaps above all evident in the historical novel. Europe was in need of historical retrospect. The emphasis was on war, depicted as a grand adventure, there was a conspicuous element of chauvinistic self-esteem and a correspondingly distorted image of the international opposition. Now and then educationalists and an enlightened public would voice their disapproval of this kind of historiography, but their protests would be silenced by regularly recurring major wars. Only since the end of World War II has it been possible to discern any significant change in this respect. Pacifist tendencies were first expressed by religious books with their message of peace on earth and in utopian visions of the future. Sunday school stories, which were enormously popular throughout the world between 1800 and 1900—my own country imported any number of Sunday school tracts from the Anglo-American market—contained early ventures in antiwar propaganda and pacifism. Books describing conditions on the home front did not as a rule evince any great delight in war, either, though the spectacle of a devastated home often inspired descriptions of a brutal, inhuman enemy. The background was seldom gone into.

Wars have been waged almost uninterruptedly in the world and new generations have constantly had to be prepared to fight in them. The Austrian writer Bertha von Suttner, née Kinsky (1843–1914), was one of the first people to labor in word and deed for peace in a concrete manner. Before her marriage to Arthur von Suttner she had been Alfred Nobel's private secretary in Paris and later she and her husband got in touch with a peace organization, the International Peace and Arbitration Organization, which was led from London by Hodgson Pratt. Bertha von Suttner had seen the horrors of war at close quarters in central Europe and when in 1889 she came out with her pacifist novel *Die Waffen Nieder* (published in English in 1892 under the title *Lay Down Your Arms*), she had great difficulty in finding a publisher: the novel was considered politically risqué and tendentious. It came out in several languages and special editions for young people were also published. It has not been reprinted for a long time, although its content is still very much up to date. Permit me to quote a passage which many news bulletins have made familiar to us:

The village is ours . . . no, it is the enemy's . . . and ours again . . . and the enemy's again . . . but it is not a village any more, just a pile of smouldering ruins . . .

Every age has felt the need to provide new instructions in its children's books on how life is to be lived. Thus children's books do not merely reflect the contemporary social scene and the problems of adult life, the simplified manner in which they treat their subjects also makes them something of magnifying glasses. Many people have defined the political function of books, among them George Orwell. He says in "Why I Write":

Political purposes—using the word "political" in the widest possible sense. Desire to push the world in a certain direction, to alter other people's idea of the kind of society that they should strive after. Once again, no book is genuinely free from political bias. The opinion that art should have nothing to do with politics is itself a political attitude.[4]

Orwell, who has given a more vivid portrait than anybody of the future we have to expect if we do not do something about it in time, has critically examined children's books in a variety of contexts in his essays, which are well worth reading.

Responsible people in the new socialist states set up after the First and Second World wars realized from the very outset the function of the children's book as a means of political education. In contrast to the western democracies, who operate under the cloak of education, the eastern countries made children's books a matter of state and the subject of express directives (with the author's union as the deciding body) concerning both subject matter and its treatment.

The socialist children's book evolved in the USSR after the First World War and in a series of other eastern European countries together with China after the end of World War II. I feel that a great deal of effort, above all new effort, is needed to extend our knowledge of this form of children's literature. The meagre material available in the west is of little use owing to its pre-eminently antagonistic attitude—there

[4] *The Collected Essays, Journalism and Letters of George Orwell;* ed. by Sonia Orwell and Ian Angus, v.1, *An Age Like This,* 1968, p.26.

may be a few exceptions—and the few glimpses we get of this children's literature are generally biased. This of course is due to the world situation and the ideological boundaries—a corresponding bias exists of course in the east with regard to our western children's literature. But is it not time, as Boris Pasternak has put it, "in these days which are so heavy with suspicion to try to clear up some of our misunderstandings?" If we are willing to attempt real co-existence at an ideological level in the sphere of children's books, we will have to surmount many prejudices and we will have to renounce the fond idea that unpleasant problems can be avoided so long as they are not mentioned. If we are to succeed in opposing the socialist or Marxist children's book we must begin by learning more about it. A retrospective view generally helps to open and broaden the horizon. The children's literature of the USSR did not spring fully grown from the October Revolution of 1917—literature cannot be geared to new criteria in the twinkling of an eye—the theoretical basis of this literature began to take shape far earlier, before and around the turn of the century, as the revolutionary movements in Europe began to acquire definite contours and well-defined objectives.

In October last year, while I was attending the symposium of the International Society of Children's Books in Frankfurt, West Germany, I spent part of my Saturday walking round the campus of the Johann Wolfgang Goethe University. Among other things I visited a Marxist students' bookshop—one of a chain which is represented in a number of European capitals, including Paris and Zürich. Children's books were ranged on a special counter—I recognized some of our exports. But my interest was caught by the name of Hermynia zur Mühlen, whose "tales for the poor" were reissued in West Germany in 1970 and 1971. She was an Austrian socialist who before and after World War I made an important contribution together with her husband Stefan J. Klein by translating stories on social subjects from Hungarian into German. Her own stories for proletarian children—*Märchen der Armen*—appeared during the 1920s in Berlin. One of the illustrators of the series was George Grosz, who fled to this country when the Nazis came to power and was granted asylum here. It was the encounter with this new edition that gave me the idea of the theme of this lecture and it was my conversations in East Berlin with Horst Kunze and Heinz Wegehaupt which brought some of the problems of internationalism within the world of children's books into focus. Together these two men embody a formidable knowledge of the historical and Marxist aspects of children's literature. It was Horst Kunze who raised the question of fragmentary and one-sided knowledge of children's books in his justly famous foreword to *Schatzbehalter*, an anthology of children's literature in Germany from the mid-eighteenth century up to 1914. This hundred-page foreword, modestly entitled, "Ein Wenig Theorie," gives a clear and consistent argument concerning children's books, claiming that existing bibliographies and surveys have generally been compiled to suit traditional or personal preferences. Kunze feels that the time has come for a historical and sociological elucidation of the development of the children's book and that due place must therefore be given to the great consumers' literature for children. His review contains a great deal worth pondering, discussing, and, of course, contradicting.

In this foreword Horst Kunze also provided a sketch of the work done on children's books by the social democratic movement, and he established that children's literature figured on the agenda starting with the second party congress held in Dresden in 1871. Children's books were regarded as part and parcel of the political education of the young and the course of the debate can be followed in considerable detail in the German labor press down to the 1920s. It is an interesting debate, many of the leading political figures of the movement warned their followers not to publish proletarian children's books (tailor-made socialist children's books). But the first venture appeared between 1893-95 and in 1900, namely, *Bilderbuch für Grosse und Kleine Kinder,* published in four parts in Stuttgart. This was criticized, however, in the journal *Die Neue Zeit* (1893/94, Jahrg. 12, no.11) by Karl Kautsky, who felt that children's books should not be concerned with propaganda or with the fundamental tenets of socialism. Children's books should be character forming. Kautsky has been severely criticized on this account by later theoreticians in the field of children's literature, especially in East Germany. But many of his contemporaries in the social democratic movement were against the idea of tailor-made socialist children's literature, on the grounds that this would put them in the same boat as the producers of religious and chauvinistic children's books. Nor should we forget that it was the social democrats who were quick to dissociate themselves from the crude chauvinism of the patriotic books for children and young people which flourished in Imperial Germany before the first war. This was the seedbed of the Nazi children's books which were to leave such a mark on the years between 1933 and 1945.

By far the most lucid argument put forward within the social democratic movement on the subject of children's books came from Clara Zetkin (1857-1933), an active protagonist of women's rights, an issue which she regarded as a social problem and, accordingly, inseparable from the general political struggle. She was for many years the editor of the social democratic women's publication *Die Gleichheit.* At the social democratic rally in Mannheim in 1906 she gave a speech on child education which has come to rank as a classic and which is often quoted in eastern Europe on the subject of children's books. In fact many of the leaders of the German social democratic movement emigrated to the USSR after World War I and again with the advent to power of Hitler.

They made valuable contributions in Russia until they were silenced forever by the Stalin régime.

This debate is not mentioned in many of the standard German histories of children's literature published in the west, but some of it is described in Hermann Köster's *Geschichte der Deutschen Jugendliteratur,* published in 1927 (reprinted in 1968). Köster realized the significance of this discussion and it was no coincidence that he was suspended from his post as educational administrator as soon as the Nazis came to power. We know very little as yet about the part played by social democracy in children's literature outside the German language area, but in view of the watertight compartments that segregate the world of children's books in German from that of America one would probably be hard put to it to find any reflection here of the debate begun by Heinrich Wolgast and the contribution he made in the German "Jugendschriftenbewegung." A great deal of the contemporary West German or central European debate on children's books, which is so alien and incomprehensible to the Anglo-American side, began with Wolgast. Heinrich Wolgast was a teacher in Hamburg who was passionately interested in the "Kunsterziehungsbewegung," i.e., educational work designed to teach the masses to appreciate art. It has been said that Wolgast's polemical essay on the decline of literature for the young, *Das Elend unserer Jugendliteratur* (1896), transplanted this movement to children's literature. His main thesis has been an abomination to many: "A book for children and young people must be a work of art. Literary works of art are a part of literature in general, so that literature specifically designed for children and young people should not be allowed to exist." Many people contradicted him, among them Erwin Ackerknecht, one of the leading liberal librarians in Germany, in what is now a classic work of German literary criticism, *Jugendlektüre und Deutsche Bildungsideale* (1914). Well, children's literature survived and Wolgast's book, the most recent German edition of which came out in 1950, was meant to sound the alarm. The tocsin was heard across the continent of Europe and as far away as Scandinavia. Happily to relate, Heinrich Wolgast was spared the true misery which children's literature could be plunged into: the Nazi children's book came after his time.

German histories are extremely reticent about this kind of children's book too, while on the Anglo-American side it is passed over in almost complete silence, apart from sporadic mentions in journals of children's literature. Here I would like to mention an important documentary work by Peter Aley, *Jugendliteratur im Dritten Reich* (1967). The author has tried to outline the vicissitudes of the children's book during the Hitler era using documents and published materials. He draws no conclusions and offers no comments on his own behalf: instead the terrifying material is left to tell its own story. Klaus Doderer, the leader of the institution for children's books in Frankfurt, who headed this project, remarks that Peter Aley has succeeded in capturing not only the enforced official attitudes of Nazi children's literature but also its triviality and mediocrity. The author has given us a glimpse behind the Nazi scene and shown that the process of cultural impoverishment was not confined to contemporary children's literature—there were hardly any translations to be had except from the Aryan north, great scope being given to the Norse sagas—but also left its mark on adaptations of earlier children's classics. Thus in the case of *Robinson Crusoe*—a book which has been revised or condemned in the most varied connections—the Nazis required and obtained an adaptation which accentuated the human gulf between Robinson and Man Friday in the name of racial purity. And the unfortunate Spaniard who remained alone on the island was not permitted in the orthodox Nazi edition of Robinson to marry a native woman. We may laugh, but the laughter dies in our throats when we see some of the cruel and prejudiced books that the Nazis produced for their children. Peter Aley's documents show how purges of schools and libraries were begun as early as 1933 and how new principles for the writing of children's books were established in Germany. Once one has seen how the methods worked, the defense of the liberty of the printed word seems a more urgent task than ever. The entire debate on children's literature was swept under the carpet in Germany, the authors held their peace or emigrated. Erich Kästner stood and watched as his books were burned in the street. Now there are two Germanies which have gone their separate ways in the world of children's literature. Western Germany has opened its doors to the entire world, Eastern Germany has followed the tune of eastern Europe. But here too a remarkable change is in progress.

If we turn our attention to the USSR we encounter two names of paramount importance, Maxim Gorky and Kornej Chukovsky, both of whom, on somewhat different premises, have left their mark not only on the ideas current in the USSR concerning children's books but also in the socialist states—those of the Eastern bloc—established at the end of World War II. Perhaps we should also note that the view of children's books developed in the USSR has spread further afield as a result of new political constellations, e.g., into the socialist countries of Africa, Asia, and Latin America. It seems to me rather late in the day to try to understand what this view of children's literature is based on. Chukovsky's famous book *From Two to Five* is available here in an abridged and somewhat adapted translation, it has also been published in the eastern European countries. A comparison of the American and East German adaptations provides considerable food for thought. Gorky's collected essays on children's books have been ignored in the western world, although they are mentioned in bibliographies. There are two East German editions, the most recent of them published in 1968 under the title *Über Kinder und Jugendliteratur*. His ideas on children's books are axiomatic in other east European countries as well, and it is difficult to arrive at a proper appreciation of children's books in Russia without having read Gorky's essays.

The Russian literary critic Vissarion Belinsky (1810–1848) has also come to play a part in the theory of children's literature in the eastern countries, and in recent years there has been a revival not only of his educational writings but also of his critical works on children's literature, published in Russia during the 1830s. People in the eastern countries are fond of quoting what Belinsky once wrote in a devastating review of an excessively didactic children's book: "A well-brought-up child should be neither a domestic pet nor an adult but a child." He was well ahead of his times.

Our various historical outlines devote very little space to Maxim Gorky and the influence he came to exert on cultural policies after the October Revolution and his long work of preparation for the new children's book. He had already taken an interest in children's books at the turn of the century, working with—among others—the Tsarist Ministry for Education and Family Affairs and compiling—again, among other things—a checklist of children's literature as well as founding a children's library on a philanthropic basis. By 1910 he had defined the new realistic children's literature as he wished to see it. During the First World War he wrote a series of articles in which he vehemently condemned the chauvinistic wartime literature for children published by both sides. When the October Revolution broke out Gorky was well prepared for the contribution he was to make, namely, the foundation and development of Soviet children's literature. Gorky became the leader, theoretician, and, above all, the tireless critic of this literature. The pioneers of the first socialist state were confronted with the task of building up a new form of culture, the culture of the workers. The thirteenth party congress in 1924 adopted a resolution to the effect that a corpus of children's literature was to be brought into being under the close supervision and direction of the party, thus initiating the children in the idea of the class struggle and promoting proletarian internationalism and the collective endeavor. It was Gorky who coined the expression "socialist realism," which he considered very much a part of children's literature. This realism entailed a positive, heroic depiction of the course of social development. Literature was to serve a didactic purpose and children's books were to be given a pre-eminent political and social function. The collective was to be described first and foremost, one should avoid the detailed descriptions of the small problems of small people or the insignificant conscience troubles of the propertied classes that prevailed in the west. This is not the place to go into further detail concerning the complex battle of ideas that was fought out in the Russian literature of the twenties and thirties until the Stalin epoch cast its shadow across every sector of the arts, particularly the printed word. We know that this resulted in paralysis, stagnation, and personal literary tragedies of enormous dimensions. Many books were written in accordance with the official recipe.[5] It is difficult to hear any living pulse in those works, the authors did not dare to set their personal mark on their material, the main thing was for them to preach the right ideas. The Stalin epoch was followed by the thaw, and we know that Russian literature today is on the threshold of a rebirth. Let us hope that this will also benefit the children's book and let us keep a weather eye open for the new children's book when it comes.

In the definitive edition of Gorky's essays and letters concerning children's books we can see how he defended the fairy tale and the freedom of the imagination. Thus, contrary to what we are often led to believe, his essays are not confined to theses on the importance of the children's book in the construction of a socialist community. Some editions of these essays in the west would do a great deal to improve our knowledge of the contemporary Russian children's book.

It is important for us to get to know not only the theoretical view adopted regarding children's books and the way in which it was expressed at top level but also the working methods of children's and school libraries. After all, it was the librarians who had to put the orders into effect. One of the leaders of the library system was Lenin's wife Nadeshda Krupskaya, who was the author of many publications concerning children's literature. She led a number of book purges soon after the October Revolution, when she held a senior position in the Commisariat of Education, book purges as drastic as those of Hitler's Germany. A great deal vanished from the children's libraries, bringing voluble protests from Gorky. It is extremely interesting to read about the difficulties of one Madame Smushkova, then chairman of a Central Library Commission, who had to write a special article on the topic "On the Problem of the Removal of Literature." You can read about these early Russian librarians who were so reluctant to take part in the campaign for removing books in *Survey, a Journal of Soviet and East European Studies* (1969, no.72), the article written by Bertram D. Wolfe. For the twenties witnessed a discussion which we should have kept track of before so many voices were silenced forever. Anybody interested in the present official Russian approach to library work with children should read Mme. N. B. Medvedeva's *Report on the Various Types of Research into Children's Literature and Children's Libraries.* The report was first presented at the session of the section of library work with children of the International Federation of Library Associations in Moscow in 1970. May I personally add one thing: Whenever we receive an east European children's book

---

[5] Thus one of Lucy Sprague Mitchell's stories was published in German in Moscow in 1929: *Lied der Neuen Lokomotive. Für den Kindergarten* (Moscow: Zentral-Völker-Verlag) , 11p.

of which we feel critical, we should remember the position of authors in those countries. They have to decide whether to write or be silent.

Chinese children's literature provides another example of writing steered by political considerations. Lu Hsün, who was a senior functionary in the Chinese educational system during the 1930s, is not altogether unknown to us. He also published a collection of essays on children's books and his career resembled Gorky's in more ways than one. Lu Hsün also rejected the bourgeois literature of the west—with the possible exception of classics and fairy tales—and called for a children's literature that would help to fit people for the classless society. He achieved posthumous importance when Mao Tse Tung exalted him as the foremost Marxist-Leninist literary critic in China.

But now we are beginning to receive reports on the children's literature of present-day China. Here I am thinking of Jean-Pierre Diény's study, *Le Monde est à Vous. Le Chine et les Livres pour Enfants,* published in France in 1971 and almost immediately reviewed by a literary critic in one of the leading Stockholm dailies. I am told it is now in the course of translation here. Diény, who is a sinologist, was in China during the cultural revolution, attached to a college of education there, and when he returned to France he brought with him 180 Chinese children's books which he had purchased between 1964 and 1966. He has analyzed this material in terms of themes and subject treatment, as well as going into format and illustration. The children's political development is the main consideration, the principal aim being to arouse their class consciousness. Since the younger generation never knew the oppression of the prerevolutionary society, children's books serve an important function by helping them to realize the differences between the China of yesterday and today. One regularly recurring theme shows how the peasants used to toil under the tyranny of the landlords or the contrast between workers and factory owners. Imperialism has been dealt with in many books, and the work of the missionaries is portrayed in an equally unfavorable light. We find here the same heroics and panegyrics concerning the collective as in the children's literature of Soviet Russia. The People's Liberation Army is one of the central themes. A presentation is given not only of former social conflicts but also of China's relations with the rest of the world. Diény shows that the ancient folktales and fables tend to be left aside since it is feared that they might sow heresy: an idyllic portrayal of the past could make readers forget the actual class conflicts which were a part of it.

Here again we have a children's literature on the march which has abandoned literary and aesthetic criteria and given pride of place to political objectives. Probably it will be a good many years before there is room for anything else. Now that so many rapprochements have been made between China and the west, we must not neglect the opportunity of finding out more about this literature. What we need—and as quickly as possible—is more impartial and authoritative reports like Diény's. Opinions and attitudes must not be allowed to stand in the way of information. Conversations across the frontiers are made easier by a knowledge of other countries' premises and objectives, not least in the field of children's books. And free access to information and facts is considered one of the democratic virtues of the western world. The best way to deeper contact, to a scholarly and intellectual interchange, is through a widening of our lingistic skills. We can no longer allow everything to be filtered through two world languages. International understanding in any concrete form must be based on knowledge: knowledge of language, knowledge of the cultural and ideological values of other nations. Let us try some new door openers for international understanding. Let each of us in our various posts and countries do what we can to advance the positions of the children's book. Here are some of the ways I believe in:

1. Let us try to adopt new perspectives and ways of thinking, e.g., a literary-sociological perspective. Let us learn more about the dependence of children's books on social structure, culture, and ideas and about those by whom and for whom the books were written. More research is needed into the formation of attitudes by reading, e.g., attitudes to social groups, minorities, other countries. Let us find out more about the way in which educational policy in the democracies of the western world influences children's literature. One thing is sure: literary patents are not the monopoly of the eastern countries.

2. The world of children's books employs a phraseology which may have emerged during the pioneering years of the children's libraries but is now fairly obsolete. Now that our knowledge of the world of children's books is expanding, we should throw away such postulates as: If children in Poland or Ceylon read Perrault's *Contes* they will love La douce France as long as they live. Love is not that easy.

3. We need to collaborate with the largest possible number of branches of science using children's books as research material, e.g., the social and political sciences. We should welcome as much elucidation as possible in as many disciplines as possible. For years now the world of children's books has been clamoring for an academic interest in the subject, and now that this interest is beginning to emerge we find the world of children's books adopting a critical and standoffish attitude towards it. If we are criticized we must learn to take it. We have been quite introspective and isolated, we have moved in narrow circles. It is true that literary studies have neglected children's books and that this must be rectified. But have not we for our part tended to an excessive degree to shut ourselves off from literature as such? We must keep abreast of literary trends in order to understand the influences at work in children's

literature. Let us welcome greater cooperation between children's libraries and the academic side. Few can rival the children's librarians in their knowledge of their material, but we must cure ourselves of the habit of continually retracing the straight and narrow paths of selective methodology.

4. We need comparative research into children's literature. This requires a knowledge of languages together with both national and international teamwork. We can begin near home, e.g., by journals on children's literature in our various countries reserving an annual feature issue for the international sector. This could cover the publication profiles of different countries, as well as translations, theory, methodology, and matters concerning children's libraries.

To avoid unnecessary duplication the chief editors could join forces. The children's press is a large concern which few of us are able to view in general terms and isolated articles are hard to collate. For instance, why has the Czech periodical *Zlaty Máj* never been presented here or in Sweden to show what aspects of children's books were discussed in Czechoslovakia in 1971? I hope you do not think this sounds as deadly dull as writing annual reports. That is not my favorite occupation either, but there is one thing to be said for it: you can see what you have really been doing during the past year. And don't let's start yet another journal which we never have time to read: instead, let us expand and improve some of those we already have.

5. Library schools the world over need to elucidate the international aspect by means of obligatory courses. They must concentrate on things that are important, by which I mean things at grass roots, not on sporadic reports from international conferences. Many of these conferences have been important but they have been reported irregularly and diffusely, sometimes rather naively. Workers in the vineyards must also have a sense of involvement, a feeling that this concerns me. The results of the international conferences should be put into practice on the domestic plane. More languages must be studied in order to expand librarianship.

Conclusions

Internationalism within the field of children's books means patient work day after day, year in year out. International organizations help. IBBY, IFLA, and UNESCO provide a groundwork, scholarships help, workshops help, tours to foreign countries help, translations help. We need far more knowledge, reevaluation, and renewal. I regard the children's book as an incomparable instrument and a significant meeting point for people of different ages, different nationalities, and different convictions. But the world of children's books is not one; there are many.

Quoted and Consulted Literature

Aley, Peter. Jugendliteratur im Dritten Reich. Dokumente und Kommentare. Mit einem Vorwort von Klaus Doderer. Gütersloh: Bertelsmann, 1967. 262p. (Schriften zur Buchmachtforschung, 12).

Belinski, Wissarion G. Ausgewählte pädagogische Schriften. Herausgegeben vom Deutschen Pädagogischen Zentralinstitut. Berlin: Volk und Wissen Volkseigener Verlag, 1953. 347p. (Über Kinder- und Jugendlektüre p.234–79).

Chukovsky, Kornej. Kinder von 2 bis 5. Berlin: Der Kinderbuchverlag, 1968. 211p.

Chukovsky, Kornej. From Two to Five. Berkeley and Los Angeles: University of California Press, 1963. 163p.

Darton, Frederick Joseph Harvey. Children's Books in England. Five Centuries of Social Life. Cambridge: University Press, 1958. 367p.

Diény, Jean-Pierre. Le Monde est à Vous. La Chine et les Livres pour Enfants. Paris: Gallimard, 1971. 155p.

Doderer, Klaus. Jugendliteratur Heute. Eine Querschnittsanalyse des Jahrgangs. 1964. Frankfurt-am-Main: Institut für Jugendbuchforschung, 1965. 64p.

Doderer, Klaus. Klassische Kinder- und Jugendbücher. Kritische Betrachtungen. Weinheim-Berlin-Basel: Julius Beltz Verlag, 1970. 162p.

Escarpit, Robert. Sociologie de la Littérature. Paris: Presses Universitaires de France, 1968. 127p.

Escarpit, Robert. "Creative Treason" as a Key to Literature. Bloomington, Ind.: Yearbook of Comparative and General Literature, 1961, no.10, p.16–21.

Gedicke, Friedrich. Gesammelte Schulschriften. Berlin: Johann Friedrich Unger 1789, v.1, p.422–66.

Gorkij, Maxim. Über Kinder und Kinderliteratur. Berlin: Der Kinderbuchverlag, 1968. 242p.

Kaiser, Bruno. Zur Geschichte des Proletarischen Deutschen Kinderbuches, in Almanach für die Freunde des Kinderbuchs. 1949–59. Berlin: Der Kinderbuchverlag, 1959. p.33–41.

Kautsky, Karl. Editorial addendum to Das erste sozialdemokratische Bilderbuch by E. Erdmann. In Die Neue Zeit, Jahrg. 12, 1893/94 no.11, p.340–43.

Klingberg, Göte. Hur synen på barndomen förändrats, in Fataburen. Nordiska Museets och Skansens Årsbok, 1971. p.9–18.

Kunze, Horst. Schatzbehalter vom Besten aus der Älteren Deutschen Kinderliteratur. Berlin: Der Kinderbuchverlag, 1965. 444p.

Kunze, Horst. Lieblings-Bücher von Dazumal. Eine Blütenlese aus dem Erfolgreichsten Büchern von 1750–1860. Zugleich ein Erster Versuch zu einer Geschichte des Leserschmaks. München: Ernst Heimeren, 1965. 438p.

Köster, Hermann L. Geschichte der Deutschen Jugendliteratur in Monographien. Unveränderter, berechtiger Nachdruck 1968 der 4. Aufl. von 1927. Herausgegeben und mit einem Nachwort und einer Annotierten Bibliographie Versehen von Walter Scherf in Zusammenarbeit mit der Internationalen Jugendbibliothek, München. München: Verlag Dokumentation, 1968. 571p.

Literatur der Arbeiterklasse. Aufsätze über die Herausbildung der Deutschen Sozialistischen Literatur (1918–1933). Berlin and Weimar: Aufbau-Verlag, 1971. 799p.

Lu, Hsün. Den sanna historien om Ah Q och andra berättelser. Malmö: Bo Cavefors Bokförlag, 1972. 190p.

Ludwig, Nadeshda. Die Grundlegenden Wesenszüge der Sowjetischen Jugend-literatur einer Literatur des Sozialistischen Realismus (diss., Humboldt-Univ. Berlin). 1955. 296p.

Medvedeva, N. B. Report on the Various Types of Research into Children's Literature and Children's Libraries. International Federation of Library Associations. 36th sess., Sept. 1970, Moscow (mimeo) 24p.; also summary in YLG News, v.15 (1971), no.1, p.3–6.

Mitchell, Lucy Sprague. Lied der Neuen Lokomotive. Für den Kindergarten. Moscow: Zentral-Völker-Verlag, 1929. 11p.

Märchenbuch für die Kinder des Proletariats. Berlin: Baake, 1893. 157p.

Orwell, George. The Collected Essays, Journalism and Letters of George Orwell; ed. by Sonia Orwell and Ian Angus. 4v. Harmondsworth, Middlesex: Penguin Books, 1968.

Pasternak, Boris. Doctor Zhivago. London: Collins and Harvill Press, 1958. 510p.

Rousseau, Jean Jacques. Émile, ou de L'Education. 1–4. Amsterdam: J. Neaulme, 1762.

Schenda, Rudolf. Volk ohne Buch. Studien zur Sozialgeschichte der Populären Lesestoffe 1770–1910. Frankfurt-am-Main: Vittorio Klostermann, 1970. 607p. (Studien zur Philosophie und Literatur des Neunzehnten Jahrhunderts. Bd. 5.)

Solzhenitsyn, Alexander. Cancer Ward. New York: Bantam ed., 1969. 559p.

Staël-Holstein. Germaine de. A Treatise on Ancient and Modern Literature. Illustrated by Striking References to the Principal Events and Characters That Have Distinguished the French Revolution. 2v. London: G. Cawthorn, 1803.

Staël-Holstein, Germaine de. The Influence of Literature upon Society. 2d ed. 2v. London: Colburn, 1812.

Suttner, Bertha von. Lay Down Your Arms. The Autobiography of Martha von Tilling. London: Longmans & Co., 1892. 435p.

Wegehaupt, Heinz, comp. Kinder– und Jugendliteratur der Arbeiterklasse von den Anfängen bis 1945–eine Auswahl, In Beiträge zur Kinder- und Jugend-literatur (Berlin DDR). November 1970, p.102–10.

Wolfe, Bertram D. Krupskaya Purges the People's Libraries, In Survey. A Journal of Soviet and East European Studies (London), 1969, no.72, p.139–55.

Wolgast, Heinrich. Das Elend unserer Jugendliteratur. Ein Beitrag zur Künst-lerischen Erziehung der Jugend. 7. ed. Worms: Verlag Wunderlich, 1950. 351p.

Zetkin, Clara. In Protokoll über die Verhandlungen des Parteitages der Sozial-demokratischen Partei Deutschlands Abgehalten zu Mannheim vom 23. bis 29. September 1906: sowie Bericht über die 4. Frauenkonferenz am 22. u. 23. September 1906 in Mannheim. Berlin: Buchhandlung Vorwärts, 1906, p.347–59 (Title: Sozialdemokratie und Volkserziehung: Zetkins Korreferat).

Zur Mühlen, Hermynia. Was Peterchens Freunde Erzählen. Märchen. Mit Zeich-nungen von George Grosz. Berlin: Malik, 1921. 31p. (Märchen der Armen. 1.)

Bettina Hürlimann

88 Bettina Hürlimann, the daughter of two publishers,
grew up in Germany with a knowledge of and love
for books. She worked in publishing and later
established, with her husband, the Atlantis Verlag
in Switzerland. She has written several books for
children, but is perhaps better known for her
professional books: *Picture-Book World* (World
Publishing, 1969), *Three Centuries of Children's Books
in Europe* (World Publishing, 1968), and the
autobiographical *Seven Houses* (Crowell, 1977).

Particularly active on the international scene,
Bettina Hürlimann was one of the charter members
of the International Board on Books for Young
People, serving on its award jury and on the jury
for the Biennale of Illustrations Bratislava. As an
editor, she has been a pioneer in bringing to the
West books for children that had been published in
Japan and India, and in introducing authors and
artists of the West to the wider world of
international children's books. Her lecture,
"Fortunate Moments in Children's Books," was
presented in Kansas City, Missouri, by the Kansas
City Public Library and the School of Education,
University of Missouri, on April 27, 1973.

Fortunate Moments
in Children's Books

I COME FROM FAR AWAY TO YOU—from a country which is, like yours, a very old democracy; from the country where Rousseau and Pestalozzi were born and exercised tremendous influence, in educational and other affairs, upon the whole of Europe; from the country where the *Swiss Family Robinson* was written by a very education-minded father; and from the country where a severe-looking lady wrote the story of *Heidi* which, depending on our age, was the book with which our mothers, grandmothers, or even their mothers grew up. I was very happy to receive this invitation for the Arbuthnot lecture, especially since I knew Mrs. Arbuthnot's books. One was already on my shelf before I came to the United States for the first time, and it was one of my first guides to this country, the first door I was able to open. You are all foreigners to me, and I do not know what you expect of me. Children's books have to be, as Jella Lepman, the founder of the IBBY, used to say, a bridge, a bridge of international understanding. She meant it amongst children. This time it must be amongst grown-ups, amongst grown-up people who may even use children's books not only for children, but also as a medium for themselves and as a source of enjoyment. They may enjoy poetry

meant for children as poetry for themselves; they may receive knowledge and information about the life of children in foreign countries
or in bygone times from books written for young people.

For me, books (not only children's books, even pure fiction) are always a mirror of the country from which they come. When I went to
Russia for the first time last summer, I had the great figures of Tolstoy's
novels in my mind as well as those of Pasternak and Solzhenitsyn.
Through children's books I knew also about those eager, clear-eyed Russian children, tidy and well-behaved, who call themselves *pioneers* and
are so devoted to their country. The extraordinary thing was, that
through those books, the old and the new, I was quite well prepared for
what I found in reality, for the great Russian soul as well as for the
children of today. These tidy clear-eyed *red-ties* in Russia may be our
friends or our enemies in years to come, and it is good to know and understand them as well as we try to understand our own long-haired and
sometimes untidy young people who, in their way, strive also for a better
future.

My original intention was to show you how children's books were and
are a mirror of the child's position in society. Fortunately I read, before
I started on it, Mrs. Ørvig's brilliant lecture of last year about a rather
similar theme, which made me give up my ambitious plan. Instead, I
would like you to follow me into the past, where I shall describe to you
a few fortunate moments, or, as one would say today, a few "happenings," in the history of children's books, which seem to me typical and
significant though you may find my choice very personal. For me, the
history of children's books is very much alive. It has not become an abstract sort of science yet, and most scholars, i.e. the historians and the
professors of literature, do not include children's literature in their program, though one or the other may have discovered that certain books he
read when he was a child are masterpieces of poetry. So what I am going
to tell you now may not sound scientific; it is just a result of much reading and some imagination.

I am conscious of the fact that I am the first Arbuthnot-lecturer coming from the German-speaking world. I come from Switzerland—I am
Swiss—but I was born in Germany, in Weimar, the town where Goethe
lived. So I am connected with the German language in many ways. This
is not only the language of Goethe, Kant, the brothers Jakob and Wilhelm Grimm, of Thomas Mann, and of such people as Freud, C. G.
Jung, and Einstein, whose thoughts changed the outlook of our world,
but also the language spoken by Hitler and his companions. Nevertheless, or for just this reason, I shall take my examples, the stories I want
to tell you, chiefly from the German-speaking world. There are a lot of
reasons for this. If we believe that literature, especially children's litera-

ture, may be a medium of understanding amongst nations, real knowledge about each other's books is necessary. This mutual knowledge is still very small. And it must first exist amongst grownups, who may pass it on to children. In the indexes of Mrs. Arbuthnot's and other American books I have seen how few German names are mentioned. Our knowledge about each other's children's literature may even be wrong or at least one-sided. If you think how much sympathy and love amongst nations was created by children from books like *Heidi* (about which Mrs. Arbuthnot wrote some very beautiful lines) or from *Tom Sawyer* and *Huckleberry Finn,* who are so immensely loved and known in Europe, you realize there cannot be *enough* knowledge about each other's children's books, even about books less well-known than those just mentioned. For example, *Little Women* seems still to enjoy great popularity in your country, yet is completely unknown on the European continent. *Uncle Tom's Cabin* and shortened versions of *The Leatherstocking Tales* are not even mentioned in Mrs. Arbuthnot's books, which means they were not regarded as books for the young. In Europe, especially in German-speaking countries but also in others, they were for nearly a century the most beloved American books. The success of the popular editions of Cooper's books, for example, was the beginning of a whole genré of literature, *Indianerliteratur,* which was extremely important and formed our "image" of America. On the other hand, perhaps many Americans conclude from some of the most famous German fairy tales or from *Slovenly Peter (Struwwelpeter)* that there is a cruel element in most German children's literature, but this would be an equally false image. As you can see, there are curious and rather irrational relations among nations concerning the literature for children. Only real knowledge about books and their backgrounds, the real life behind it, can help to avoid errors, errors which may even be the beginning of prejudice and hate. Thus it is with a certain intention, but also out of love for my own language, that I choose most, but not all, of my examples from the German.

I start my tale in the century when your nation came into existence. Life in your country was so hard that there was no question of any real literature for children and still less of pictures. There was nothing but religion in the purest Puritan style. In 1646 a book for children came out which was called *Milk for Babes Drawn out of the Breasts of Both Testaments.* I mention this well known date for a special reason. The life and education of children was not much better on the European continent although Catholicism and Lutheran Protestantism allowed a little more color in the life of children. On the other hand, this was the same decade in which education and with it the story of children's literature took, here and there, a few steps forward which were fortunate for children. About two of these steps I want to speak now.

Comenius' *Orbis Pictus*

Let us enter a poor schoolroom in a village of Hungary. An elderly teacher, a foreigner, is the schoolmaster. The time is about 1650. Maybe the village people do not all know that their teacher with the sad face is a famous pedagogue of his time named Comenius who has written books like *Didactica Magna* or the *Janua Linguarum Reserata* (the open door of languages). He had also been the Bishop of the Bohemian Brethren, "Brothers in the Law of Christ," who had adopted an ethical system based on Christianity as well as on humanism. During the Thirty Years War his community was more or less extinguished, but lived on through the Moravian Brethren even in your country and in Germany through the Pietism of the eighteenth and nineteenth centuries. This movement was also much concerned with educational questions and literature for children. This old man from Bohemia, Comenius, had lost through the war everything a man can lose, all his belongings, his family, and even his community. What he had before him were poor children in a part of Europe which still suffered from the consequences of the long war. But this great humanist was still able to think about the children and what they needed most. He thought of the pious people who made their children suffer by teaching them the languages of the Bible, Greek, Latin, and Hebrew, when they were four years old, quite a natural thing to do at that time. And he thought of the girls and boys sitting in front of him who had no books at all, perhaps not even paper to write upon. He wanted the children to learn many things about God and the world He had created, about plants and stars, about clouds and rain, about sun and moon and geography. He included girls, the future mothers, in his teaching. He was for clean, well-aired classrooms and for physical exercise, and instead of making the children memorize abstracted knowledge he went out with them to observe nature. This was a very new thing to do. When he returned with them to the classroom he put their experiences into clear and very simple sentences which he wrote down for the children. Maybe he even made little drawings on the blackboard or on a piece of paper to illustrate his words. One is not sure about this, but if you think what he did afterwards you can well imagine that he did what most modern teachers find quite natural to do. Naturally most schoolchildren of that time had to learn Latin, so things were written down in Latin as well as in the children's own language. It was an amusing and poetic way to learn this old language. Comenius must have thought so himself, otherwise he would not have written down the simple sentences and taken with him the sketches of a little book which he called *Orbis Pictus* or *Painted World*. He was on the way to the last station of his life, to Amsterdam. Perhaps on his way he passed by Nuremberg and talked with its famous printers and his own publishers about the illustrations for his little book. Even very clever experts have not found out for sure whether Comenius drew the illustrations himself or simply made sketches or merely instructed artists as to what to do. One knows the artists who did the final woodcuts. In any case the pictures are in wonderful harmony with the text, and the book was to become for more than a century the most popular book with children of all classes.

We have left our village-classroom by now together with the teacher, who lived until 1670 in Amsterdam, saw his *Orbis Pictus* coming out in 1658 in different languages, and would probably have been very satisfied had he foreseen that his little book would be used a century later by a small boy called Johann Wolfgang Goethe and that more than 300 years later reprints of this old book could be enjoyed. Children today, learning Latin still find the book amusing. But the story of this book and its influence on future publications is a story in itself.

Conrad Meyer's *Sechsundzwanzig nichtige Kinderspiel*

Let us move to another place. A year before *Orbis Pictus* came out (1657), in Zürich, Switzerland, a very different illustrated book for children appeared. It was about children's games and the moralizing text had been written thirty years before by a Dutch poet. A man of Schaffhausen, Johann Heinrich Ammann, translated it into German and gave it to his painter and publisher friend Conrad Meyer from Zürich. Conrad Meyer had been a benefactor of children for ten years already, and this is another curious story. An old custom demanded that members of all sorts of learned or public bodies of the town should contribute toward the cost of heating their local drinking and meeting places. Called *Stubenhitzen,* this was delivered each year on the day of St. Berchtold (January 2) by children. In return they were treated to a rock-hard pastry and Veltliner wine. In the Society of the Town's Library one year (1646), mind triumphed over materialism and the children received, instead of pastry, a wonderful folded picture-sheet about table-manners illustrated by the painter Conrad Meyer. These picture-sheets became a tradition which has endured up to our time. For many years to come it was Conrad Meyer who did the engravings. They were mainly filled with historical information, morality, portraits of famous people and music, and being produced by good artists and famous writers they now are among our national treasures.

Meyer's book about children's games shows that children, even in the most puritan times, were really children. You see them chasing through the town, over the fields outside the city walls, playing all the games children played before traffic stole the streets from playing children. Under the word *ludus,* the Latin word for play, Comenius in *Orbis Pictus* also provides simple descriptions of the games with primitive little illustrations, explanations of games recognized by Comenius as healthy occupations for children. Conrad Meyer's book, *Sechsundzwanzig nichtige Kinderspiel,* is in comparison already a real picture-book with full-page illustrations for every game. The texts, though done in amusing verses, have a terrible tendency to warn that games symbolize the more primitive instincts and inclinations of mankind which must be overcome. Similarly John Newbery wrote a hundred years later in his *Little Pretty Pocket-Book* (1767):

> Leap-Frog
> This stoops down his Head
> Whilst that springs up high,
> But then you will find,
> He will stoop by and by.
> The moral
> Just so it's at court
> Today you're in place
> Tomorrow perhaps,
> you're in disgrace.

Comenius is certainly more progressive here. Meyer's pictures, on the other hand, are the first artistic illustrations for children I have ever seen. It is a very rare book, though a facsimile was printed in 1969. A lovely French book of very similar character came out in the same year, but the engravings by Jacques Stella show, instead of the well-dressed children from Zürich, very gay looking naked, putto-like children.

Children's portraits by great painters of that age also indicate that the discovery of the child as a being in his own right was not far away. You must only look at the paintings by Velasquez and Murillo or at those of the great Dutch and Flemish artists of the time. Children were no longer "grown-ups." Here were faces with the special quality of childhood, its innocence and beauty. This did not mean that the really fortunate time for children had arrived yet. For decades to come they still had a hard life. They were dressed in stiff materials which must have been difficult to wash. They died like flies from the lack of hygiene. The school-reform of Comenius had not yet taken effect, and these children had no or very few books of their own. Yet the time was not so far away when the Frenchman Charles Perrault in 1697 would bring out his famous collection of fairy tales, the first collection printed for children; when Anton Galland in 1704 would start the first translation of *Mille et une nuits* from the Arabic; and when *Robinson Crusoe* would appear in 1719 to bring delight to people of all ages and to bear, in a sense, children of its own.

Johann David Wyss' *Swiss Family Robinson*

It is to such a "child" of Robinson Crusoe we move in our next scene. Berne, Switzerland, is the neighborhood of Heinrich Pestalozzi, the great

Swiss pedagogue, in whose thoughts family-education with the mother as a central figure is a decisive element. There were even schools at the time organized according to the principles of family life. The head of the school was called *father* and it was in such a school in the north of Germany that Johann Heinrich Campe, famous writer and teacher of children, told, sitting with a group of children under a tree, the famous version of Robinson Crusoe called *The Younger Robinson* (1788), which changed Defoe's story definitely into a very didactic children's book, introducing each chapter by a conversation between the children and the father-teacher.

From here it is only a step to *Swiss Family Robinson* whose genesis is both an original episode and a moving family story as well.

We meet outside Berne a family going for their Sunday walk. Sunday walks were and have been since that time a habit with continental families, not always liked by children. The family we are going to meet seems rather happy about their walking tours. The head of the family, Johann David Wyss, a former field-parson, now pastor in Berne, made these promenades very useful and entertaining affairs. Everything they saw was used for interesting information. When it seemed that every visible thing around them had been explained, the much traveled field-parson started to unfold his knowledge about foreign countries, and, still living under the overpowering influence of Jean Jacques Rousseau, who thought *Robinson Crusoe* the only book worthwhile for children, this pastor-father dressed up all his information into a wonderful Robinsonade, where a whole family is shipwrecked and saved in the most adventurous way.

For many weeks one could see him walking and talking with his children. At home questioning and answering was continued, probably in the presence of the mother, who plays her special part in the future book. In the evenings the family conversations were written down, fortunately on good paper and with good ink. One day the father started to add very accurate drawings and shortly afterwards the third son, Johann Emanuel, began to illustrate the manuscript with beautiful sepia-drawings. As the whole book consists more or less of conversations, in which the father takes the part of the chief narrator, and as the handwriting changes occasionally, we can assume that the book was a family co-production. A great-grandchild of the Wyss family, Robert I. Wyss in Berne, presently in possession of the manuscript, seems to think so. I personally have the impression after seeing the manuscript and studying the first printed editions that the father Wyss must have been the chief author after all, much as he is the leading person in the story. He had the four volumes bound in thick leather bindings, wrote the title, *Charackteristick meiner Kinder in einer Robinsonade,* on the first page and put it aside. Many years later, when all the boys were

grown up and the father was an old man, one of the sons, Johann Rudolf Wyss, professor of philosophy at the University of Berne and one
of the correspondents of the Grimm brothers for fairy-tales in Switzerland, took out the book again and found it still alive, though more than
fifteen years had gone by. He edited it, called it, because *Robinson* was
still a very fashionable name, *Der Schweizer Robinson* and gave it to
one of the famous publishing firms of his country who had it illustrated and published it in 1815. Its success was an immediate one in many
languages and to study the changes it underwent in different editions is
extraordinarily interesting. In Switzerland today it is very seldom read
by children, but it seems more popular in your country. When I was last
in America I saw the Disney film of the story. At first I was horrified,
but afterwards I wondered if perhaps this sort of metamorphosis is necessary from time to time to keep things alive. Even *Grimm's Fairy Tales*
are transformed nowadays in the most strange ways. That they stay what
they are is a proof of their vitality. And this leads us to another place,
again to a spot on our globe from which much happiness came to the
children, to Kassel in West Germany.

Jakob and Wilhelm Grimm's *Kinder-und Hausmarchen*

Two persons who lived and worked there, Jakob and Wilhelm Grimm,
were linked by many strings to other places, other times, and other people. We are in the second decade of the nineteenth century. The French
revolution has produced a bourgeois world, very different from the aristo-
cratic eighteenth century. The Napoleonic wars which were not finished
by then had caused strong patriotic feelings. Both the bourgeois mentality and the patriotism, tendencies a little suspicious nowadays especially
when connected with the Germans, were something new and fresh and
gave strong impulses to the life and to the books for children.

These two young men in Kassel, born in 1785 and 1786, grew up together, nearly like twins, slept in the same bed, worked at the same table
and, though of different taste and character, were to work together all
their lives. They had sisters and brothers and a widowed mother and
spent most of their days together working as librarians. Both were scholars and their work with language and grammar made them the founders
of modern German philology. This had great influence on their later
career at the University of Berlin, but first there were other things for
them to do. Inspired by their friends Clemens Brentano and Achim
von Arnim, the romantic poets who had about ten years earlier (1804)
published the collection of popular poetry and nursery rhymes *Des
Knaben Wunderhorn,* they started to look around for German fairy
tales as an ancient expression of the German language and mentality.
They did it at first purely as scholars and as explorers. In the year 1812
the first volume of the tales, a small, rather cheap looking, green book

of 400 pages, was lying under the Christmas tree of Bettina von Arnim in Berlin. It was dedicated to her and to Achim von Arnim's first child, Johannes Freimund. Arnim had been their most devoted friend though there had also been differences of opinion and Arnim had been the first to say this was no children's book. But the dedication showed that this book, though it had a learned and very interesting commentary of 60 pages, was meant for children, for the house, for the family.

It was called *Kinder-und Hausmärchen*. Your words for it would be "Household Tales." Up to that time fairy tales had been called "Feen-und Ammenmärchen." Fairies had been the driving force in most of them; they were told in the kitchen and maybe at the bedside of children at night, in better houses by the servants who usually came from the country. They were, though loved by the children, not taken seriously by educated people. Now it became suddenly fashionable to collect them and the two brothers got such tales from all sorts of people and from different parts of Germany. They were very careful and critical in their selection, especially as they had a most authentic source of information next door to them. This was the family of a pharmacist named Wild (originally a Swiss from Berne), who lived in a big house on the same street and had many children. Two of them, a girl called Dortchen (Dorothy) and her sister Gretchen, were probably the Grimm brothers' first link to this house, which proved to be a true fairy tale house. Both girls were good story tellers, as it was a habit in this house to tell stories and to tell them well. But although Dortchen and her sister are generally believed to be the chief source of about twelve tales of the first volume, it was also clear from which source the girls had them. Most came from Marie the nurse and housemaid who must have had a great number of them in store. Ten years later Wilhelm Grimm married Dortchen Wild and their son Hermann, also a philologist, has given us a most warmhearted report of everything connected with the family tradition.

Naturally (and now comes the most important part of it all) the brothers, delighted as they may have been about the story-telling of these lovely young girls and others, did not just write down what they heard. Even for the first edition they did a lot of revising, comparing with other sources, and trying to find a simple language which was at the same time full of character. With time and with later editions it became clear that Jakob, the more scholarly, tried to keep the tales in the most simple, original form, more or less as they had heard them, and that Wilhelm, more of a poet, was for retelling them in a new form with regard to the children. The first volume contained a great many of the most famous stories, amongst them *Der Froschkönig* (The Frog Prince), *Brüderchen und Schwesterchen, Hänsel und Gretel, Aschenputtel* (Cinderella), *Frau Holle, Rotkäppchen* (Little Red Riding Hood) and *Al-*

lerleirauh. There were eighty-five tales, a most delightful treasure for reading and story-telling.

For the second volume the brothers used many new sources from different parts of Germany, amongst them a wonderful storyteller from Zwehrn in Hessen. She was a farmer's wife called Frau Viehmännin who had a rich knowledge of popular tales and knew how to tell them. She was able to speak slowly too, so that the brothers could write everything down, word by word. More than thirty of the second volume were her tales. The brothers had met her just in time, because, though she was only about fifty, she died in the same year (1815) the second volume came out. A beautiful woman with a face full of character, her portrait, drawn by the third brother, Ludwig Grimm, was added to the second edition of 1819.

As you know, this second edition was more or less the definitive one, though as long as the brothers lived, wherever a new edition came out, certain corrections, which were not always improvements, were made. The second edition changes were chiefly concessions to the children: some pictures by Ludwig Grimm were added, and the learned commentary was removed or banished to the third volume of the second edition which was a scholarly affair.

This second edition was the book which became one of the most popular children's books of the world, illustrated by hundreds of artists in many countries, and which has been discussed, loved, and attacked, especially in our time. But though there have been such wonderful editions of all sorts it is still an adventure to study the first edition with all the traces of fresh information and research, to let your imagination follow the brothers on their visits to the young sisters Dortchen and Gretchen and to their kitchen to hear Marie the maid, or to wander with them to Zwehrn, the village in Hessen, where they listened to their best storyteller, the *Viehmännin,* with the beautiful lined face.

None of their sources seemed incidental. With the marvelous instinct they took the right path and were able to give to what they found the right linguistic form. This would never have been the same had there not been two of them with different approaches to the language but with equally good will in finding the best solution.

I must bring to an end this episode though there is much more that could be told, e.g., of the brothers' interest in and discovery of the old Italian tales by the Neapolitan poet Basile of the seventeenth century which are partly included in the second volume of the first edition; or of their later encounter with Hans Christian Andersen, a story in itself; or their relations to the movements of contemporary literature. The brothers were liked and esteemed by many great people of their time. Their book became a family book. It was no longer regarded in bad taste to read fairy tales to children. As a consequence other collections appeared, not only in Germany, and appropos to the new age, after the French Revolution, the tales had changed their face too. There were no longer so many princes and kings and fairies, though they did not disappear completely. There were tales of poor children, bad and good people, malignity and justice, not told as sentimental stories but with the special impersonal quality which belongs to fairy tales only. Children of that time were a fortunate generation in connection with books, and this not only in Germany and other German speaking countries. You realize this special quality which is so timeless if you compare it to the more didactic and at the same time sentimental books for children filling slowly the book shelves of an educated family of the era to follow.

Heinrich Hoffman's *Struwwelpeter*

Again we move to another time and to another spot of Europe. It is a doctor's household in Frankfurt, and it is the year 1844. Though now we have many books for children on the market—fairy-tales, nursery rhymes, sentimental stories about very good or very bad children—there are still parents who are not quite satisfied. There was this young doctor, for instance, who went to town to buy a book for his first child and came back with a paper-covered empty book. "Everything is so deadly serious, nothing funny to laugh about," he said to his wife. "I shall try to paint a book myself." And so he did. His wife knew well that he could do it, for when he was examining the pulse or the throat of a little patient who was crying with fear, the tears stopped as soon as the young doctor took out his notebook and started to draw a tidy little boy on the paper. When the tears did not stop after that the doctor continued to draw, gave the boy hair which grew longer and longer and longer, also made his fingernails longer and longer and longer until the children saw on the little piece of paper a wild looking creature which looked more like the Indian god Shiva than like any boy of any picture book the children had seen. Naturally the little patients were so astonished that they stopped being afraid of this doctor at once. (By the way, the similarity to the god Shiva was not so surprising, because Dr. Hoffmann was founder and member of a club of artists called *Die Bädr des Ganges*. It seems that the members were interested in Indian gods.)

Young Dr. Hoffmann, after he had bought the copy-book, spent all his free time drawing picture stories which could amuse his three-year-old son. He did it with pen and ink, and he left some space for the rhymes which he added later. They were easier for him as he had always been a satirical poet and had some training in verse-making. He was no experienced painter however, for when he started painting, the ink of the line drawings ran into the color, and he had great difficulties in finishing the book in a satisfactory way.

But there it was under the family Christmas tree, and the little son was delighted. So were all his family and friends who saw the extraordinary little book. It contained several stories: *Die Geschichte vom bösen Friederich* who was beating his dog and got bitten; *Die Geschichte von den schwarzen Buben* in which three boys were thrown into an inkpot because they had teased a little Negro boy; *Die Geschichte vom wilden Jäger* who was nearly shot by the little hare; *Die Geschichte vom Suppen Caspar* which ends tragically with a cross on a grave; and the horrible story of the *Daumenlutscher*. On the last page came *Struwwelpeter* (Slovenly Peter) as a sort of identity-card of the author, who did not give his name. In later editions more stories were added and *Struwwelpeter* put on the first page.

Amongst Dr. Hoffmann's friends was also a publisher, who at once was very excited about the book. He took it away from the little boy, had it copied by lithographers, printed, and handcolored by young girls working at home. Hoffmann controlled everything however. He was a modern man who did not want his funny figures idealized in the fashionable way of the time, nor did he want sweetish colors. His drawings were very spontaneous but also very original and his colors clear and fresh. He knew exactly what he thought good for children. Even the psychological aspect, which made the book so famous but also much disliked by later generations of pedagogues and parents (never by children)—the burning child, for instance, the starving and dying *Suppen-Caspar* and the cut-off thumb of the *Daumenlutscher*—was conscious to him. It was a new thing at that time, not to forbid things but to show by examples in stories and pictures what could happen if you were not careful with fire, if you did not eat your porridge, or if you were staring into the sky instead of looking on the road before you like *Hans Guck in die Luft* who was drowned in the river. His examples were very drastic indeed, but Hoffmann, a general practitioner at the time, would become, a few years later, one of the pioneers of modern psychiatry, someone who built an asylum for epileptics and lunatics according to modern principles. In one of his money-raising articles he explained why he wanted his home for the poor lunatics in a similar surrounding and style in which the rich people of the town built their country houses. The astonishing thing was, that he got his asylum, that it was built in New Gothic Style, and Hoffmann became a sort of international expert in this field. At the same time he continued to produce the most lovely books, first for his children, later on for his grandchildren. None of them had this so-called cruel element and none of them was as successful as *Struwwelpeter*. He remained famous as the *Struwwelpeter Hoffmann*, a fact that angered him sometimes, because for him, *Struwwelpeter* had only been an episode in his long life, which was dedicated to sick people and to his family. He also lived long enough to see what strange things happened to his long-haired hero, when he traveled round the world and his author lost control of him. *Slovenly Peter* was changed in many ways, misused for political satire, printed and colored badly, and translated in many languages the doctor did not understand.

By writing *Struwwelpeter* its author, by nature quite a normal citizen of his home town Frankfurt, became the best known German author outside his country and an important pioneer of picture stories. For a generation now, many modern parents have tried to hide the book from their children, but the children nearly always discover it somewhere. Modern mothers are also against stepmothers and evil witches of the Grimm tales, but if you ask children: "What is your favorite fairy tale?" they still might answer *Hänsel und Gretel* which contains all this in the purest form. But this would be another topic.

I hope you have received from these last two episodes a vivid picture of the pure or even idealistic intentions of these three people, Jakob and Wilhelm Grimm and Dr. Heinrich Hoffmann, who happen to be the most famous authors of children's books from Germany. Like the Grimm tales, *Struwwelpeter* too has to suffer strange revisions at the moment.

Johanna Spyri's *Heidi*

Let us now turn once more to Switzerland. I do not think I can speak to you, coming from Zürich, without mentioning Johanna Spyri. Her life is too near to let imagination play, yet on the other hand, it is especially necessary here, since she destroyed, before she died, all her personal letters and documents which could be helpful to a later generation.

We shall take a boat from Zürich, one of the many small ships called Swallows which take the traffic along the borders of the lake. In Johanna Spyri's time it was still an old-fashioned steamboat, and in her childhood the chief transport was by coach. We shall stop with our Swallow at Horgen, a big industrial village, and go uphill until green fields surround us and the mountains look as if they had come a little nearer. You recognize snowy peaks and on both sides of the country road you see the most lovely pointed hills, each with a tree on top, looking like an umbrella for the shepherds and their flock. You walk on and you come to the highest point, from which it goes downhill again to another Swiss canton, to a different landscape. Here a village is spread over the rolling country, where the fields, the trees, and the houses lie open to wind and sun and weather. The village is called *Hirzel* and it is the place where Johanna Spyri was born and spent her childhood and youth. The house in which she lived is a little apart from the others and contained, besides herself and five brothers and sisters, the mother Mela Heusser who was a poet and the father who was a marvelous country doctor.

Much misery entered this house from the countryside around, and the children of the family got their impressions of real life and its difficulties from it. But at the same time they had a wonderful childhood full of freedom and natural beauty. It was here that Johanna Spyri came in contact with human beings of all sorts, and it was here that she experienced the strength of love and compassion as her parents practiced it. Here also was born her conviction that country life was better than town life and that nothing was better for children than to live in the open air of the countryside.

Although after she was married she lived until her death in the town of Zürich, when she wrote or told stories she was the country doctor's daughter again, and this remained the source of her strength forever. The rustling of the big old trees, described so vividly in *Heidi* that you never forget it, was a childhood experience of her own, and so were many other things. In each community there lives somewhere in a desolated hut or house an old man full of bitterness and hate against everybody like the Alm-Öhi. Each village knows some motherless children as we find them again and again in Johanna Spyri's stories.

To understand the real value of Heidi's creator, a popular poet who knew exactly her limitations because she knew so well the poetry beyond those limits, we have to follow her to Zürich, which became her home for nearly fifty years. Here, Johanna Spyri née Heusser, was the wife of a very cultured man, a high official of the town. They lived together on the upper floor of the town hall in the midst of the old city, and their flat became soon a meeting place for all sorts of artists. Amongst the visitors were not only the most famous Swiss poets of that time, Gottfried Keller and Conrad Ferdinand Meyer, but also prominent German emigrants like Richard Wagner. Johanna did not like the great composer especially, but she was kind to his wife Minna when Wagner had his affair with Mathilde Wesendonck, the wife of a rich German living in Zürich. Lively and openminded as she was, Johanna soon became the hospitable center of a large circle. Quickly she had adapted to the ways of life in the city. She was liked and adored although she was critical with others and sometimes had a sharp tongue. She liked children, but not the very small ones. Like all her heroes and heroines they had to be more than six or seven years old. The little ones were sometimes even afraid of her. She wrote stories, poetry, little plays, all for private use, and educated her most beloved only son Bernhard with great care. Only when she was nearly fifty years old did she start to write seriously because of the unexpected success of a popular story *Ein Blatt auf Vrony's Grab,*which was not for children.

When *Heidi* was published in 1881 Johanna Spyri became famous quickly. Then as a result of two tragedies she became a full time writer.

The son Bernhard died as a young man of twenty-nine and soon her husband, who could not recover from this blow, followed him.

And there she was, a strong personality, full of life, and completely alone. With astonishing energy she took matters in hand and started a new life, moved to another house, a house in the Zeltweg, which is next door to my office, so that I can see her house from my desk. There she installed herself and her maid Vreni, also a figure reappearing in her books, and went on to write books "für Kinder und auch für solche, welche die Kinder lieb haben," which means "for children and such people who like children."

All the books she would write now, though no longer known so well to children of today, were awaited eagerly by the readers of her time, though none had quite the success of *Heidi*, the most original child she had invented. All the ideas she had about childhood, all the characters she loved so well, were integrated in this book. There was the angry old man, the Alm-Öhi, an astonishing figure for a children's book; there was the orphan child going to town, going through fear, homesickness, and sleepwalking; there was the good and helpful doctor, the severe housekeeper, the ailing towngirl Klara and all sorts of persons, taken from Johanna Spyri's own life and therefore convincing. But there was also in Heidi, the little girl, something of the author herself, of her vitality and her capacity to bring happiness to others. Thousands of children in German-speaking households were from then on called Heidi after this model child of yesterday. Thousands of children from other countries would mould their image of Switzerland from *Heidi*.

I say "model child" of yesterday for I think it would be very improbable in our modern world to send a small child without parents to live with an old man with very dark passages in his past, even if it happens to be the grandfather. Heidi would have been sent to a home and the grandfather probably to a psychiatrist. Modern critics, even very intelligent ones like Professor Doderer and his colleagues of the *Institut für Jugendbuchforschung* of the University of Frankfurt, think that this book belongs in a museum and not in the hands of children, because serious social questions are solved by Christian pity and love and everything happens through God's will. Any sociological approach to such problems, as they appear in this book, did not exist for the author. The professors of Frankfurt put forth their conviction about *Heidi* and some other classics as well in a book (1969),which has a certain influence on young teachers and librarians of today, but *Heidi* has not been killed by it yet.

However one thinks about *Heidi* as an episode in the history of children's books, the book is very important. Heidi introduces the natural child of the country into the stuffy bourgeois atmosphere of the nurseries of the time. The effect must have been tremendous and also the influence on the literature to come. You see here again, that this success is not incidental. It derives from strong personality with a rich life behind it. Though a most successful writer of her time, in constant contact with other well-known authors, and living in a town where at the university the first German and Russian female students were finishing their studies, Johanna Spyri was strongly opposed to women's emancipation, though not against good schooling for girls. She thought of the future mothers as the heart and center of the family, and this shows again the influence of Pestalozzi, the great pedagogue whom no Swiss writer for children can escape. It leads us back to Pestalozzi's famous popular novel, *Lienhard und Gertrud* where Gertrud, the wife and mother, is the central figure; it leads us even back to *The Swiss Family Robinson,* where the mother is shipwrecked with the men and the children and takes over the government of the famous tree house. It leads us also to modern Switzerland where women, though they are rather powerful even in certain public domains, only two years ago received the political vote and even that against some protests.

Jean de Brunhoff's *Babar*

Let us now leave this extraordinary writer, whose life ended in 1901 and thus brings us into our own century. If anything in the history of children's books is typical of the twentieth century it is the growing importance of picture books and their role in preschool education. So let us add to the six episodes about children's books a seventh one of how a book, perhaps the most human picture book of our century, at least in Europe, came into existence.

There are naturally many epoch-making moments I could describe to you in Switzerland. I think of Ernst Kreidolf, whose lovely picture books were, like those of Crane and Caldecott in England, pioneers of the artistic picture book for the German speaking world, or about Alois Carigiet, who created in *Ursli with the Bells* a modern pendant to Heidi. Outside of the country I think of such a great figure as Jiri Trnka from Prague (the same country as Comenius) who came from puppets to children's illustrations and brought more fun and happiness than any other artist of any other country to the children of his own unhappy nation. But none of these would be as universal as the figure I have chosen. I said it would be the most *human* picture book. I stick to this, though the hero is an elephant.

There was in 1931 a human family: the mother, a pianist in Paris with her two little sons, the father, the painter Jean de Brunhoff, living for the time being in a place called Montana, a Swiss spa where he was undergoing treatment for tuberculosis. Bound to a quiet life, lying on the balcony of his room, his thoughts wandered. Letters from his wife were lying on his lap; he read them again and again. In them the mother was reporting what the little boys had said, she was talking about her life and work, she was writing about the children being ill, as children are from time to time, and about the stories she told to keep them quiet, and how they loved a special story about an elephant which she had to retell again and again. That was something for him. This elephant started to fascinate the grown-up father too. Getting up from his deckchair, he fetched pen and paper and his next letter was full of elephant-drawings, to the delight of the children. A grown-up person was also delighted, Jean's brother, the publisher of a magazine *Jardin des modes*. He knew his sick brother was depressed that he was not doing any useful work or earning money. So the publisher-brother commissioned a picture book using the elephant story the mother had begun with the children.

And so a little elephant was born in a big forest. He was called *Babar*. His mother loves him very much; she is rocking his cradle, which is a hammock, with her trunk, singing softly. But a hunter kills her and little Babar, running away from the hunter, who shot his mother, comes to the town of the human beings. He meets an old lady who makes a civilized person of him, teaching him all the good things the human race has invented. One day his cousins Arthur and Celeste arrive in town and after they have become humanized too, they and Babar return to the elephants, leaving the wonderful old lady behind. The king of the elephants has just died and Babar, who marries Celeste, becomes king of the elephants.

In the second volume, on his honeymoon, Babar has the most wonderful and terrible adventures, painted brilliantly by Brunhoff, and the old lady joins him as wise adviser. In the third volume he is a king and a general who has to fight in wars and make peace with everybody in the end, a very political chapter about an ideal state. Another volume is filled with his adventures as a father, and the last volume, only partly finished before Brunhoff died in 1938, was about Father Christmas.

Between the different volumes Brunhoff had returned home to Paris and looking at the book *Babar en Famille* you find a happy family self-portrait, perhaps the most moving ever created in a picture book.

Here again everything is done against the rules. Dressed up animals in picture books were at that time (1931–1938) and still are, not liked by many intelligent people, and they are right. But then a miracle happens and this elephant comes into the world and as there is a stroke of genius in it, all the rules and theories become null and void.

Taking leave of these seven episodes and places I visited with you, I think that each attracted me because a warmhearted personality was be-

hind the scene: A human pedagogue like Comenius trying to make learning a picture book pleasure; the Swiss painter Conrad Meyer creating
one of the first amusing picture albums for children as early as 1656;
the wonderful brothers Jakob and Wilhelm Grimm, so clever and at the
same time so devoted to children; the amusing Dr. Hoffmann of Frankfurt, a great benefactor—not only for the children; and the energetic
parson of Berne, who changed the tree, on which the first Robinson was
merely hiding from fear of wild animals, into such a memorable tree-
house, which made him famous round the world. There is also Johanna
Spyri, who used so well what she received as a child, a wonderful background of nature and human beings; and last but not least the painter
Jean de Brunhoff, who died so young and yet made innumerable children happier and wiser. We could add many others from many countries. To collect the stories of famous books and how they came into existence would make a wonderful storybook for children and grown-ups.

It was a great pleasure to me to live with these extraordinary books
from the past once again for a few weeks. I owe this to your invitation,
which made me descend to the roots of our own children's literature
again. Without these roots and without a lively tradition, our children's
literature of today would not be as rich and many-sided as it is. This we
should not forget.

Ivan Southall

Ivan Southall, who worked for a newspaper before
entering military service (where he was awarded the
Distinguished Flying Cross), is not only Australia's
most honored writer of children's books, but also
the winner of the British Library Association's
Carnegie Medal for *Josh* (Macmillan, 1972). He
received the Australian Children's Book of the Year
Award for *Ash Road* (St. Martin's Press, 1966), *To the
Wild Sky* (St. Martin's Press, 1967), *Bread and Honey*
(Bradbury Press, 1970), and *Fly West* (Macmillan,
1975). He was also the author of *Sly Old Wardrobe*
(St. Martin's Press, 1969), illustrated by Ted
Greenwood, which won the Australian Picture Book
of the Year Award.

A prolific writer, Southall has used Australia as the
setting for all his fiction for children and young
people, while some of his nonfiction writing and his
work for adults has had other settings. His lecture,
"Real Adventure Belongs to Us," was presented on
May 10, 1974, in Seattle, Washington, under the
aegis of the School of Librarianship, University of
Washington.

Real Adventure
Belongs to Us

Tonight I hope to relate the simple tale of a boy who searched the world for a book to read and found it in a moment on a mountain. This does not mean it is a tale for children, though dreaming up stories for children to read is the labour of my life. There is no compulsion, of course, either way, that I should write or that children should read. Perhaps no book of mine ever has been genuinely read by a child—I accept my reassurance on trust—even if I have letters expressing the delight of this child, the doubt of that child, the perceptive criticism of a few, and occasionally the compliment of a request for photographs, please, for the classroom gallery, by return of mail: "It's not that we go for your books much, Mr. Southall, but we're collecting photographs of things. Last week it was old steam engines. This week it's you."

It is a truth, I have never witnessed with my own eyes any child, freely, in his own time, without compulsion—except one adoring daughter—actually at it. Once, in a bookshop, I stood behind a likely-looking lad at the brink of decision, *had his hands on a Southall*, but changed his mind and bought *Zip Magee and the Mud Monster* or something of the kind. One day I shall sit in a railway carriage and it'll happen. Out of the pocket of someone's jeans shall come a dog-eared copy of a familiar masterpiece and this kid will curl up in the corner with it and there it will be. Perhaps I'll lean across and tap him on the arm. "Do you *really* like it? What do you really think of it, hey?"

And he'll look up, and shift his gum to the other cheek. "It's for kids, Dad. What's it to you? You'd never understand."

Perhaps I wouldn't. As the man I am without the pen in my hand, perhaps I wouldn't.

Amongst the letters (I risk the parody the confession invites), are those that begin, "Dear Ivan." Not "Dear Sir" or "Dear Mr. So-and-So." From children who ask, "Why is it so? What am I to do? I know you'll know what I mean." Turning to me as if I were a brother a little older, far enough ahead to have gained a little wisdom, but close enough to touch, not knowing me as I am, a grandfather many years and a thousand miles or ten thousand miles removed. They picture me as Josh or Michael or Max or Matt—or Frances or Jan or Abigail. Are they victims of a delusion? Or am I? There are grown-ups who say, "Southall doesn't write for kids; he writes about them to exorcise his hang-ups."

I begin my tale knowing I cannot bring you to a reasonable end. Is there ever an end? Is any answer permanent? Is any conclusion final? Ideas and men grow only through change.

Beginnings

Books were not easy to come by when I was a lad. I lived at the fringe of an Australian city where settled suburbs lost definition, and orchards and horse paddocks and bushland began. We had patches on our pants, not because it was the "in-thing," but because bare skin would have bloomed otherwise. There were magpies warbling in the morning and kookaburras laughing and long queues of unemployed. We had heard of wireless sets that spoke out loud, but did not own one. Nor did anyone else we knew.

Money went for food, mainly. Public money, what there was of it, went for bridges and roads and drains. There were no libraries for children. I used to walk a mile or so to the library to borrow books for my parents. There wasn't a book in the place for a kid to take away, that anyone told me about. Libraries were for grown-ups, for real people. You know?

Kids read penny comics—full of stories, not pictures—printed in England three months earlier. For us in the Antipodes they were always out of date and out of season and all the competitions and free privilege offers had long before closed. No Australian story comic ever lasted more than an issue or two. If it were of Australian origin everyone supposed —from a century or more of indoctrination—that it would have to be second-rate and because of this conditioning it usually was. Good things came from England and we were expected to accept this as natural, and we did accept it, although everything was different and bore little resemblance to the life we lived at the bottom of the world. Hence we grew up in a kind of limbo—second-class or third-class English children displaced, out of context, out of tune, deep down doubting the rightness of being where we were.

In the stories we read, English children played in the snow at Christmas time; we had never seen snow and Christmas was a hundred in the shade. English children played soccer; we knew nothing of the game. English children went to boarding schools; what on earth were they? These things would not have mattered if it had been possible to identify—there *is* a universal language greater than these differences, but our stories missed it somehow. The English were always the goodies, the Germans were bad, the Americans were called Yanks and made a lot of noise. Australia never got a mention except as the wilderness to which profligate cousins were sent and out of which lost uncles came. To be Australian in the old British Empire was to be born with a raging inferiority complex (millions of those Australians are alive today), and national life at the adult level was a fierce struggle to prove to the English that at least we could beat them at games. At everything else they were supreme and frequently let us know.

From our English comics we learnt the fundamental truths of life: for instance, people with yellow skins were inscrutable and cunning, people with brown skins were childlike and apt to run amok, people with black skins were savages, but, if tamed, made useful carriers on great expeditions of discovery conducted by Englishmen. It was in order for black people to be pictured without clothes; after all, they didn't know what clothes were. But white nudity was unimaginable. The white body was so sacred it was not proper to look at your own.

Childhood in the Twenties and Thirties was a kind of comic culture, for us an alien culture built upon the products of overworked hack writers which kids bought and sold and traded and exchanged until they were tattered beyond further use, until the print from excessive reading practically faded from the page. These comics were imbued with blunt simplicities (the writers had no time for subtleties), with unquestioning loyalty to God and the British Throne, with the absolute morality of good or bad, bravery or cowardice, truth or falsehood, adventure or sloth, British or non-British. Death for God and King, they were synonymous, was the ultimate virtue.

Books for children, conceived with artistic integrity and emotional honesty, to help balance this lopsided culture, were not to be found, largely, I suppose, because writers had been formed in the same mould, taught not to think but to believe, unless by uncommon virtue of intellectual merit or by fortunate accident of birth they were of the elite.

Education for the elite functioned in another dimension. Those liberated souls or the brave ones or the honest ones I had not heard of, and they were not to be found among the writers who spoke directly to my generation. The voices of the brave did not get through to the boy or girl sitting up in bed reading the comics of forty or fifty or more years ago. This is not to imply that the old British world now gone was all bad. For some, as their literature reveals, it was a form of Utopia where they lived and loved in fine houses and exercised their talents at leisure, while masses of the population existed on the breadline, their status little better than serfdom. For us, the colonials, despite our inferiority complexes, we did know where we had come from and where we were going; God was in his Heaven, the King was on his Throne, and we believed. To be British was enough; what greater birthright for anyone could there be?

Libraries for children, those years ago, from which some sort of choice could be made, had not reached the bottom of the world. There was a library—that's what it was called—on the lower shelf of a cupboard at school, the cupboard where the chalk dusters were put away. Open the door and sneeze. Take a book home and sneeze. I sneeze now, out of respect, as I write it down. Books bound in purples and golds and adorned with flowers and scrolls, bestowed upon the school by someone's grandmother cleaning up a room; books published about the turn of the century in England, designed specifically to improve, with titles like *Daniel's Good Deed* by Richard Righteous and *The Best Girl in Form Four* by Patience Virtue, didn't impress me much, I fear.

I was handling all the improvement I needed. I used to leave home on Sunday mornings at 9:30 for Junior Christian Endeavour, stay on for 11 o'clock family worship, and then go back for Sunday School at 2:30. More often than not I was there again with my parents for evening service at 7:00—kept me off the streets—*for sure!*

I had an ambition as a lad to be steward at the church door. The steward met your family on the steps, issued hymn books to those old enough to read and trustworthy enough not to make paper darts for aiming at the choir, and escorted you with dignity to your pew. At half-time he brought the plate to collect the pennies, then quietly closing behind him the swing doors, retired to the porch to "keep an eye on things" while everyone else inside enjoyed the sermon. The older I became the better sense it made. When I grew up I would be the steward and sit out *there*.

The bench that bore the imprint of the steward's backside was, in fact, the lid of a box as long as the breadth of the porch; underneath it, hiding there, was the Sunday School Library. This consisted largely of books, multiple copies I must suppose, written by Arthur Mee, all of which, I am reasonably sure, were designed to improve. I can recall with something approaching totality those areas of my childhood I concentrate upon. I have concentrated hard upon books by Arthur Mee. Nothing stirs. The curtain remains down. Does this mean I was a Philistine, that I never read one through?

There was another source of books; oh, a rich source for the village genius. Every year the same kid was dux of the class at school and won the big prize, a book with lots of pages in it, along with the history prize, the geography prize, the arithmetic prize, the scripture prize. You name it; whatever it was he got it. That's what made him dux. Winston was his name. Every time I drew near him I felt myself to be in the presence of the elect. If he spoke to me I'd start stammering.

In the Third Grade I fell in love with Miss James. Every other boy in class fell in love with her too; Winston as well, I suppose, unless elementary responses were beneath his plane. Saddest hour of my young life, I think, came on the last school day of that year, 1929, because we were going up next year, all of us except her; we were leaving our beloved teacher behind. The immensity of these tragedies when you're eight years old, going on nine.

Half-way through the summer holidays a removal van came up our street and stopped at the empty house opposite ours. Guess who got down? Guess who opened the squeaky iron gate and walked up the path with the key? My love. It was she.

First day of the new school year there was I, at 8:40, tapping at her door. "Hullo, Miss James," I said, looking way up there, worshipping her, "may I carry your case to school? Please."

Where did the courage come from? A borrowing from later years? Imagine my joy when she agreed, and try to picture the magnitude of my bliss when I learnt she was going up with us into Grade Four. Picture her bliss, too. She had all of us for another year.

Every morning at 8:40, excluding a one-month break for measles, there I was proudly bearing her case away, walking beside her, adoring her. That year I won my only school prize, the Progress Prize, for exactly what I am not sure. I have it still, chosen by her, *Tony's Desert Island* by Enid Leale.

One other source of books was open; one requirement only needed, sainthood.

Sunday School prize-giving came round once a year. To be in at the kill you were required to sustain over fifty-two successive weeks, the kind of self-discipline and self-denial that makes heroes. Each Sunday Southall arrived at 2:30, dead on time, wet or fine, fit or all but totally incapacitated, catechism word perfect, text known to the last dot over the last "i," wearing his neatest home-mades and his most charming manner. Five marks you gained for an impeccable performance in all departments, one mark each for attendance, punctuality, behavior, catechism, and text. I was impeccable. Holidays were a problem if you were lucky enough to get them. Sunday School never went into recess. You could always catch up on catechisms and texts, but if you did not attend, for any reason, even banishment to an infectious diseases hospital, you lost your attendance mark, your punctuality mark, and your behavior mark. Every week of absence sent you three marks more down the drain. For holidays I dared visit no one but my Great Aunt Susan in the country, despite my enormous fear of snakes and my loathing of the Throne Room at the bottom of the garden. Great Aunt Susan was the most daunting, the most exciting, the most eccentric, the most magnificent, the most loved adult of my boyhood outside my own home. She lived in the land of wooden trestle bridges and cow-pats and asparagus and mine shafts and pine trees and empty buildings and strong children. From her Sunday School class I was able to secure those vital marks firmly initialed on an official card as evidence beyond dispute of my unbroken endeavor. Year in, year out, until I was sixteen, I sustained this feat to win each March the prize, that I might have a book of my own, that I might have a book to possess. I have them still, and all but two of strong religious content (a sinking disappointment *they* were) are adventure stories set in exotic climes. The only books for a boy to read I ever really saw, the only ones I ever really read—over and over and over again —yet it is not hindsight to observe that something always was missing, the *possibility* of believable identification. In any situation I read about I could see myself only by suspending belief in myself. I wouldn't have put it into those words at the time, but I knew.

The "Hero" Enters

The hero, inevitably, would be fair-haired, blue-eyed, English, incredibly brave, incredibly good, incredibly handsome, clean-cut, wholesome, masculine, modest, brilliant, called Nigel. Nigel is dux of his class, captain of the cricket team, a total abstainer from cigarettes, swearing, girls, and all other evil. In the books I read only bounders smoked cigarettes behind the rose bushes, only cads and sissies associated with girls of any kind, except mothers, sisters, and aunts. In all honesty, despite my huge religious experience and my public face of shining innocence, there was always the certainty that my only possible relationship had to be with the cads, the bounders, and the cowards.

Nigel's mother of sacred memory has been dead three years, and his father, Professor Armstrong-Manly, has vanished in darkest Africa. There, at the moment of discovery of a lost city lodged in the interior walls of a once-dormant but now active volcano, deserted by his faithless carriers, he has slipped from his exploration of the rim, that knife-edged bit that goes around the top where one must balance with great care if one is an English professor in an adventure story for boys. Down he has slipped to lie trapped on a ledge fifty feet below, out of reach of the top, out of sight, an appalling plight. But he survives, fed by friendly apes on breadfruit and coconut milk, kept in good heart by diamonds brought daily by the apes from the lost city, and warmed at night by the gentle bubbling of the lava far below. At length, he teaches Yang Youtang, king of the apes, to carry a message bottle to the great river that sweeps down to the sea. Months later the bottle is swept ashore at Land's End, there to be found by fifteen-year-old Tom Sykes, an honest apprentice coal miner who has just ridden a bicycle from Yorkshire to prove that coal mining is good for you. Tom leaps back on his bicycle and rides to Manly Manor to deliver the bottle into Nigel's hands.

"Come at once," the note says, giving the map coordinates in code, "I am in terrible danger. The volcano must erupt at any moment. Beware of a tall man with a black eye-patch and a guttural accent. Signed, Professor Armstrong-Manly, your long-lost father."

"My goodness," Nigel exclaims, "I must sail for darkest Africa without delay. Come with me, Tom. Be my faithful friend and who can tell what your reward may be."

"To the death," Tom vows.

Hastily packing his portmanteau and placing in his left breast pocket a photograph of his mother and in his right breast pocket a leather-bound edition of the Holy Scriptures, Nigel sets off. Thanks to sharp-eyed, loyal Tom, a man with a black eye-patch is eluded on the boat train and again at Southampton as they board the S.S. *Windsor Castle*. The voyage to darkest Africa is a battle of wits against treacherous Chinese crewmen in the pay of Black Patch who travels incognito disguised as a Lutheran missionary. Meanwhile, back at the volcano, Professor Armstrong-Manly has lain trapped on the ledge these past two years and is but a husk of his former self, withered by the fierce equatorial sun and by gusts of heat rising from the evil depths of bubbling lava, weary unto death of breadfruit and coconuts, no longer able when conscious to recall the English tongue, though when delirious crying his son's name in a loud voice which issues eerily on still nights from the crater giving rise along the Congo to the legend that the volcano is haunted.

Nigel and Tom, fighting their way into darkest Africa, forever fearful their faint-hearted carriers may desert, attacked by lions and pygmies with blow-pipes, trailed by Black Patch despite every manoeuvre to mislead him, come at last to the volcano from which rises smoke and sulphur fumes and cries of Nigel's name. The earth shakes—sounds like thunder roll in the heavens. A major eruption is imminent. As foretold, hundreds of apes abandon the lost city and rush blindly into the night never to be seen again. The faithless carriers flee to their deaths, falling into fissures, drowning in rivers, eaten by tigers, strangled by boa constrictors. Patch appears at the jungle fringe, revolver in hand.

"Courage, Tom," cries Nigel, and together they scale the slope, Patch after them shooting wildly, as great boulders shaken by earth tremors break loose. Nigel races along the crater rim shouting, "Father, Father, it is I," while Tom engages Patch in hand-to-hand combat. From his portmanteau Nigel takes a fifty-foot length of rope, slaps the grappling hook over the lip of the crater, shins down into blistering heat and suffocating sulphurous gases, throws his father across his shoulders, and climbs the rope again as it begins to burn in his fingers. Patch, screaming his guttural last, is overcome by Tom and drops from the lip a great depth into the fiery pit. The heroes reach a cave by the river as the volcano blows up and the lost city is destroyed forever. The professor, already growing stronger, shows them a million pounds' worth of diamonds, a bulging bag of diamonds. "All thanks to loyal Tom," declares Nigel. So Tom is given a diamond of his very own and a job for life in the kitchen at Manly Manor.

How does a run-of-the-mill colonial kid, or anyone else for that matter, identify with characters like Nigel? Shinning up and down ropes and rescuing fathers from volcanoes, when you're not *allowed* to climb a ladder and the only time you climb a tree it takes half a day to get down again because of vertigo?

So brave, so noble, so true, so strong, so clever, so generous, so pure, so rich, so English, when you're a skinny streak of thirteen selling newspapers at the railway gates after school to help the family, though hoping to fiddle a penny on the side to buy a hot potato cake, only passing your exams when you can cheat a bit, worried by strange things happening in your body and to your thoughts that no one grown-up will tell you about, except to infer that it's dirty and inhuman, sure you're a coward because you're scared of tough kids and high trees and deep holes and all that dying stuff that goes with wars, though marching off to war, cheered by all the girls and singing because you're so happy about it, is being British to the core.

Did you ever read about a completely believable boy or girl who spoke your language and thought your thoughts and had your problems and experienced your fears and was sometimes bad or stupid or troubled or irritable or sexy or frightened half to death, but could be a nice kid too? If you were an Australian in my day I am all but certain you could not. If you were an ordinary working-class English child, I am sure you were not much better served *and* for reasons that might have been more disturbing. If you were American at least you had librarians who liked children, and you did have, even then, wonderful libraries and there were books to borrow, though whether their authors faced life or ran from it or distorted it I am unable to say; I was down underneath, too far away to know, hanging into space by my feet, my brain addled by English super heroes.

There were movies, of course, to add variety to the culture, if you could nag the money out of Mum once in a while or slip in the side door at interval time, but they didn't count much. Forgive me, ladies and gentlemen, but most of them were American, so one did not need to believe them. You cheered the serial like mad, Buck Jones and Tom Mix, but they were grown-up characters and identifying with them never came into it and when you went outside into the fierce daylight you left them behind you, behind the door, in the house of make-believe.

Your books and story comics were different. They were at home under the pillow. Open them, any time, and the English public schoolboy hero was inside. The motive at the source, if motive came into it, was to present what were supposed to be high ideals and high principles, to encourage you to be big and brave and bold for God and King and Empire (God and Empire also being interchangeable, with blasphemy embracing all three), and to prepare you to die to preserve the status quo; but all it achieved, if you were sensitive, was to hammer home the humiliating truth of your weakness whilst misleading you wholly about the true nature of real living English public schoolboys.

"I had done nothing but grow up"

I know this is a simplification. I know many factors in depths of time and history contributed, but all were related, I believe, and I cannot accept my own obvious invitation to pursue them or we shall be here for the rest of the night. Instead, let me jump to conclusions. If, over a long period, you never hear the other side of an argument or a proposition, you don't know about it. If, over a long period, you are taught that your mother country and its allies are honorable and of noble intention and others are dishonorable and selfishly motivated, it would be surprising if you did not accept it. If, over a long period, you are taught by inference in church and school and everywhere else to feel sorry for people with skins of a different colour, not because their rights as human beings have been taken away, but *because* their skins are different, can you be judged for false attitudes? If, over a long period, no one gives you good books and you can neither borrow them nor buy them and you do not know they exist, how are you to be influenced by their values? How are they to add richness and understanding to your experience if they are not accessible? And the great literature compulsorily administered like medicine at school speaks a language the ordinary child finds

difficult to understand, and that it *is* taught at school, sometimes clumsi-
ly, alienates it from your spirit perhaps for all time.

A proportion of the human race doesn't give a damn about anything
but appetites, I know that; some people never have raised their eyes and
are not likely to; but man has come to where he is, culturally as distinct
from materially, because sensitive people have cared; or have accepted
a truth because they have confronted it face to face; or have been compelled to search for it because of inner disquiet; or, instinctively, have
created it out of their own souls, sometimes unawares, sometimes despite
themselves, and have been able to express it in the language of their day.

Simply from looking at myself as a boy and being aware of effects, I
know that the words children read for recreation are of prodigious importance. No matter how you regard this material, as an opportunity to
present life to children honestly, without sentimentality or intentional
bias, without denying man's humanity or glorifying it or belittling it—
or whether you see it as an opportunity to distort or indoctrinate or pervert or enslave—the degree of influence is not something you can put a
measure on. The ultimate influence, on the course of adult taste alone,
may well be permanent unless the process is reversed by firm re-educa-
tion. If you raise a dozen children or a million children or ten million
children on falsehoods and phonies and trivialities—through your own
ignorance or indifference or deliberate intention—you end up with a
substantial number of grown persons who need to be sustained by lies
and illusions and cheap sentimentalities because they cannot live with
truth or be bothered by the effort of comprehension art demands. Switch
on the box at almost any hour and there it is to see. In terms of human
wastage you dare not even think about it.

At fourteen I was out working full-time and never encountered literature in an atmosphere or situation where it had a chance or I had a
chance. As a youth, life was largely work at my trade as a process en-
graver and attending night school to learn my trade and a frantic spare-
time endeavor to appease the fever to write. This was usually done
against the clock as if tomorrow I were to die and a million things were
to be written down. But a million things were not to be written down except the most trivial absurdities. There was nothing else I knew and my
own experience was unsuitable as raw material to draw upon. I had done
nothing brave or noble or exciting. I had done nothing but grow up.

I wrote in clichés throughout my youth as I had read throughout my
boyhood—of swashbuckling deeds, of non-stop cliff-hanging physical adventure in which the baddies spoke with guttural accents and the savages
were black or brown and the cunning heathens were yellow, putting into
effect my long and thorough briefing. There was nothing else I knew ex-

cept the Bible. It, too, was full of super heroes and hostility between races and high and bloodthirsty adventure. There were other levels in the Bible, and I knew them intimately, but they were not for writing about if you were a boy. Perhaps for thinking about, but not for proclaiming. The boy, even such a short while ago, was the warrior in training from the day he focussed on his mother's smile. The gentler parts of the Bible were for girls. Boys went for David and Goliath, and Joshua and Jericho, and Samson and the ass's jawbone, and Moses and the drowned Egyptians, and Meshack, Shadrack, and Abednego. And a thousand more like them. . . . Wonderful stories. . . . How incredibly violent everything is. Is the struggle lost at the source before we begin?

Struggle at the Source

My turn came. The boy frightened in a tree, the boy who had never hurt a friend or an enemy with his hands, learned to accept the thunder of flying-boat engines in his ears and the warring world of sea and space into which he flew many times. Fear was a part of every day, none more total than on the night he fulfilled and justified his briefing. An explosion of violence in the air and on the Atlantic directed by me. So I was decorated for qualities I admired in others but found wanting in myself. I was given a ribbon to wear under my wings and a silver cross in a leather case that I have kept along with *Tony's Desert Island* by Enid Leale.

How was it that a coward came to wear a hero's badge? Or had I been misinformed? Was fear not cowardice? Was fear-sickness not cowardly either? The sickness that shook you, that possessed you, that filled you with dread of dying so young, so soon. Were there no such people as the heroes of my life-long indoctrination? Were decorated men scared and ordinary like me? Was being brave—for lack of a better word—something a frightened lad could be?

I did not allow those improper thoughts to be publicly viewed. I held up my head and played the hero with the self-effacing manner best suited to the role, but was never over-reluctant to go without my coat that the glory of my jacket might be seen. True, I was a nice young fellow and didn't boast or brag or grossly misbehave, but I missed a chance to mature before my time. I simply joined the club, but should have baled out from conformity then and there. So for fifteen more years in my series books for boys I went on perpetuating the myths of my growing years.

Simon Black was my hero, developed from stories I had written in adolescence. He was the first character I came up with after I set out twenty-seven years ago to take on the world, abandoning my trade and what security it gave me. Cutting adrift. Going it alone.

Simon, this character of mine, was a decorated air force officer, a former flying-boat pilot who had flown in the Battle of the Atlantic, brown-eyed, black-haired, lean, six feet tall, Australian, wholesome, modest, incredibly good, incredibly clever, incredibly brave, incredibly handsome—me! The super me. Same person, of course, as the super you.

Nothing was too difficult for Simon. Getting to Mars back in 1952 might have been tricky, but he made it in the end in a spaceship designed in his spare time between rushing all over the earth solving problems beyond the wit of presidents and kings and the capacity of armies. I didn't write these stories to cash in, they were not an exploitation—my wife and young family quietly starved along with me—nor did I write deliberately to pervert or subvert or indoctrinate or perpetuate the status quo; I thought it was the proper and only thing to do. I was much too busy trying to scrape together a living, working twelve to fifteen hours a day, to waste time reading what my contemporaries were writing—and to this moment I still don't know.

Each day, whether the book on hand was for children or for adults, the attitude of mind was the same—a strenuous search for bigger and bolder and more breathtaking deeds. Talk about racking my brain. Talk about stretching every winning post to a mile. Used to wear myself out from the stress and strain. Used to stagger off to bed emotionally mangled, at the end of invention. Next morning, with some fresh absurdity, off I'd go.

I knew something was wrong, as I had always known, even when I used only to read the stuff, long before I started writing my own. But in my own life only the war was worth drawing from. Nothing else had happened to me and I was much too poor and underconfident and insecure to risk earning time on literary experiment—*if* it had occurred to me.

I wrote a comic strip once, for a woman's magazine; only regular income we saw in years except for bits picked up from laboring here and there. We stepped lightly for a while; I believe my wife owned a second pair of shoes; but editorial policy changed and our strip disappeared. No protest. No deputations to the editor. No heartbreak, except my own, marked its passing. You'd have thought one kid somewhere would have raised a cry. But no. Every newspaper you opened, every weekly magazine, had its strip or its several strips or its dozen strips on exactly the same theme. The super-man theme. *Mike Manly* I called mine.

With the Heart of a Lion

We lived thirty-two miles from town, up the mountains, over the top, and down the other side; a pocket ignored by progress and time. Eight and three-quarters acres of bushland and four acres cleared falling from a pot-holed red earth road to a creek in a fern gully several hundred yards below; all ours; with a clumsy house of rough-sawn timbers then about fifty years old, and tumbledown outbuildings with harness over rails, and leaning chicken pens though the chickens roosted in trees, and a brooder house and incubators worked by kerosene, and spring-tine cultivators and harrows and ploughs rusting outside. $2,400 the lot. We paid ten dollars down, created a few hundred, and borrowed the balance from a bank manager who said, "My God; you've got the heart of a lion."

Behind us the world stretched eastward out of sight across valleys and forests and mountains and sky and cloud. On autumn mornings the sun came up behind a plateau of mist fifteen miles wide with such brilliance it was more than eye and spirit could stand. Eucalyptus forest hedged us on the south, dark and tall and sometimes unnerving. It began a hundred yards from the house and I never walked into it. Shout at it and the echo cracked back. For a while we called it Echo Farm, but dropped the name; perhaps it was an invocation of the wrong kind. On the north boundary, a quarter of a mile across paddocks, lived an old man; well, he seemed old to me. Fifty years he had been there; had pioneered a block when he was thirteen. A small man, bow-legged, hard, kind, with a body like wire. He cut his wrist once with an axe, with the nearest doctor a walk of eight miles. Held himself together with his other hand and climbed the hill to the house for aid. His wife fainted. His daughter fainted. Two of them out like corpses on the kitchen floor. So he put the kettle on and boiled water and sterilized a needle and a hair he plucked from the draught horse's tail and stitched himself up again. Hail to thee, old friend, now gone. What a man.

Twenty-five years ago there we began. A burnt-out one-fire stove to cook on, a sheet-iron fireplace on wooden stumps to keep out the cold. Termites in the foundations, termites in the walls. A thousand-gallon tank was all the water on hand. Numerous other tanks rusted out with holes stood around. No water on tap from the town supply, though a large reservoir was a mile away. No electricity; candles and lamps with mantles and hissing sounds. No local services except a grader once a year down the road. No sewerage—and no night man to call to take away the pan. A one-holer fifty feet from the back door, full of spiders and scuttling lizards and pulse-arresting pauses—one was so defenseless there. But we had a bathroom, by name; fourteen feet long and three feet wide—a passage resumed. At the narrow end a tap from the tank outside poked through the wall. The bath was of sheet-iron, huge and old with feet of ball and claw. The water heater was a Malley, a black cylindrical object of sinister appearance—like a depth-charge—one foot wide and three feet tall standing on the floor at the distant end between the bath and the outside wall. All conveniences, as it were, in single file. Getting to the water heater or to the tap or into the bath was rather like negotiating the corridor of a crowded train.

Let me tell you about the Malley: a little funnel on top to receive water trickled from the tap, and a large sooty hole (a venturi) through which you poke paper and sticks and bark and the burning match. There is a pregnant period—and that *is* the proper word—then BOOM, you leap back, eyebrows scorched, and the Malley takes charge, BOOM, BOOM, BOOMING in rhythm, belching light and heat and sparks and flame, all but literally jumping up and down, shaking the house, terrifying everyone around not accustomed to the sound. First time my wife fled outside, snatching up our young son on the way, and crept back later to see if I was alive. Then, out of the spout of this marvelous machine, comes a thin, thin stream of scalding hot water, a kind of mystical experience. But you cannot turn it off until the fire dies down and the water runs cold, not an embarrassment unless you've climbed in too soon.

There I squatted one night, feet drawn up under me at the high end away from the ferocious spout, compromised, cooking like a crayfish. I could have escaped over the back, I suppose, at the risk of slipping a disc, but made a long forward step to turn the tap on full to flood the bath with cold and went out through layers of paint and rust, out through the bottom, and away poured everything into the house.

We were too poor to buy another bath and for four years went without. We used the concrete wash troughs under the plum tree instead. The drill was to half-fill both troughs, put your rear end in one and your feet in the other and pray for solitude. That we achieved it for four years unobserved I doubt, but what you don't know about you don't worry about.

Several adults were in the house one night, long ago, my mother-in-law among them, conversing with the spirit in the glass. Not my kind of entertainment—an old English pastime you might have heard about. A load of old rubbish, I thought, while that glass rushed in circles around my table with a message allegedly from my father, dead fifteen years by then, a good man, a gentle man, an impressive man, worn out at forty-seven from hard work begun when he was eight, and the whole thing troubled me a bit. But the glass persisted and one does not offend the guests. "Ask it questions," they said, so I asked, "How is it I survived the war when every day I was sure I couldn't last?"

"I flew beside you," the glass came back.

For pity's sake. What do you do about a thing like that? So I said, "Will I survive as a writer?"

"Yes," the glass spelt out. "Have faith."

My next question was even more out of character. All I wish for the future, then as now, is that it should happen in its own time, but I asked, "What will I be doing in a month?"

"Digging for gold," the glass spelt out.

"It's stupid," I said, "the whole thing's stupid." But the glass went on. There was gold, it said, £60,000 worth (half-a-million dollars in the values of today) at a depth of sixty feet, at the bottom of a· shaft sunk sixty years before by Chinese prospectors who had died from misadventure. If I would proceed along a given line for a given distance, then turn left at right angles for forty-two feet, the shaft would be mine.

Next morning my mother-in-law was up at about six. "Come along," she said, "everybody out. Let's find it." Truly, I wanted none of it, but after breakfast we were in the bush with surveyor's tape and compass and blackberry slasher and axe. Getting through that jungle took half the day and at precisely the given point, in the midst of rampant blackberries and scrub of fierce growth, we found the shaft. Brimming with water. I swear it.

I plumbed it to about forty feet, I think, with lengths of half-inch pipe screwed together—that was all the pipe I could handle—and took specimens from the top where rock appeared to have been dropped and hammered them to powder. If it wasn't gold we were looking at I cannot imagine what. But I took weeks to think this through and turned cautious and stubborn. I viewed it as a choice between the easy way and the hard way, between gold or fulfillment. It might have been something else entirely, but that was how I viewed it. So the bush grew back and the shaft is lost—I made sure of it. There are no regrets.

We grew our own food, vegetables in rotation all the year round, a small plot within a wire fence; it was that or starve to death. We added eggs and poultry meat, though getting that poor cockerel's head off each Friday night was too much for me in the end. Fourteen years later the survivors and their descendants still staggered about, the oldest domestic fowls on the face of the earth. Even tried farming for a few cash crops. Started off with green peas, but had to plough a half-acre first.

We had Jack, of course, the horse. He came with the place. Largest living thing I ever had communion with. Didn't have any proper fences so he had the run of the estate. Come dinner-time he'd thrust his head through the window and whinny for tid-bits, giving my mother-in-law hysterics. On bright nights he used to gallop, thudding, round and round and round the house. Trying to catch him for work was an intellectual feat. As soon as he saw leather he'd take off, down the hill and into the bush, kicking up his heels, making explosively vulgar noises from his propulsion end. Hitched him at last to the plough (reading how from a book) and away we went, but not along the contours as hoped. Straight down the hill again at an incredible rate, through all obstacles, and I was lucky to escape with my neck. Next time I hitched him to the spring-tine cultivator and when he tried to bolt I dug the tines in about a foot deep. Between us we tore that half-acre apart and Jack never forgave me.

I planted my peas from the gardening book, though it was not a packet in my hand, but a sack. Seeds two inches apart, rows a foot apart, each pea individually *put*. Took about a week. Up came the crop like a lawn, a wonderful sight. Several times daily I'd orbit it admiring the angular effect. Even wrote to the seed company expressing my joy; never had germination like it, I said, which was correct. But it was a long, dry summer. The peas grew stoutly to six inches, turned yellow, and that was that.

I planted lemons and passionfruit for long-term prosperity, three-quarters of an acre of each. Couldn't buy more; I was too much in debt. "Is it safe to plant them?" I asked the old man next door. "You know, frost and all that?"

"Frost," he said. "Here? You're on an easterly aspect, lad. The sun's warming things for you hours before it's up. That aspect is money in the bank."

In they went, in their beautiful rows, a picture to behold, all measured up, and it was a record cold year to succeed the drought. We even had snow. I rushed frantically from vine to vine and tree to tree covering them with everything I could grab, even the clothes off my back, but never picked a passionfruit, never sighted a lemon.

Raspberries came next. A quarter of an acre was all I could afford. In stools of three, six feet apart all ways, a sight to see. Everyone grew raspberries so I couldn't go wrong, I couldn't lose. Came spring and they burst gloriously into leaf.

One stormy night at half-past two that young woman said to me, "It's now, it's now, it's now." We charged away in our clapped-out baby car, twelve miles through lightning and thunder and mountains and torrential rain for the birth of child Number Two—Number One having gone to his grandmother fortuitously.

Home at daybreak, on my own, looking around. It was an awful old house, a dreadful old house, that I was trying to rebuild as I learnt to use tools. But I was appalled that morning as I looked around; it simply would not do.

I bought paint, enough for every room, and worked like a madman, pausing only in the evenings to drive to the hospital and back again. It didn't look bad after those seven hard days, and I hadn't told her, for her it was to be a surprise. But for a week I had not viewed the estate, the daily intoxication of the heavy-footed stride, the man of property, thumbs in pockets, glowing with pride. Hadn't seen Jack much either, though he had come up for oats each night when called. Incredibly voracious creature. Twelve and three-quarter acres to ravage at will, oats thrown in. He liked raspberries too. My quarter-acre was ruined, pulled up by the roots and chewed. Never picked a raspberry either.

Tried half an acre of French beans. They'd bring a good price, people said. "Beans do well round here." Seeds four inches apart as recommended in the gardening book, rows eighteen inches apart as straight as railway tracks. Enormous enterprise. The first were germinating before I had time to get the last in. First class season, warm and wet. How those beans shot up. Then the rabbits came. Off I rushed to the old man and practically wept.

"Well," he said, "you could fence your beans in, but I know you can't afford that, or you could sit up all night and shoo the rabbits off. . . . I'll tell you," he said, "I'll tell you what. Four gallons of night-soil and six pounds of lime stirred to a paste. Get yourself a brush, lad, and paint every leaf. That'll stop 'em. No rabbit alive'll give them a second look." It's what he said; I give my oath on the Book. So staunchly I stirred it up, four gallons of night-soil and six pounds of lime, and took my little brush. Half an acre, up and down the rows, painting every leaf. A nightmare event. And the rabbits still got them, which was just as well I think. And I still don't know whether that old man was serious or not.

Every major planting, no matter of what, came to grief. Farmers are born, I guess.

There were other little things, like foxes among the chickens, and storms smashing windows and sucking out two hundred handwritten manuscript sheets; never published, never finished. A screaming hurricane at night, the house swaying and groaning with bits breaking off, interior walls having just been removed for alterations. Pushing furniture to the front for defense, rushing round driving nails into everything, children under a table at the back of the house. . . . Drought; carrying water in buckets four hundred yards from the old man's well, shade temperatures of up to a hundred and twelve for ten successive days, pregnant wife sitting in the creek from seven in the morning until sunset. Children ill or injured, kicked by Jack, scratched by wild cats, nighttime fevers, and no doctor to consult. Every pet imaginable, silkies and bantams and pigeons and parrots and dogs and cats and mice and tortoises and white rabbits and guinea pigs and twin billy goats dying by violence, by inexhaustible bad luck. Chimneys ablaze and kerosene stoves blowing up and no telephone to call for help. A screech owl at night, like a woman under attack, inches from the bedroom window. Number One child sitting on a strip of bituminized felt blown from the roof, two deadly snakes coiled underneath. Number Two child, her head caught between the floorboard joists underneath the house: how do you get her out before she chokes? Number Four child, born unwell. Problems of relationships, of hardship and disappointment and monumental misfortune pushing faith to the brink. An uncontrollable forest fire of incredible magnitude, fire dropping from the heavens and springing up round about as if breaking out of the earth, not knowing if there can be an escape, stunned when the escape happens, drenching rain falling as if arranged by a writer to end a book. That house finished at last, after fourteen years, an environment made of materials on hand without spending money to achieve an effect, and having to give it all up from sheer impoverishment. Nothing to write about either, except swashbuckling stories for boys strenuously invented and documentary books for adults about larger-than-life adventure arduously researched, one's own experience not presenting itself as worth thinking about.

The Crest of Clarity

A journalist called, a very good journalist who had reviewed me twice. I assumed he had come to talk about my books: I mean, what else? I had written by then about twenty-five or six and was pleased that he felt they were worthy of general comment. Later, reading him through, it seemed he was more interested in the life I lived than in the work I produced. I was surprised and embarrassed. I was not obsessed by modesty, but regarded myself as an observer, not a doer, as a failure in a practical sense. I heard it said of me in those days by a local gossip that I was a lay-about who didn't know what work meant. I had bristled—what man working eighty hours a week would not?—but I had not gone after her with a stick. Had she been rude about my books I would have jumped up and down on the spot.

I am perturbed at the depths of my indoctrination, at what it accomplished. I was not dull, I was able to do things for myself and for others, able to lead and speak publicly to some effect without borrowing thoughts or opinions, but in the context of my greatest endeavor, my work, I remained blind and limp and lame. I observe there is no need to wait for Big-Brother-Watching. Has there ever been a time he has not been with us—or against us—or in us? Every voice that raises itself where children listen should look inwards, should go witch-hunting inwards, should know that the enemy has been planted within himself.

Where does awakening begin? I questioned earlier whether anything has an end. I equally doubt that anything has a beginning. Beginnings and endings are conventions of language. The specific moment that may be said to be the birth of an idea or a book or a change is too subtle to be defined by us. I was taught as a child that Creation is infinite, neither

beginning nor ending, and I am certain at this moment I was not misinformed. Yet there are opportunities, there are crests of clarity that
mark moments of revelation, there are sources that become apparent
when one is nudged. I have tonight, for instance, passed in part across
the origins of every book I am happy to own, as well as a few I would
be happy to forget. They are all there; the characters, the situations, the
conflict, the development; all are there. If you have detected one or two,
you're out in front—I needed *years* to see them for myself. Within the
same words lie originating parts of other books still to be discovered.

Each discovery made and each book written is part of the last and part
of the next.

The major crest of clarity, for me, came one wet Sunday fifteen years
back. It is as close to a beginning as I know. My brother and his wife
had added their children to ours rushing about the house. By half-past
five I was wearing thin and out of a head throbbing from noise said to
my brother, "What would happen to these kids if we were not here to
pick up the bits, say, for a year or a month—or even a week? What
would happen if they were left?"

"They'd die," he said.

They'd die? Left to fend for themselves in a world without adults,
they'd die? Or would they? Super kids would have no problems, but ordinary kids, real kids, a group of kids like ours, as we used to be ourselves,
would confront all the wonders of being alive.

Oh, the obvious truth so long in the coming. Real adventure cannot
happen to super heroes; by nature they would have to be insensitive to
it; real adventure belongs to us. Being ordinary and inept are acceptable
qualities, they give meaning to achievement. There must be contrasts
within oneself. One must know weakness to know strength. One must be
foolish to be wise. One must be scared to be brave. Adventure is simply
experience; the mistakes often enough meaning more than the successes.
I had come to my crest, unexpectedly, on a wet Sunday, or was it a door
that fell ajar and I was ready to slip a foot through? "Write it," something said to me, "you know what, boy; get down to it and write it. It's
time that kid who thought he was a coward had a book to read."

Mollie Hunter

Mollie Hunter, most of whose books are set in her native Scotland, writes historical fiction and fantasy of equal distinction. In 1973, her World War I novel, *A Sound of Chariots* (Harper & Row, 1972), won the Child Study Association of America Award; the British Library Association Carnegie Medal was conferred in 1975 for *The Stronghold* (Harper & Row, 1974). Among her other books are *The Ghosts of Glencoe* (Funk & Wagnalls, 1969), *The Wicked One* (Harper & Row, 1977), and *A Furl of Fairy Wind* (Harper & Row, 1977).

Mollie Hunter's book on writing for children, *Talent Is Not Enough* (Harper & Row, 1976), grew out of the lectures she had given the year before, primarily the Arbuthnot Honor Lecture. Her presentation, using the same title, was given on April 25, 1975, in Philadelphia, Pennsylvania, and was sponsored by the Graduate School of Library Science, Drexel University, and by seven other participating institutions.

Talent Is Not Enough

L ONG AGO, when I had to endure the kindly, adult condescension that
asks, "And what will you be when you grow up?," I used to answer,
"A kennel maid."

They smiled, reading into this only a childish desire to achieve a life-
long romp with the more playful versions of man's faithful friend. *I*
smiled, letting them have their delusion, the while I gritted my milk-
teeth on a private vision of myself as a commanding figure with wrists
of steel tautly controlling a pack of huge and baying hounds, a fearless
trainer, an expert tracker, a—

"Nonsense!" said a teacher who asked me this same question one day
and was given my usual answer. "You'll be a writer." And passed so firmly on to the child next in line of question that there was no arguing with
her decision. The idea that I could be a writer was planted in my head;
and for this, at least, I must thank that strong-minded lady—although
how she had reached so positive a conclusion can only be a guess with me
now. I was talkative, of course—I have to admit that; and even at that
tender age I was what I have always continued to be—a storyteller with
a great love for words of sweet sound and rich colouring. Yet what

neither she nor anyone else could have forecast at that time was that these drives would eventually find their true scope in writing for children; and for this, as for every other form of the art, there is a statement by Ralph Waldo Emerson which makes a shot in the dark out of any prediction for a future in writing.

"*Talent alone cannot make a writer. There must be a man behind the book.*"

"A person" behind the book would be the more acceptable phrasing nowadays, and—although I have no wish to try to improve on Emerson —it points the reference to say simply that "Talent is not enough." This much one learns in writing for children—to be terse without losing the totality of a meaning; and it is in writing for children that I see the deepest implications of the whole statement. I call a ghost to witness the initial proof of this; the fearsome, rheumaticky ghost of the man who was Granpa Cormack.

He was an acquaintance of my village childhood in the Lowlands of Scotland, this old man, and the sphere of his power was the local market garden. He was very tall and thin, with a hobbling walk aided by a long, heavy stick. His face was small and russet-coloured, heavily wrinkled by age, bad temper, and the pain of his rheumatics. Like ourselves, he used the broad Doric which was the everyday speech of the Lowlands then; and to him, we village children were always "*they blawstit bairns*"— "those damn kids."

Granpa Cormack purely hated children; yet it was to this old curmudgeon we had to apply in the summer holidays for a chance to earn much-needed cash from what we called "a job at the berries," and so Granpa was both our terror and our joy. Terror struck when he came hobbling down the rows of raspberry bushes, roaring and laying about him with that heavy stick. Joy came in the weighing-house when our berry-picking for the day was checked, wages were paid, and we all scuffled about gleefully trying to confuse Granpa's calculations with practical jokes—such as hiding stones in the baskets to increase their weight, and then stealthily abstracting the same.

It was still from Granpa Cormack, all the same, that I learned to recognise at least one aspect of the truth implicit in my theme, for berry-pickers under his rule were never allowed to do anything in half-hearted fashion. The basket for holding the fruit had to be slung around the neck so that both hands were free to work. Otherwise, like some ancient Demon King shooting through a stage trapdoor, Granpa would burst from the bushes roaring, "*Yase baith eer haunds!*"

The English of this is "Use both your hands," and it indicates the basic and very obvious sense in which talent is not enough. Even the greatest talent, lacking the craft to develop it, is no more than an itch in the mind; and the higher the potential, of course, the greater the effort needed to bring it to peak achievement.

To sustain this effort, however, means cultivating the capacity to endure loneliness—not that loneliness itself is peculiar to the creative mind. Far from that, the mere fact of being human implies an essential loneliness in each of us—microcosmic as we all are; for universe may communicate with universe, but—by their very nature—they cannot mingle.

To say, then, that the writer's lot is a lonely one, is not to complain of this, but simply to make the point that to be creative is to be different from those who are not; and so, to that extent also, to be cut off from those others. Yet, ironically, it is out of this even deeper loneliness that the writer hopes to be able to communicate to an extent denied the noncreative ones; and the irony is accentuated by his awareness that he will never really be able to tell how far he has succeeded in this.

A writer, indeed, could be likened to a person locked for life in a cell; someone to whom the mere fact of imprisonment has taught things he wants desperately to convey. He compiles a code, spends the rest of his life using this to tap out messages on the wall of his cell, and all the time he taps he is asking himself, *"Is there anyone out there listening? Can they hear me? Do they understand?"*

It may take years of experiment, too, before a writer can even be sure he is using the code which is best for him—before he settles down, in fact, to the form of writing that best deploys his particular talent; and with hindsight on my own experience, I can see nothing to choose between myself and an old shepherd to whom I gave a lift in my car, late one winter's night. He sat watching the road ahead, this old fellow, his gaze fixed on the centre-line of glass studs endlessly reflecting light from the car's headlamps. But seemingly he had not grasped that this was simply a repeated reflection, for at last he said in a puzzled voice, *"Wha lichts they?"* (Who lights these?)

I explained that the lights were only reflectors set into the road, but he was not convinced by this. Some person or other must have lit the road ahead—he was sure of that; and so it was with me at the start of my career as a children's writer. In spite of the years I had spent learning and attempting to practise the writer's art, I came late to this aspect of it, and only then because of the persuasions of my own two young children. The book they coaxed from me was expanded from stories I had previously made up for them; but for me it was also a sustained attempt at a form of language that could ring true only if it hit a particular note—a traditional note, evolved from many, many past centuries of the music in the storyteller's voice.

I took the children with me on the way to rediscovery of that music, reading the book to them by instalments in the course of its writing.

And even although I realised it was only the beam of my own imagination reflecting back at me from their pleasure in this tale, I still had the feeling of being on a road where *someone* had placed lights ahead for me.

There was one other thing that happened in the course of all this to convince me that this lit road was the one I would travel thenceforth, and always. At a certain point in the story, my eight-year-old son wept—more than that, he wept in a way I had never seen happen before with him, or with any other child. He sat bolt upright, never ceasing to listen to my reading, his gaze never shifting from me. There was no blinking, no sniffling, not a tremor of his features. The tears simply rose up, filled his eyes, then spilled over, and bounced like drops of broken crystal down his cheeks. The child seemed unaware he *was* weeping, in fact; and to me, it was a very moving thing, for spontaneous tears like this come from some suddenly touched and very deep level of emotion.

I read further on, and the tears no longer came. But duration of an emotion is no gauge of its intensity. Moreover, the range of a child's emotion has the same extent as that of an adult, and all the child lacks, by comparison, is the vocabulary to match his range—yet still there are ways of supplying this defect. So variable are the uses of language, so infinitely flexible their application, that the storyteller may turn the simplest of words into poetry powerful enough to express the deepest, most complex of emotions; and this note of strong and simple poetry was the very one I had been attempting to strike in my choice of language for that particular book.

Those soundless tears, then, did more than move me. I felt them as an honour, for the story situation that drew them was poignant beyond the child's own power to express; but he had understood my form of words for it, and they had spoken for him. And so at last, it seemed to me then, I had discovered my particular code—one that would indulge my keen delight in all the effects of sound and rhythm and meaning in language, as much as it satisfied my instinctive urge to turn everything, everything, *everything,* into a story!

A synthesis of two loves had brought me to this point—my writing and my children. Yet it does not follow that the writer who loves children can, or should be, a children's writer, any more than that a person who loves animals can or should be a lion-tamer. Love can be blind, inept, a bore. Understanding is Argus-eyed, and shrewd in realising the child's need for story-characters through whom he can identify with the rest of human kind, and so discover who *he* is, how he "belongs"—

Talking of this to my husband one day, he quoted something from his own childhood in the village neighbouring mine—Prestonpans, locally known simply as "the Pans."

"When I was a wee lad, we used to play at "War"—the First World War, with Germans on one side, British on the other; and the men of the Pans were there in the thick of it, and fighting with the best of them. Then after I went to school and had a history lesson or two, we played at "War" again—Robert the Bruce at Bannockburn, with Scots on one side and the English on the other; and the men of the Pans were in that fight too, and still among the best of them. I never had any trouble in identifying!"

And neither he had. A childhood where story was king had seen to that; and in the talent of the children's writer, the lively imagination of the storyteller is the basic and chief ingredient.

A powerful grip on the possibilities of language is also essential in writing for children. This, because selectivity must be practised in relation to the reader's age—which is not to say, of course, that a child should not be sent scurrying to the dictionary for help. Rather, it indicates that, out of all the choices available in a given syntax, the children's writer is constantly being forced to find the simple one which will enhance rather than diminish his text, by being at the same time the strongest, or the most vividly descriptive. The bones of language are what he seeks—spare, smooth, strong, needing no fleshy padding to elaborate a structure already inherently beautiful.

The capacity to recall the sensory impacts and perceptions of one's early years is obviously also a vital part of the talent in question; but a further dimension of recall is needed for the physical world of childhood, which—we tend to forget—is out of scale in surroundings proportioned to adults. Terror, adventure, or interest exist here in direct proportion to this distortion of scale—especially for the very young child, to whom the underside of a table may be a dark cave, a walk of a few yards along a gloomy path a journey of heroic proportions, a scuffle of dust a relief-map, fascinating in its contours, offering godlike opportunities for re-arrangement of hills and valleys.

Finally, to come full circle on the question of emotion, adult life conforms to a code that debars spontaneity, and is embarrassed by naked idealism. To scream, shout, or howl to release a feeling is considered uncivilized; to be a committed idealist is thought naive. So adults learn to protect themselves from over-painful realisations, and to blunt the first sharp edge of any emotion; with the result that uninhibited displays of childhood emotion become gradually incomprehensible to them. And so they tend to move through the causes of these with all the expertise of elephants trying to balance on the tips of asparagus fern.

The person whose nature has intended him to be a children's writer can find a way through this delicate jungle, for there is something in that nature which has preserved the child's sense of wonder, and kept alight the enthusiasms of youth. The other side of this coin is that some at least of his emotions remain as raw and vulnerable as in those early years; and thus he may feel again the first sharpness of their impact, as much as he is able to re-experience the terror of the dark cave or gloomy path, to taste and sense again with the novel faculties of youth, and to visualise once more in a careless scuffle of dust, the marvellous contours of a small, strange world.

All this may not answer to what children's writers, in fact, are; but that does not invalidate any theory of what their talent should be. The touchstone of truth is in the children themselves; and I look back with gratitude to having my own two children to inform me so. I had another good fortune at that time, however, and that was in having reached a point in my life where I was ready to rebel sharply against all the conventions which then ruled the world of children's writing.

It was wrong and stupid, in my opinion, that this should be dominated by a middle-class syndrome which was no more than a hangover from the days of Victorian nurseries; downright ridiculous that juvenile hero-characters should always be children of this class, engineered into excitement by such highly coincidental unlikelihoods as parents called suddenly to visit sick Aunt Jessie, jewel thieves in the neighbourhood, and the only policeman available being either stupid, deaf, or venal. This was pre-masticated pap, regurgitated for a mythical "child reader" by adults who were themselves examples of retarded mental development.

In my view also, all those publishers with a fixation on stories of English boarding-school life came into this same retarded category. Such stories, I guessed, were more than just alien to my native Scots tradition. They must certainly also be incomprehensible to all children not of the elite minority processed through such unnatural institutions. As a parent, I was angered by the humiliations of poor children perpetually confronted in their reading by the cruel implication that they were the exceptions to the rule of people never having to worry about the rent, or getting enough to eat, or being cold and ragged. As for the historical novels written for children, I considered it was high time someone put paid to all those cardboard figures flouncing about in period dress, and delicately flourishing anachronistic handkerchiefs.

If a seventeenth-century commoner blew his nose with his fingers, let him do that! And why not write about commoners anyway, instead of allowing an endless parade of aristocrats to dominate the scene? Commoners are the very stuff of history. The feel, the taste, the smell of history is what comes through their lives—"the rascal multitude," the *canaille*—those who beg and starve and steal, or labour skilfully if they have been lucky enough to have the chance of learning a trade; and through the centuries, die in the cannon's mouth. Let them speak, for a change!

So I argued—hotly. But of course, I was only one of a considerable number of authors who were then briskly engaged in freeing the whole scene of children's writing from its artificial conventions; and now this freedom has been so well accomplished that one finds it hard to believe these conventions ever existed. And yet, and yet. . . . It cannot be too strongly insisted that freedom is not only a state of being. It is also an attitude of mind. Lacking this, freedom fragments into anarchy—a sequence which impels us from the examination of talent to its place in context of the statement that "Talent is not enough."

"There must be a person behind the book" is the corollary to this statement; and sooner or later in a writer's life comes the situation where—like every other individual—he or she is faced with all the implications of his own personality in relation to past events and future possibilities. The confrontation is a painful one, yet without the self-knowledge it brings there can be no true understanding of other people, no real compassion for them. And to experience these feelings for others is also to experience the sole possible victory over the essential loneliness of the human condition. The victory, however, comes only very gradually, for it relates directly to the slow and difficult process of accepting one's self-knowledge and coming to peaceful terms with it. Sometimes, indeed, the process is lost sight of altogether. Yet still the trigger-point can remain clear in the mind; and I can place exactly when this happened in my own life.

October 1956. The rising of the Hungarian people against Soviet Communist rule. The last, pathetic broadcast to the rest of Europe, asking for the help that never came. The pictured glimpse of a young girl's face—round, serious, innocent, as she marched along under a banner that asked for nothing more than peace and freedom. Another glimpse of the same child—she could not have been more than fifteen—lying dead from machine-gun fire. The heart-breaking message sent with the children rushed out of Budapest and over the Austrian border—*"We are staying to fight. Please look after our children."*

We never missed a news broadcast at that time, my husband and I. The tension in our household took on an unbearable edge. Then, at the end of a bulletin one day, the Red Cross made an appeal for people to help in the dangerous work of getting those children over the Austro-Hungarian border, and suddenly I felt a great, cracking release at the very deepest level of my emotions.

Children are important to me. I look at the eyes of an eight-year-old and see a wonder shining there which, in every generation, is innocence renewed; and I am moved to tenderness. I look at the eyes of an adolescent and see there the conflicting eagerness and uncertainty of the between years; and I find myself touched by a strong compassion.

My own two children were the most important things in the world to me at that time. My love for my husband was deep. My fear of death

for myself was an obsession which had haunted me every day from the
moment when the death of my father—loved to the point of idolatry—
had shattered my nine-year-old life. Yet in that sudden moment of emotional release, nothing of all this mattered any more. My loves were un-
altered, I was still desperately afraid of dying, but I knew I had to do
something to save even one at least of those child victims—anything at
all, supposing it was only protecting the child from death with my own
body. Otherwise, I realised, I would either have to live with the memory
of a betrayal; or, like Judas, go hang myself, for I could never bear to
look myself in the face again.

I told my husband I was going straight out to answer the Red Cross
appeal. I can see yet his look of sadness; but he was—and is—a man of
conscience, and he made no attempt to stop me. And so off I went to vol-
unteer—and found my noble gesture ending in bathos, for I had none
of the special skills the Red Cross needed for their work, and another
dead body would have been only an embarrassment to them.

My offer of help was not accepted; yet still my moment of self-con-
frontation retained its value, for out of it I had learned that there are
worse things in life than dying, and that some things are worth dying
for.

I found myself looking at my life with new eyes, the eyes of self-
knowledge. I began the painful process of coming to terms with what
I saw, of developing some philosophy out of it; and because I am a writer, the maturing of such talent as I had ran parallel to this process. In
time, some aspect or other of this slowly forming philosophy became integral to everything I wrote; and so in time also, I arrived at my final
clear criteria for deciding what place to assign the terms "suitable" and
"unsuitable" in children's reading.

*   *   *

I recall an old Scots lady who told me scathingly, "Ach, books! If ye've
read yin, ye've read the lot!"

I challenge anyone to produce a comment more shattering to a writer,
or more ignorant of the true and ultimate function of books—which
is to preserve aspects of life conveyed in terms of enduring importance,
creative imagination, and artistic skill. This is the dictionary definition
of literature, but it should be remembered that these same aspects include high adventure, humour, and fantasy—as instanced, say, in R. L.
Stevenson's *Treasure Island*, Mark Twain's *Tom Sawyer*, and James
Stephen's *The Crock of Gold*. All of these were beloved books of my
own childhood. All answer truly to the definition of literature. With
them for example, it could reasonably be argued that children are as entitled as adults to the benefits of so valuable a human endeavour—more
so, indeed, for the first light of literature on a young mind does more

than illumine. A touch of glory descends, and that mind can never be truly dark again.

No such argument is needed, of course, for the child whose reading ability has outstripped his physical age. For this reader, at least, any book which yields something of literary value is a suitable one; but by far the greater number of children will find their reading pleasure in books which take account of the general limitations of childhood's intellectual experience, and which are therefore categorised as being specifically for certain age-groups.

A dual onus thus falls on those who provide the normal reading experience of children. They must ensure that this offers literature in the fullest meaning of that word, and they must bear in mind that children are—or should be—a special care, in the sense that literature is one of the mediums through which young minds eventually reach maturity. Thus also, if old conventions are to be discarded as restrictive to the true function of literature as well as being socially out-moded, they must be replaced by at least this one all-important convention—the convention of care; and the only area of debate left is the extent of this care and the manner in which it should be demonstrated.

At first sight the answer seems obvious and very simple. No single group of people has the right to ignore a consensus of thoughtful opinion on the development of the child mind; particularly where this is concerned with the comparative defencelessness of the pre-pubertal years. Some form of censorship would therefore appear to be a continuing need—a sort of gentle conspiracy, perhaps, of adults who are socially progressive, well-intentioned, and experienced in the world of children's books; but this will not do. It will never do, or we shall be back where we started with the new freedom simply re-creating the old prison in modern shape.

On the other hand, there are themes now encountered in children's books which, at first mention, appear totally unsuitable for readers of tender age. To name but a few at random—race prejudice, social deprivation, drug usage and abusage, environmental pollution—all of which are topics of burning relevancy to our society; and all of which, once the shock of first mention is past, can be seen to affect the lives of children as much as they affect the lives of adults. Inevitably, therefore, it must be accepted that children have to learn to relate to the type of situation from which such themes are drawn; but the operative phrase which defines the convention of care in this respect is that they should be enabled to do so *in a manner which raises the level of their understanding.*

Thus, for the children's writer who chooses any such theme, there is only one way of discharging his dual onus. He must create some frame of reference which will enable the reader to relate intellectually to the *significance* of that theme; and the same pattern of argument applies to subjects of an emotional significance.

A broken home, the death of a loved person, a divorce between parents—all these are highly charged emotional situations once considered unsuitable for children's reading, but which are nevertheless still part of some children's experience; and the writer's success in casting them in literary terms rests on the ability to create an emotional frame of reference to which children in general can relate.

The new freedom of the children's writer, in fact, would appear to have no problems that talent and technique combined cannot solve. It gives the impression of youth itself—expansive, strong, and vigorous. Yet the impression is mistaken, for this particular freedom is a delicate thing. Like a small, wild bird, its wings are easily broken. It can be killed by capture.

Where is the emotional frame of reference for rape? Or for "baby-battering"? More often than we care to think, the rapist's victim is a child. The incidence of children maimed or beaten to death by a violent parent has been revealed as wide-spread in Western society. Are we to infer here also that we are justified in arguing from the particular to the general—that because some children are victims of such aberrant behaviour, it may be made part of all children's experience? The examples chosen are not extreme, and it would be absurd for the children's writer to beg this question and yet still claim free choice of thematic material.

Similarly, where is the intellectual frame of reference for all the decadent aspects of our society—the hedonism, the perversions of art and nature, the dance on the edge of the grave that flaunts the triumph of sensation over sensitivity? To pretend unawareness of these is in itself a form of decadence. Not to condemn them also as being aberrations from even our wildly imperfect norm is to live without courage— worse, without hope for the future. And children *are* the future. Are we, then, justified in sending them out with minds crippled by our own handicaps?

The distinction between the normal and the aberrant—this, to my mind, is where the dividing line should be drawn in themes for children's writing, with all that lies on the side of the normal classed as suitable, and all on the other side as unsuitable. This, it seems to me, is where the convention of care must operate most strongly—particularly in those tender pre-pubertal years. Otherwise, the law of diminishing returns is immediately activated, and the writer will only succeed in rubbing his young reader's nose in the dirt of the world before the same child has had the chance to realise that the world itself is a shining star.

It could be fairly argued, of course, that there is no need for any such dividing line; the good taste of either writer or publisher, or of both combined, making a sufficient safeguard to the rights and sensibilities of young readers. I would not wish to be Cassandra in this, for it could be just as fairly argued that those of a generation ago made the same assumption on matters they considered unsuitable for children's reading; and their mould was rudely broken.

It would be a very blinkered approach which did not recognise that ours could be broken as rudely—and not least because the new freedom of children's writers has also meant new scope for talented people in every aspect of the children's book world. In effect, children's writing is rapidly rising from its position as the Cinderella of the arts, and it could be salutary to wonder whether some talented newcomers to the ball might be more concerned with dancing in glass slippers than with keeping an ear open for the midnight chime that warns, *"Children . . . ! Children . . . !"*

The law of diminishing returns will begin to operate with a vengeance then—indeed, the conditions for it seem already to have been set to some extent by the technical device so often now used to define the frame of reference for a realistic story of modern times. This is the first-person narrative, in which the limits of a young narrator's grasp are set as those presumed for the young reader. The result of this device may be a story to which a reader can relate in very direct terms; but simply because of the narrator's limited vocabulary, there is no scope for the adventure in language which allows the reader's mind to soar. And overall, this is a loss.

In terms of an individual book, this net loss may be small. In terms of a vogue, or cult, in children's books, the loss could be significant; and at the present time it seems to me that the vogue in "realistic" stories for children is indeed beginning to take on the aspect of a cult. This, in turn, could spell out the danger of even greater loss than an incidental restriction on language—the danger that children over-burdened by serious themes may be made old before their time; or even, simply, that they may be denied the due meed of their natural fascination for the fantastic, the hilarious, the exotic, the adventurous, in story-telling.

These are all items that have to be taken into account before the freedom of the children's writer can be assessed for what it truly is—freedom with responsibility. They are only one more aspect of the convention of care; and it is only by respecting that convention that this same freedom can be exercised in a manner which has value to the development of a particular age-group, at the same time as it sustains the concept of literature.

One last point must be made. There can never be any question, in all this, of preaching to the young. That would not only be self-defeating, in the sense that it would produce a tract instead of literature. It would also be a useless exercise—as both argument convinces, and vivid recollections of my own childhood remind me.

I had the run of my grandfather's library then—a collection devoted to works of an "improving" nature, but the only improvement this achieved for me was that I learned to read very fast. I had to, in order to be able to pick out the action scenes from the long, moralising passages I thought of as "the dull bits." My puritan upbringing balanced the account with feelings of guilty unease over deceiving poor grandfather. Yet despite the guilt, I still resented the dull bits as attempts to lecture me about life, when what I wanted to do was to find out about it for myself. And this latter, it seems to me, is the driving urge of the older child whose basic need to identify has to take account of the expanding realisations of his adolescent years.

The world to be faced then, this adolescent becomes vaguely aware, is more complex than he had imagined in the years of early childhood. Right and wrong, good and evil, are no longer absolutes, in the sense that different groups of people have differing interpretations of these terms. Vaguely also, he senses that his very freedom of choice as an individual is forcing him to decide with which group he will stand; and here, it also seems to me, is the important area in which the convention of care must operate for such readers.

To "load" the story in favour of the writer's own standards would be morally wrong and eventually as self-defeating as preaching at the reader—who would very quickly detect any atmosphere of special pleading. And yet the children's writer who aims a story at this particular age-group is opting out of his responsibilities as a person unless he acknowledges the type of dilemma which can face its members. And once again, any talent which cannot make this acknowledgment in story terms must yield any claim to create literature.

I recall one book in particular which faced me with problems on all the counts I have mentioned, but specifically on this last one. It concerned certain true incidents of witchcraft in sixteenth-century Scotland, and was published at a time when witchcraft was much in vogue as a subject; but this last, so far as I was concerned, was simply coincidence. My interest was in the personal and historical motivations behind these incidents; yet how could I convey this interest to young readers either through people so depraved as the witches themselves, or as brutal as those who eventually brought them to justice?

I found the key to my problem in two characters. Without loss of historical accuracy, I could picture one of the witches as a young girl drawn unwillingly into conspiracy. Without any distortion of actual events, I could create the fictitious character of a boy through whom her story was told. By using this latter device, moreover, I would be projecting through a character who was only an accidental witness to the activities of the witches; and so, without in any way minimising the degree of their depravity, I could be selective in terms of the incidents witnessed and the nature of such incidents.

Thus far the technical expertise of my craft had carried me; yet still I knew that to write this book in terms of incident only would be a sterile exercise—the very manipulation of acquired skills I so despised. I had to get behind the eyes of my characters, find the little threads of common human feeling that bound them to me, not as a writer, but as a person. I had to discover from this something that was worth writing about, or the book would not be worth writing at all.

What sort of people were my girl, Gilly, and my young fellow, Adam? I had visualised her as a victim, a gentle creature without the courage to fight against her fate. I had made him sullen, aggressive; someone who believed he could survive his own brutal circumstances only by treating pity for others as a sign of weakness in himself. What happens when the lives of two such youngsters become entangled?

Would not Adam then face a choice? Would he not have to show himself more than ever ruthless; or, even if it meant lessening the chances of his own survival, to allow himself to feel compassion for Gilly? As a writer, I knew I could achieve greater depth of characterisation for Adam if I had him choose the latter course, and that this would also create insight on all the other characters involved with him. As a person, I had learned that only in compassion is true strength; and thus Adam's struggle towards the same knowledge became the pivot on which the whole plot turned.

I enjoyed writing that book. There is a particular exhilaration in voicing a belief passionately held; an exquisite pleasure in practising a craft learned only very slowly to the point where the skills are confidently handled. I was confident enough at that time to feel I could give my story the bite and pace it needed to make its impact, and through the reluctant growth of Adam's compassion for Gilly, I spoke out loud and clear.

But to what purpose? Was there anyone out there listening? Could they hear me? Did they understand?

One looks around in schools and libraries at children in the teen years, and the exaltation of writing is overtaken by forlorn realism. In general, one must acknowledge, the minds of these children are pre-occupied with the myriad trivia of their days. In particular, the physical uncertainties of adolescence have brought each one to the peak point of self-obsession normally experienced in an individual life. What time or inclination have they for an appreciation of literature? How capable are they of such an appreciation?

The honest answer to both questions is that the majority of these young people will always read at the superficial level, and it will always be incident which has the predominant impact on their minds. The characterisation which dictates course and development of incident will always be taken for granted, *but*—and here, ah here, one may soar again! Even the most superficial reader will follow the incident by identifying with the character concerned in it; and so, willy-nilly, there comes a point when reader and character are involved in the same emotions.

The experience does not last, of course—how long does it take to read a book? Yet even so, the reader will at least have glimpsed a reflection of himself in another young person caught in a situation that demands the enunciation of some value, the setting of some standard. Temporarily at least, he will have had a sense of participating in the decision taken, and the process of thought set subconsciously in train may yet surface in his mind. Moreover, if the writer has done his job properly *as* a writer, story will still be king. And so the reader will still be essentially free to formulate his own eventual philosophy; but the convention of care will at least have shown him something of what may be implied by the choices occurring in those adolescent years.

"It all sounds very moral." This was the comment made to me in a rather dismissing manner on another occasion when I put forward these ideas; and yet what is their obvious alternative? The theory that the artist owes allegiance to nothing save his art?

This is no more than a time-worn excuse invented for the credulous by the inadequate, for the essence of creativeness is the ability to produce a work which is more than the sum of its parts. The artist's own life is only one of the many lives which form these parts, and the basis of his achievement is in realising and accepting his involvement with those others. Its significance is in having transmuted this acceptance into a form which has beauty and meaning for them also.

Any other claim for the artist is sheer humbug, for not to accept involvement is to admit to a talent too feeble to direct the true springs of creativity. Where children are concerned, it is pernicious humbug, for children have no experience against which they may assess the artifice of such a claim. They have not yet learned what it is to ask for bread, and be given a stone. And so, perhaps it *is* all very moral; yet not, I think, in the way the commentator implied.

The eye of self-knowledge informs me that such values as I have are not mine by right. Nor have I done anything to earn my basic abilities as a writer. All these are part of something life has given me; therefore something I owe. And what I owe I must give back, along with the natural increase due to experience. This, it seems to me, is merely what honesty demands; and true honesty is itself the only true morality. I find my way of giving through children, because I am a children's writer, and because no comment on childhood has ever moved me so much as these lines:

> Have a myriad children been quickened,
>   Have a myriad children grown old,
> Grown gross and unloved and embittered,
>   Grown cunning and savage and cold?
> God abides in a terrible patience,
>   Unangered, unworn,
> And again for the child that was squandered
>   A child is born

>   (G. K. Chesterton, "The Nativity," in *The Collected Poems of*
>   *G. K. Chesterton* [Cecil Palmer, 1927])

What a catalogue of blame! And what a note of grace at its end.

The child that was myself was born with a little talent, and I have worked hard, hard, hard, to shape it. Yet even this could not have made me a writer, for there is no book can tell anything worth saying unless life itself has first said it to the person who conceived that book. A philosophy *has* to be hammered out, a mind shaped, a spirit tempered. This is true for all of the craft. It is the basic process which must happen before literature can be created. It is also the final situation in which the artist is fully fledged; and because of the responsibilities involved, these truths apply most sharply to the writer who aspires to create literature for children.

Especially for this writer, talent is not enough—no, by God it is not! Hear this, critics, editors, publishers, parents, teachers, librarians—all you who will shortly pick up a children's book to read it, or even glance idly through it. There *must* be a person behind that book.

Jean Fritz

Jean Fritz, a notable author of children's books who specializes in American history, historical fiction, and biography, was the first American author to contribute to this lecture series. Since the United States was celebrating its bicentennial year, her comments were particularly meaningful. She said, in a letter to the editor, "I spent the first thirteen years of my life in China, going to a British school, playing with German neighbors, and trying to figure out what an American was." Among the books in which she has found some answers to her question are *Brady* (Coward-McCann, 1960), *Early Thunder* (Coward-McCann, 1967), *Who's That Stepping on Plymouth Rock?* (Coward-McCann, 1975), *Will You Sign Here, John Hancock?* (Coward-McCann, 1976), and *Stonewall* (Putnam, 1979).

Mrs. Fritz, who lives in Massachusetts, has been a librarian, a teacher, and a reviewer. In 1979 she received the annual prize given by the Children's Book Council of Washington, D.C., for the body of an author's nonfiction for children. Her lecture, "The Education of an American," was given on April 9, 1976, in Los Angeles, California, and was sponsored by seventeen libraries, library systems, and universities in the area.

The Education
of an American

L ADIES AND GENTLEMEN, your invitation to me to be the May Hill
Arbuthnot lecturer this year when our nation is celebrating its 200th
anniversary and when the American Library Association is celebrating
its 100th anniversary is such an honor, I long for old-fashioned, phrase-
flying rhetoric. If I were only twelve years old again, I might be able to
do the occasion justice. In those days I seldom suffered over language.
Knowing my own was never grand enough, I appealed to poetry to mark
an occasion, rich nineteenth-century poetry with which, fortunately, I
was from an early age well furnished. So it was in the spring of 1928
when I returned to America after a childhood in China that I prepared
myself for what seemed to me to be a peak occasion, the fairy-tale point
of my own story. My long exile was over, the loneliness behind me, the
trials overcome, and when on the deck of the Robert Dollar liner, the
President Taft, we came into sight of American soil—the Golden Gate
no less—I was ready to live happily ever after. I was "The Man Without
a Country" (and I knew the story well) but *I* was returning home. I
strode to the railing of the deck and I addressed the passengers who had
assembled to watch our approach to land. "Breathes there the man, with

soul so dead," I cried, "who never to himself hath said, 'This is my own, my native land!' " The passengers looked, as I reconstruct the scene, somewhat nonplussed, my parents looked decidedly embarrassed, but in the background the ship's band struck up "California, Here I Come!" Perhaps the band merely wanted to forestall further theatrics, but I felt the moment had been well served. I was satisfied.

As a child, I spent an inordinate amount of time puzzling over what it meant to be an American. How was it different from being another nationality? Would I, having lived twelve years of my life abroad, be less American than my cousins? In the international community where we lived, 500 miles up the Yangtse River, my friends and classmates represented many countries—German, English, Italian, Russian, as well as American; going into their homes, celebrating their holidays with them, I had a miniature exposure to a wide world. I could see the different life-styles of each country and enjoy them, yet I knew with the passionate chauvinism of an expatriated child that America was best. My friends, of course, were just as passionate about their loyalties. And I am afraid that we all felt fortunate that we were not Chinese because in those days to be Chinese might mean that you were impoverished to a degree that was hard to conceive even when the evidence was before your eyes. Every day as I walked to the British school that I attended, I passed lines of ragged, miserable, sick, filthy, often monstrously deformed beggars and I remember the confusion of emotion that never failed to sweep over me—pity, shame, repulsion, helplessness, wonder that human beings in such a condition could still be human beings, but always I ended up feeling guilty but lucky. Supremely lucky to be an American. Such a scene could never take place in America because there were two things I knew with certainty: America was the land of opportunity and America was moral. More moral than other countries. I suppose I learned this in so many ways, spoken and implied, that it became embedded in my consciousness as, indeed, it has been part of Americans' collective consciousness for much of our two hundred years. Historically, money and morality have been the twin concerns of Americans, driving us first across an ocean and then across a continent—our morality sometimes holding our acquisitiveness in check, sometimes disguising it so cleverly, we believed, no matter what we did, that we were simply engaged in the self-congratulatory process that we call progress.

But of course at this stage of my life I knew none of this. I didn't grasp, nor do I believe the average citizen today truly grasps, the unique story of our country. To come to grips with what it means to be an American (and I don't care how recent an American) requires a person to wrap his mind around the enormity of the discovery of America itself: to feel what it meant psychologically to a civilized world to have a new undeveloped continent suddenly at its disposal. A new chance, an escape from corruption, a fresh slate, a place to begin again. "We shall be as a citty upon a hill," John Winthrop said; "the eies of all people are uppon us." As long as there was new land, there was new hope, and it was but a step for the hope for regeneration to turn to a conviction that regeneration had taken place. And it was another step to the desire to disseminate our morality and our Americanism, which at times became almost indistinguishable. That I was indirectly involved in this business of dissemination, that my parents were missionaries, seemed as natural, as inevitable to me as the fact that Sunday came every week. But observations came later. In my childhood I took all precepts on faith and if I had a hero, I suppose it was Woodrow Wilson because he was my father's hero. Recently I came upon a statement of Wilson's that strikes at the heart of what has traditionally been one aspect of our national self-image. "Sometimes people call me an idealist," Wilson said. "Well, that is the only way I know I am an American. America is the only idealistic nation in the world."

Avidly I read books by American authors. How American was I? I wondered. If I had taken the reading too seriously, I might have been disheartened. America was obviously a masculine country dominated by boys, sometimes mischievous but always enterprising. Even the men could never quite surrender their golden boyhoods—wild, free, and raw as the country had once been wild, free, and raw. No matter where they lived, they went on acting, at least in books, as if the frontier were just around the corner and at any minute they might strike gold. You couldn't hold a good man down in America, the authors seemed to say. Or a bad one either, for that matter. If a man was clever enough to fool the world, Mark Twain was not the only one who was willing to hand it to him. The country was built, I gathered, not so much by men caught up in the grim reality of survival but by men, rascals and heroes alike, out-witting and out-talking each other for the sheer fun of it.

One major branch of children's literature right down to the present day is in this Mark Twain tradition and I revelled in it, appreciating the vicarious opportunity to light out for the Territory and escape the determined domesticating pressures of Aunt Sally, who was present in female form in most of the books I read and certainly in the society I knew. What I found strange was that the adult world, which in real life was unfailingly on the side of Aunt Sally, nevertheless accepted every kind of high jinks that appeared on paper or had taken place in the past. "Boys will be boys," was the affectionate way adults threw up their hands and held on to their past. It was the Mark Twain tradition, so closely related to America's frontier folk literature, and indeed it rang absolutely true to me, for my father's boyhood, as he recounted it, was filled with tall stories, practical jokes, robust humor, escapades that involved bloodhounds at night, cows in belfry towers, schoolteachers outsmarted. When I asked my father to make up a story, invariably he gave me a spur-of-the-moment Chinese adaptation of Paul Bunyan—a Yangtse Valley giant who strode down from the hills at night and with one easy step crossed the five-mile-wide river. "And what would you do if you met a tiger walking up to you on the street?" I asked my father. It was my favorite question as a very young child because I adored the answer. My father would laugh as if he didn't have to think twice about that. "Why, I'd just reach down that tiger's throat," he would say, "and turn him inside out so he would be going the other way."

In 1900 my Great-uncle Henry, who was at the time moderator of the Presbyterian Church, wrote a half-joking prescription for education that seems to me to carry the same flavor of the nineteenth-century down-to-earth American style that I heard in my father's stories and that I found in so many books. "They may talk all they want," he wrote, "about their new-fangled fads in education but I submit if our family is not a proof that buckwheat cakes in winter, sour apples in summer, and pumpkin pie and the Shorter Catechism the whole year round, do not produce a pretty hardy generation after all."

This is a long way from the style of the intellectually oriented eighteenth century. Patrick Henry subscribed to a barefooted boyhood, but among our Founding Fathers he was one of the few who was not making out formal, hour-by-hour schedules of study for his sons and daughters. In the meantime, of course, Andrew Jackson had come along, the west had been opened up and settled, and the Common Man was riding so high that even an educated man like my Great-uncle Henry, who had written a book with the formidable title of *The Cosmos and the Logos,* could with tongue-in-cheek gusto proclaim that the simple life, the homely virtues, and a full stomach were the backbone of America. This was the tone of nineteenth-century America; it has changed course over the years but it has persisted, sometimes for better, sometimes for worse.

It was for the worse when just thirty years after the publication of *Huckleberry Finn,* Booth Tarkington came along with the Penrod books. At the time I first read these books, I suppose I enjoyed them and I remember my parents' enthusiasm. On a recent re-reading, however, I was astonished that the books could once have been so popular. I don't know whether Booth Tarkington, writing in the early twentieth century, had simply lost the vigor of the preceding generation, or whether the Common Man, or in this case the common small-town, mid-western boy, had been reduced to a stock character, loved for his very commonness. This was Main Street, U.S.A., junior style. There were certain things you could count on here: schools, for instance, existed for the sole purpose of developing ever more exquisite techniques for boring the young; the rich highfallutin people who lived in fancy houses existed for the pleasure that everyday folks derived in bringing them down a peg; animals,

black people, and the majority of girls existed for the benefit of an author who liked to play tricks and make sly jokes. All of this passed as
good, clean American fun. The critics who find current children's literature immoral because it includes an occasional four-letter word or acknowledges the existence of sex should re-examine the basic morality of
some of the so-called wholesome books of forty and fifty years ago.

Happily, we have more appealing books of recent vintage in this same
comic small-town, callow-boy genre. *Homer Price* and *Henry Huggins*
carried the tradition into the 1950s and, of course, are still read. And on
the television screen we have had their counterparts. Joyce Maynard,
writing about the 1960s, said that in her girlhood, watching "Leave It to
Beaver" was like "taking a course in how to be an American. . . . I
watched that show every day after school," she wrote, " (fresh from my
own failures) and studied it like homework, because the Cleaver family
was so steady and normal—and my own was not—and because the boys
had so many friends, played basketball, drank sodas, *fit in.*"

I read for the same reasons. Not all the boys I met in American fiction fit into the average, small-town category, but they were all resourceful and persevering. And this, I had understood from my first introduction to books, was the American Way. The Little Engine That Could
was in my mind unquestionably an American engine whose example, if
I wanted to be a good American, I was expected to follow. Nothing was
out of reach of the person who was good, hard working, and determined, for in America the poor boy might not wind up marrying a princess but he could (and sometimes did) wind up as president. In books
he was apt also to wind up wealthy, for there were few authors who had
the heart to leave a hero without first endowing him with a handsome
legacy, whether the hero was a down-and-outer like Huck Finn or whether he was a model of hard work like Horatio Alger. The promise of
gold that had once caused a stampede across our continent and later
quivered at the end of every Hollywood rainbow was irresistible even to
a high-minded author like Gene Stratton-Porter, one of my favorites as
I was growing up. Certainly Mrs. Stratton-Porter's Freckles was too good
a boy to *want* to be rich, yet richness would come to him because it was
a necessary ingredient in fulfilling the American Dream. Starting off in
life as a foundling with one hand missing, Freckles aspired only to support himself and win the respect of his boss, which were impressive
ambitions when you considered his handicap, his inexperience, and the
physically forbidding Michigan lumber camp in which he elected to test
himself. But the fact that he succeeded and in the bargain won the girl
of his dreams was not enough for Mrs. Stratton-Porter or her young audience. In the end he discovered his long-lost and loving family who, by
a marvelous stroke of luck, just happened to be wealthy members of the
Irish nobility.

Even now as an adult re-reading an old favorite, I don't begrudge

Freckles one particle of his good fortune, but when I come across a current book from this same American stock (poor boy overcoming great obstacles by dint of courage, perseverance, and ingenuity), I am disappointed if the author is too prodigal with his hero, especially if the book is as fine as Walter Edmonds' *Bert Breen's Barn*. The mystery of hidden treasure is, of course, basic to Mr. Edmonds' plot, introducing the necessary villains and the necessary danger. Still, all through that book I worried—not that Bert would fail (I knew he would get that barn moved one way or another), but that he would end up not only with the barn but with the money too. In Mr. Edmonds' capable hands, the old pattern works as well as it ever did except, I think, for that treasure which does indeed go home with Bert. In today's world, a happy ending is about all that I can accept; a perfect ending, complete with pot of gold, seems not only gratuitous but seems, at least to me, dated. Even in my childhood, when I was eager to suspend belief, I knew that the pot of gold was an invention, but I was not sure that adults knew. There were so many things that adults said that did not match up with my experience. I did not, however, forsake books or entirely discount the word of adults or even undervalue my own experience. I was simply puzzled. Not until I began writing books for children did I commit myself to the proposition that to the best of my ability my words would correspond with my experience.

Now back to those boys' books. I had one problem with my growing conviction that America was primarily a boy's world. I was not a boy. Nor could I, no matter how determined or hard working, become a boy, although I did spend one lazy summer daydreaming with a Montgomery Ward catalogue, figuring up how much a complete suit of boy's clothes would cost if I should want to run away. The finances were so impossible, I never had to follow the logistics further, which was just as well. Instead, I played all summer on the edge of the Territory, in the shadow of the Great Wall.

There was a second major branch of children's literature, however, that gave me an insight into a more genteel side of American life—the family story. The typical, truly American family, I came to understand, was a large one, which again left me, an only child, out of the mainstream. Still, I was delighted to find in books so many large families I could repair to for that secondary, underground life that runs through childhood, paralleling the visible life, compensating for it and fortifying it. And here at last there were girls on center stage, and although I agreed with Rebecca of Sunnybrook Farm that "Boys always do the nice splendid things, and girls can only do the nasty dull ones that get left over," I found the girls a spirited and able lot. Generally they were making up for absent husbands or fathers: men like Mr. March, who

was away at war, or like Mr. Wiggs (of the Cabbage Patch Wiggses),
who "had traveled to eternity by the alcohol route," or like Mr. Pepper,
who had simply died, leaving a family of five children so destitute they
did not know what a Christmas was like.

All the families had one thing in common: they were poor but they
had such a jolly time of it, I wondered how under any circumstance
they could be happier. Yet wealth invariably came, as it did in the boys'
books, fortuitously—a matter of grace granted by an omnipotent author
to deserving characters. Just so, Mrs. Pepper's future was assured when
she discovered that she was related to her rich employer. But here the
case for poverty had been so well stated, I resented the outcome. The
five little Peppers, I felt sure, would soon be homesick for the Little
Brown House, which seemed to me the warmest, snuggest, most secure
place I had ever known. Poverty enriches, Louisa May Alcott said, and
certainly in the literature of this period the poorer the family, the more
loving it was.

Poverty also ennobled, the female in particular. Although both sexes
worked equally hard, girls were not only more virtuous but, young men
being what they were, young women were duty bound to be more virtuous. Indeed, according to Louisa May Alcott, it was up to women to
raise the standard of manhood. Fortunately Miss Alcott's heroines were
so honest, they have survived what she herself called "the moral pap" of
her day, yet her ideals for feminine behavior ruled my childhood. "I am
angry nearly every day of my life, Jo," Mrs. March admitted, "but I
have learned not to show it and I still hope to learn not to feel it." It
took me a long time to overcome the idea that anger itself is sinful,
whether acted upon or not.

Happy families, said Tolstoy, are all alike, and although there have
been in children's literature happy families that are unforgettable—the
Marches and the Wilders, the Melendys and the Austins and the Moffats—there was until recently the widespread notion that every family
should be happy in much the same way. Pollyanna was, of course, the
last word in happiness. She made such a business of it that she actually
succeeded in not feeling anger or disappointment or sorrow or in fact
much of anything. Fortunately children today not only have happy families to read about but families like those created by the Cleavers, by
Mary Stolz, by Betsy Byars and others—families happy and unhappy in
their own special ways.

If my father's family represented the expansive frontier spirit of
America, my mother's family—six children (five girls and a boy)—fulfilled the happy family pattern established in the books I knew. The
stories of her girlhood were so much like the stories of the March family that to believe one was to believe both. My parents' reminiscences and
the fiction that I read so supported each other that when I came back to

America, I was well prepared. It was a nineteenth-century world that I had heard about and it was essentially a nineteenth-century world that I found, for eras do not come and go in clear-cut slots as they do in history books. The nineteenth century was a powerful one and even today it persists in pockets and hugs the roots of our national consciousness, sometimes a source of strength, sometimes an impediment. Certainly in 1928 it was still going strong in western Pennsylvania and I was swept up in the wonder of everyday American life: the largesse of my grandmother's table; the regenerating quality of my grandfather's laughter; the generosity of uncles, slipping me a nickel for a soda now and then; the attentiveness of aunts, instructing me in household chores which were a new and temporarily exhilarating experience for me. In China we had had servants, but here I was, just like the Peppers, sweeping, pumping water from the well, feeding chickens, drying dishes. When I detected friction beneath the surface of family life, I tried to suppress it for I couldn't bear to spoil the picture that had been painted for me.

There was one aspect of America, however, that I found strange: the relationship of people to time. In China members of the foreign community might keep their fingers on the past but they kept their eyes steadily on the future, looking forward to the day when they would go home. Now we *were* home, yet the conversation, I found, invariably turned on the past. Indeed on the front porch of my grandmother's house the past was ground out, recycled, and ground finer. Whereas once the old stories had provided me with a bridge across a wide space, now the space had been spanned and I resented the long reach of time which somehow excluded me. My time was *now* and I felt very much like the fifth-grade boy whose paper I saw recently on a classroom wall. He had drawn a series of three pictures which he titled: "What Makes Me Mad." The first picture was of a woman at a stove. Under it he had written, "Mommy's cooking and she is tired." The second picture was of a man at a desk. "Daddy's working," he wrote, "and he's tired." The third picture was of two old, bent-over people. "And in a couple of years," he wrote, "they'll both be saying, 'Those were the good old days.' " Here certainly is a stunning insight into the human condition. Go through our history, read the old letters, and you will find the phrase recurring generation after generation: "the good old days of our forefathers," "the good old days before the French and Indian Wars," "the good old days of 1775 when our people were united."

Although this is a universal phenomenon, there is a special quality to American nostalgia. We mourn not only the loss of our individual youth, we mourn—subconscious though it may be—the loss of our country's youth, our uniqueness, our innocence, our bravado. Our vision. With the disappearance of our frontiers, we have on the one hand fallen in love with our past, so much so that at times we seem unable to acknowledge that the past is actually passed. So, on the political stage we break by fits and starts into a grandiloquence that, for all its twentieth-century style, still smacks of the old half-horse, half-alligator river talk. On the other hand, we lean toward "presentism" and are just as likely to reject history altogether. This also is a nineteenth-century legacy, an echo of the fierce individualism of a Davy Crockett and the stubborn self-reliance of an Emerson, who defined himself as an "endless seeker with no Past" at his back. More than any one person, perhaps, Mark Twain expressed both sides of our national paradox. He could in one breath be so homesick for his boyhood that he would long to see even a dog he knew from the old days so that he could put his arms around his neck, tell him everything, and ease his heart. In the next breath he could rail against what he called "the melancholy, the romance, the heroics, of sweet but sappy sixteen. Man," he said, "do you know that this is simply mental and moral masturbation?"

Well, it was the "good old days" that was being replayed on my grandmother's front porch behind its latticework of honeysuckle. Those good old days were exactly the ones I had been prepared for, yet I was restive. My life was not going to be lived on my grandmother's porch in the drone of bumblebees. I did not know that the Great Depression lay around the corner and in a short time we would all be shaken out of our rocking chairs. I learned then how important that pot of gold really was to America, for grown men threw themselves out of windows when they lost their pot. Others (my uncle and his family among them) turned cross and bitter when life sent them not up the ladder of success but down the ladder; they were not at all cheerful in their adversity, the way the Peppers were.

In his old age Henry Adams bemoaned his education, which, he claimed, had not fitted him for his times or allowed him to feel at home in his century. I question whether education can ever prepare a person for his times, but it might at least prepare him for change and develop his imagination to meet the unimagined problems. Too often, however, there is in the educative process an unspoken assumption that with minor fluctuations life not only will but should go on as it is. In any case, prepared or not, I began trying to find my identity as an American in new terms. I was not alone. Americans, farther advanced into the twentieth century than I, were seeking to define themselves in a way that would be appropriate to different circumstances and a more sober mood. Leaving children's literature behind, I waited along with others for the Great American Novel to tell us who we were. In those days we believed in the coming of the Great American Novel as the residents of Hawthorne's little New Hampshire community believed in the coming of the prophet who would be known by his resemblance to the Great Stone Face. One final definitive work of literature would appear and make us feel unique again.

Less naive today, we no longer look for one great novel or even one all-inclusive definition of ourselves. We have accepted our diversity and as Americans we are presently engaged in trying to establish our identity on a smaller scale; as blacks, as women, as Spanish Americans, as southerners, as Jews, and on and on. Children's books, to which I joyfully returned in the 1950s, reflect our long-overdue recognition that, in spite of our talk about equality, we have been a discriminatory nation. Our books also reflect the psychological orientation of the times. When we talk about individualism now, we are no longer applauding the simple do-it-yourself, do-it-or-die virtues of the nineteenth century; we are talking about complexities of character, paradoxes of human nature, conflicts between the individual and his society. Although children's literature still provides that compensating second world so important to childhood, it also offers a more realistic world. We have fantasies that are romps into the make-believe but we also have fantasies that are soundings into truths too illusive for the strong light of day. We have probing historical novels that question whether our history actually had to be played out in the manner that it was. And we have a few brave books, like those of Virginia Hamilton and Robert O'Brien, that take us right to the precipice of our times and ask the hard questions: Can we survive? Can we bear the truth? Can we start over with what we have? Can we transform society? Where do we begin?

The best of our children's fiction, if we paid attention to it, could lead the way to a re-thinking of our educational process. But if we expect our children to be able to consider the hard questions, we must back up their trial flights into new territory with a grounding in old territory. They cannot know where they are going until they understand where they have been. And American history as it is taught in the classroom has not kept pace with the times. I grant that there have been changes, but it is not enough to say, as some courses of study do, that the purpose of teaching history is to foster pride. Indeed, in setting the record straight, a feeling of pride may well be fostered. Dignity must be restored to people who have been denied it, and of course the past offers many moments of which we can all be proud. Still, history is the story of all human behavior, the stage for every kind of action; let us not shuffle through it in the interest of limited goals. We may have revised our history to correct certain injustices; we may have exposed violence and greed that we were once unwilling to admit, yet we continue to misrepresent areas of our past in a way that simply muddles our future.

The eighteenth century, which is receiving our special attention this year, carries the burden of many misconceptions. Let me read you a portion of an essay that recently appeared in the *New York Times,* written by Scott Moss, a high school student on Long Island.

"Ever since I was a small boy," Scott writes, "I have admired some of our men in politics. Now that I am older, 17, I find myself wishing to become a politician. When friends, relatives, or complete strangers hear what I would like to do with my life, their reactions are identical. First, they laugh. . . . Upon hearing that I plan to remain honest I receive rounds of 'Ha! Impossible.' Or the response that I despise the most, 'You are still young and idealistic—you'll change.' "

"Many of us wonder," he goes on, "why the United States was so fortunate to have so many great leaders during the late eighteenth century. . . . In years past, when your politicians were considered to be statesmen and granted much respect and admiration, men of the caliber of our Founding Fathers were as attracted to public service as metals are to magnets. These people were treated as heroes; they were the ones that others wished to emulate."

Scott Moss has not been served well by the adult world. Not only has he been discouraged about the prospect of working for his country, he has been grossly misled about the experience of the Founding Fathers. Indeed, it was not until the beginning of the nineteenth century that Scott's heroes were elevated to their pedestals by a floundering young nation desperately in search of fathers. As the century proceeded and the country became big with conquest, the heroes grew accordingly. Now in the troubled latter half of the twentieth century we cling to our Founding Fathers as symbols of security in a society that often confuses and disappoints us.

During their active careers, however, the Founding Fathers were not the unqualified heroes that young Scott imagines them to have been. Washington, Hamilton, Jefferson, Franklin, and the others received as much abuse as any of our national leaders has ever received. Sometimes the abuses in the press were so personal and so shabby that by modern standards they are shocking. As First Lady, Abigail Adams was enraged by the repeated reference to her husband as that "old, querilous, Bald, blind, Toothless Adams." Nothing, she said, but a sedition act would stop such virulence. Furthermore, the Founding Fathers were all subjected to stories of scandal, sometimes substantiated, sometimes not. They were all victims of political plots and dirty tricks, perhaps not as crude as those we have recently witnessed but just as deadly.

The experience of these early leaders was not, of course, unrelieved aggravation; they had loyal supporters and many moments of glory. Still, every one of the Founding Fathers was bitter about the misunderstanding, the slander, the ingratitude, and the day-to-day friction he had to endure. Washington said that he had been misrepresented in such indecent terms "as could scarcely be applied to a Nero . . . or even to a common pickpocket." Nor did these men look upon each other as heroes. Patrick Henry called Jefferson a coward; Adams claimed he never knew when Franklin was telling the truth; Jefferson said that in some things

Adams was absolutely out of his senses. Far from feeling that they had been rewarded for their efforts in public life, the Founding Fathers retired with an immense sigh of relief. "Politics," John Adams said, "are an ordeal path among red hot ploughshares." And if young political aspirants today are not hardy enough to thread their way among those ploughshares without crying for encouragement from the sidelines, they had better not set foot on the path. Certainly they should read their history first.

The current cynicism which this Long Island high school boy so bitterly resents is a response to bitter experiences. But hard times have always elicited cynical response. I think often of the hard-pressed Massachusetts farmer, suffering under the burden of heavy taxation imposed by his own state shortly after the Revolutionary War. "Why," he asked, "were we so uneasie under George?" I think it is well to remember this farmer; to forget him, to nourish the idea that the eighteenth century did not have its share of despair, only heightens our own disillusionment. A sentimental glorification of the past breeds a cynicism that is equally as sentimental.

An exalted view of the eighteenth century, however, is fairly common. As a nation, we have been protective of our Founding Fathers. Although they have, of course, been subjected to scrutiny in academic circles and have been presented to the public in increasingly realistic terms, they have not yet in the popular mind or in the schoolroom been accepted as people, each in the fullness of his own personality. They have not really rejoined the human race. I suggest that there is an anti-intellectual strain in our national psyche that does not want them to rejoin. It may be a kind of Santa Claus syndrome at work.

On July 4 last year a columnist in a Dayton, Ohio, newspaper wrote: "The same educational plants which taught you and me that American revolutionaries were noble to the man and sinless as the angels are now equally adamant in finding . . . that our Founding Fathers had feet of clay up to their chins . . . King George was a pretty good guy after all . . . George Washington wasn't precisely your basic genius when it came to being a general. . . . It is unlikely that our history teaching establishment could teach so long on the one hand that the American Revolution was practically a holy war, then turn to today's labored cynicism and be believed on both counts. . . . There are wire service features about how many AWOL troops took off and deserted back in Valley Forge days. . . . Where does this leave us?" the writer asks. "How are we supposed to feel about patriotism when our most cherished notions are being attacked by everybody?"

We all know how history is distorted for propaganda purposes by totalitarian regimes. This newspaper writer seems to recommend that we adopt the same tactics; it is unpatriotic, he says, to examine the past too closely. In short, he is asking us to substitute mythology for history, which seems a rather shocking suggestion for a self-proclaimed patriot to make in a democratic society. In a more wistful vein, a college student in Michigan recently told me that her friends wanted history to be romantic. I assume she meant that they wanted it to be better than life. More ideal. Costumed. Prettier. I can only conclude that those who criticize or evade a realistic reading of history can, themselves, have little appetite for life or else they have no sense that the past—being longer—has more characters, more experiences, more diversity, more adventure, more tragedy, more comedy than any one person can possibly meet in one lifetime.

Actually a realistic look at the eighteenth century should help to restore our confidence. After most of his New England army had gone home at the end of 1775, George Washington wrote, "We must make the best of mankind as they are, since we cannot have them as we wish." It was a brave statement in a moment of supreme discouragement. The eighteenth-century man was a realist to the core and deserves an honest accounting. His accomplishments are all the more impressive when his shortcomings as well as his strengths are told. The writing of the Constitution, which Catherine Drinker Bowen so aptly called the Miracle at Philadelphia, can be appreciated only after one has grasped the strength of resistance to a national government, the depth of distrust—state against state, the limitations of the representatives, and the threat of anarchy that finally brought disparate men to what they all agreed was an imperfect compromise. During that long hot summer, America's leaders were facing squarely the relationship of citizen to government, of government to citizen. I suggest that they succeeded for many reasons but one of them was the special quality of their education.

I'd like to speak for a moment about the eighteenth century and the character of its education. The eighteenth-century man (and I use the word generically) was grounded in history. He read not just because he was supposed to but because he wanted to. In their youth the Founding Fathers and many of the Founding Mothers doted on Sir Walter Raleigh's *History of the World*. Here was history in the way they conceived it, a recurring story with a single theme: kingdoms rose, they became greedy for power, they succumbed to luxury, they fell. One of the first Pilgrims, Robert Cushman, had expressed their sentiments a century before: "A Commonwele," he said, "is readier to ebb than to flow when once fine houses and gay cloaths come up." The Founding Fathers may have had fine houses and gay clothes; nevertheless they accepted the principle. Men were naturally and incurably selfish, they believed—themselves included; they should not be exploited nor should they exploit. Their business was to devise a government that would protect people against their own baser instincts. At the root of eighteenth-century thinking lay the complicated questions that have plagued mankind through the centuries: When must an individual insist upon his rights? When must he sacrifice his good for the good of the whole? As the Founders read history, as they studied philosophy, as they practiced religion, these were the questions they turned over and over. In the popular mind today these leaders are best remembered for their articulation of individual rights, yet their success at the Constitutional Convention was surely due to their highly developed sense of community.

The educator Herbert Muller states that there has seldom been too much freedom for society. "Given the long historic record of oppression," he writes, ". . . the natural conservatism or inertia of mankind, the immense force of custom and convention, the fast reserves of ignorance and prejudice . . . the final stress should be on the claims of the individual." Certainly throughout our history as Americans we have fought the forces that have threatened our individual freedoms; certainly we feel the threat today, yet I would suggest that along with our sense of self, we need and lack that large sense of community that supported our eighteenth-century leaders.

Our literature has been for the most part on the side of the individual against society. It is not only the rebel we celebrate (and who usually deserves celebration) but more often than not our heroes have been lonely figures who find their answers not in society but in lonely places. They take to the open road, they ride over the hills, they sail into the horizon. Once they could afford to do this; our sense of space was unlimited. And even now that space is no longer as available nor escape as easy, we still need psychological, if not physical, elbow room to which we can repair. Yet the ghosts of nineteenth-century individualism continue to haunt us and both in books and out of books we tend to seek a personal salvation that does not necessarily commit us, in the eighteenth-century sense, to society.

Children's books are particularly concerned with personal needs and rightly so. Children have to establish themselves as individuals before they can find their way into the community. This does not mean, however, that children's books cannot sometimes be addressed to the double-edged question: Who are we? What is our part in society? And indeed there are many books that have done just this. Take Jean George's Julie, for instance, who turned her boots away from the world of wolves back to the world of people. Take Robert O'Brien's rats, who were uneasy in their smooth-running technological society and decided to try for something better. Or take Virginia Hamilton's M. C. Higgins, who stopped dreaming of escape from the slag heap slipping down his mountain and began to build a wall. Neither Julie nor the rat Nicodemus nor M. C. Higgins found solutions, but each made a commitment to try; each rejoined his world.

I don't believe that we could ask more for our children than that they should take this message to heart. But to give them an ever larger sense of community, we must also, I believe, give them a sense of history. They must understand the past in order to know what to hold on to, what to let go. For myself, I have long ago given up trying to define what it is to be an American. But over the last years as I have immersed myself in the study of American history, I have felt my roots sinking into soil that nourishes me in a way that it must have nourished our friends in the eighteenth century. And I am persuaded that if our children can feel themselves a part of this arduous, continuing adventure we call history, they will find the courage and, I hope, the creativity to save their future.

Works Mentioned

Adams, C. F., ed. *The Life and Works of John Adams.* Vol. 9. Boston: 1854. p.338–40.

Alcott, Louisa May. *Little Women.* New York: Crowell, 1955.

Cheney, Ednah D. *Louisa May Alcott: Her Life, Letters and Journals.* Boston: Little, 1928. "moral pap," p.246.

Edmonds, Walter D. *Bert Breen's Barn.* Boston: Little, 1975.

George, Jean Craighead. *Julie of the Wolves.* New York: Harper, 1972.

Hale, Edward Everett. *The Man Without a Country.* Boston: Little, 1906.

Hamilton, Virginia. *M. C. Higgins, the Great.* New York: Macmillan, 1974.

Hornberger, Austin, ed. *Mark Twain's Letters to Will Bowen.* Austin. p.23–24. (Quoted in Warren, Robert Penn. *Democracy and Poetry.* Cambridge, Mass.: Harvard Univ. Pr., 1975. p.17.)

Keasler, John. "Nitpickers Making Patriotism Difficult," *The Daily News* (Dayton, Ohio), July 4, 1975.

Maynard, Joyce. "I Remember," *New York Times,* July 21, 1975.

Mitchell, Stewart, ed. *New Letters of Abigail Adams, 1788–1801.* Boston: Houghton, 1947. p.47.

Moss, Scott. "Attracting Today's Jeffersons and Hamiltons to Office," *New York Times,* Nov. 22, 1975.

Muller, Herbert J. *The Uses of the Past: Profiles of Former Societies.* New York: Oxford Univ. Pr., 1952. p.61-62.

O'Brien, Robert C. *Mrs. Frisby and the Rats of Nimh.* New York: Atheneum, 1972.

Padover, Saul, ed. *The Washington Papers.* (Universal Library Edition) New York: Grosset, 1967. p.90–91.

Rice, Alice Hegan. *Mrs. Wiggs of the Cabbage Patch.* New York: D. Appleton-Century, 1937. p.4.

Sidney, Margaret. *The Five Little Peppers and How They Grew.* Garden City: Nelson Doubleday, 1954.

Stratton-Porter, Gene. *Freckles.* New York: Doubleday, Page & Co., 1904.

Tarkington, Booth. *Penrod.* New York: Doubleday, Page & Co., 1904.

Taylor, Robert J. *Massachusetts: Colony to Commonwealth.* Chapel Hill, N.C.: Univ. of North Carolina Pr., 1961. "Why were we so uneasie . . . ," p.69.

Washington, George. Letter to Major General Philip Schuyler. December 24, 1775. (Quoted in *Bartlett's Familiar Quotations.*)

Whicher, Stephen E. *Selections from Ralph Waldo Emerson.* Boston: Houghton, 1957. "Circles," p.176.

Wiggin, Kate Douglas. *Rebecca of Sunnybrook Farm.* Boston: Houghton, 1925. p.12.

Wilson, Woodrow. Address at Sioux Falls. September 8, 1919. (Quoted in *Bartlett's Familiar Quotations.)*
Winthrop, John. "A Modell of Christian Charity," in Massachusetts Historical Society, *Collections,* 3d series, Vol. 7, p.47. Boston: Little, 1938.
Wish, Harvey, ed. *The Pilgrims in America.* New York: Putnam, 1962. p.49.

Shigeo Watanabe

Shigeo Watanabe, who taught for eighteen years at Keio University in Tokyo, has lectured extensively in England and in the United States. One of the leading translators of children's books in Japan, he is also the author of many books for children, among which are *Yamanba!* (*She Is a Witch!* Gakken, 1971) and *Mori no Henasoru* (*A Funny Dinosaur in the Forest,* Fukuinkan, 1971).

The author of myriad articles in English and in Japanese, Mr. Watanabe has been active on the international scene and was elected a vice-president of the International Board on Books for Young People in 1979. His lecture, "One of the Dozens," was presented on April 28, 1977, in Boise, Idaho, at Boise State University and was sponsored by the university and several other state and local institutions.

One of the Dozens

THERE ARE TWO WAYS to make a trip to a place where you have never visited before. The place may be a village, a town, or even a country. It may be the site of a ruined civilization, a house where a famous poet once lived, or even a garden where a tale of fantasy took place. One way to visit such a place is to make a thorough study beforehand, the other is to go there without any preparation except for your genuine interest in the place.

I have gone both ways but my personal preference is the latter because I can enjoy the trip far better if I go unprejudiced. If I visit a place thoroughly informed, I will see almost everything as I expect to see and feel it, as if I am confirming everything I know. I gain only the satisfaction of having visited the place and seen the things with my own eyes. I had this kind of trip to the U.S. Library of Congress, Stratford-on-Avon in England, the Acropolis in Athens, the Toshogu Shrine in Nikko in Japan, and a few other places. None of the places was as striking as I had expected. The Library of Congress was smaller than the one I had dreamed of. Shakespeare's birthplace was exactly as I had studied it in a guide book. The Acropolis blurred by smog was indeed a distressing sight. At the Toshogu Shrine in Nikko I was more interested in watching the foreign visitors.

But a trip without any prejudice or any expectation will give you the genuine pleasure of finding things which in themselves will reveal many things to your eyes: they are hidden treasures, hidden beauties, hidden histories, and hidden meanings. I was awe-struck by the history of the Tower of London. I was astounded countless times by the beauty and the power of the works of fine art at the British Museum. I was speechless when I saw the people who were living practically in the water of the Menam in Bangkok. I was horror-struck when I thought about the end of the pueblos at the top of Mesa Verde National Park in Colorado. I was angered to the bottom of my heart for the sake of the proud Indios when I thought about the fall of the Inca Empire at Cuzco and Machu Picchu in Peru.

You won't be able to cry or be awe-struck if you are prepared. But if you cried or were awe-struck by what you saw, then you will never forget the incident or the situation which moved you.

I think I am still too young to recount my past but it is the fate of any lecturer who has to talk about something connected with his life and work. I have traveled my life, like my trips, to different places without making a solid preliminary study or keeping a detailed record afterward. I have not tried to memorize everything I have encountered or to write it down in my notebook. Pamela Travers, the author of the "Mary Poppins" books, said in her lecture, "Only Connect," "Once you write things down you've lost them. They are simply dead words on dead paper."[1]

So, please let me relate my simple story, "one of the dozens" from my memories of a few events of my life.

To begin with, I'd like to quote a few passages from one of the most impressive Christmas stories I have ever read. This story was written by the late Hannah Hunt, a professor at the School of Library Science, Case Western Reserve University, before her retirement. She was a devoted school library specialist and had taught at several library schools in this country and abroad. The story was written shortly before her death, in December 1973. She had known her death was near for years because she had been operated on several times for her illness. These are the few passages from her "Christmas Remembered":

Christmas 1951 found me in Tokyo where I was one of a team of librarians sent by the American Library Association at the request of the Japanese government to establish a library school in Keio University. My delight in the opportunity was somewhat deflated by the Army Medico who processed me in Chicago.

1. P. L. Travers, "Only Connect," in Sheila Egoff, ed., *Only Connect; Readings on Children's Literature* (New York: Oxford Univ. Pr., 1969) , p.184.

Jabbing needles in both of my arms, his irritation erupted with, "Of all the things MacArthur needs over there I'll never understand why I get orders to process a half-pint librarian on the double." But by Christmas we had been in operation almost a year. We were learning as we taught—our students would be faculty to train others and the administrators of libraries throughout highly literate Japan. A Christmas party had been planned by the students for the faculty but our director had asked them to allow room in the program for a surprise visit from Santa. Where in Occupied Japan he would ever find a Santa Claus suit to fit his six foot broad-shouldered frame was a well kept secret, but at the appointed time with a "Ho, Ho, Ho" and a well filled bag he appeared. But the surprise was on us as the entire assembly burst forth with "Joy to the world, the Lord has come" in obviously carefully pronounced English. Santa paled beneath his beard but recovered sufficiently to jingle his bells so loud they prevented a second verse. We had learned a bit about saving face so the party continued through the composing of poetry woven about our names, the magician, and the juggler imported for the occasion. As we left, the campus "Santa," the rumpled suit under his arm, murmured to each of us—"Brief faculty meeting tonight, my room 9 o'clock." Though not a churchgoer he was a deeply religious man and when we were assembled said, "How can we handle this? Obviously we can't embarrass our hosts after the elaborate plans, catering, etc., of the party. Yet I think as educators we have a responsibility here. If we shrug it off we're guilty of infecting them with the same confusion about Christmas that exists in the U.S.A. Who has the first class tomorrow morning?" It was my class in storytelling that was on the spot and he said, "Perfect! I'm sure you can handle it" and his homework was done.

I asked for our best interpreter and rewrote the lesson for the day weighing each word. With no reference to the party I worked from how the library story hour could acquaint children with Christmas customs around the world, noting that in many countries it was still primarily a religious holiday, and confessing that perhaps only in U.S.A. did we allow the legend of a Saint to become materialistic and completely overshadow the religious significance. Since most students by this time read and spoke English fluently I excused the interpreter and closed by reciting the biblical story from St. Luke. Many a year at home I had recited that with a background of "Silent Night, Holy Night" played softly. I was on familiar ground and could pace it slowly for their better understanding. Curiously, that hastily prepared lesson was evidently remembered better than some I had labored over longer, for it was mentioned in their letters even after I had returned home.

I do still remember her elegance and dignity in telling the biblical story from St. Luke. I had not known, then, that my very first translation of American stories for the Japanese children which I did years later was to be "A Visit from St. Nicholas," by Clement Moore.

A few years later, I was sitting in classes conducted by another dignified teacher, who was really as fine a lady as one could be, at the library school in Case Western Reserve University where Miss Hunt was back again and teaching school library courses. The name of this teacher was

Harriet Long, the author of *Rich the Treasure*. I don't think either Miss Long or the late Miss Hunt had ever suspected that the short male student from Japan in their classes would be chosen as a lecturer for the May Hill Arbuthnot Honor Lecture twenty-two years later. Had they suspected, they would have introduced me to May Hill Arbuthnot, who was teaching on the same campus.

I was very tense then coming from a faraway country, and not comprehending everything spoken to me in English at the school. I did not know how to behave in the unfamiliar atmosphere of the classes specializing in literature and services for children. Every time I entered the classroom I waited at the door until all my classmates had entered. When the class was dismissed I stood at the door just like a doorman again until all my classmates had gone out. Some classmates smiled at me and said "Thank you." Some classmates did not notice me at all. And some other considerate classmates said, "Oh, don't wait, you go ahead!" Even when I was told to I still felt awkward to go ahead of any one of my classmates, because I had been told when I was still a student in Japan that "Ladies First" was quite an important manner for men in the U.S.A. But in the first few classes I took at Case Western Reserve University women's liberation had gone to its extremity and I found myself the only man in these classes. My state of tension was not eased until at one of the class gatherings a classmate patted me on the back and she said, "Oh, forget about being a man!"

I myself might have forgotten being a man if the dean of the school, Dr. Jesse Shera, had not reminded me about it. Dean Shera strongly recommended that I work at the Hoover Memorial Library of War and Peace at Stanford University because it needed a staff member in its Oriental Division. But I insisted on going to the New York Public Library to be a children's librarian. Dean Shera was looking at my record, which he was holding just an inch away from his strong glasses. He said in a quiet voice, "I thought you were a man." In spite of his glasses he was not a shortsighted man at all, as you know from his outstanding contribution to librarianship, and he must have foreseen my future, then, because he introduced me to the New York Public Library.

It was very fortunate for me that he did not know one of the grave mistakes I had made during my field work at a branch library of the Cleveland Public Library. I had pushed a child away from the Children's Room when he asked for scrambled eggs. I said, "This is a library here. If you want scrambled eggs, go home and ask your mother!" He was asking for *Scrambled Eggs Super* by Dr. Seuss. I did not realize that it was a book, and, incidentally, some years later this was one of the books I was to translate into Japanese along with other stories written by Dr. Seuss.

As soon as I started working as a children's librarian in the New York

Public Library, I became rather popular among my small patrons. I liked them very much. To my surprise, they were very friendly from the beginning. They were much more sociable and talkative than children I had known in Japan. They bombarded me with questions Japanese children would never ask an adult whom they met for the first time, such as "Where are you from?" "What's your name?" "How come? You're a man!"

To the first question I answered, "I am from Tokyo." As soon as a child heard my answer he said, "I know Tokyo. My uncle has been to Tokyo, you see. Tokyo is a big city in China."

To the second question I said, "My name is Mr. Shigeo Watanabe." To this answer the children responded differently. "What?" said one. "That's a funny name!" said another. "Mr. Wantang?" said still another. This sounded to me like a kind of Chinese soup.

What a cultural difference, I thought while these questions and answers were going back and forth between the children and me. In a tightly closed community like Japan's, we would never directly ask a stranger or a newcomer where he is from. Until he introduced himself we would wait or try to find out from somebody within our circle who knew him, or not ask at all but gossip about him among ourselves. This means that a newcomer must try to find a way to integrate himself into the new surroundings. Everybody knows or is supposed to know each other in the old society where classes, status, families, friends, enemies, and prejudice have lived together for centuries. In old established communities in Japan, we used to greet each other by saying "Good morning." Then, instead of "How are you?" we used to say "Where are you going?" Since then, urbanization in Japan has been drastic, however, and many folks left their hometowns, moved to so-called new housing projects, and started asking each other, "Where are you from?"

But from the question where I was from, I sensed instantly that the children were ready to accept me, and I thought that it must be a cultural trait naturally inherited by these children.

My name, both given name and family name, is popular in Japan like John Smith or David Brown is in this country. But the unfamiliar sound of my name must have surprised or puzzled the children. They were more intrigued when I wrote it down on a piece of paper both in the Japanese alphabet and in *kanji*, which is Japanese writing using Chinese characters.

Language is a vital example of cultural differences. Any language can be effective only when all the effects of sound, rhythm, and meaning are worked out in balance. In our languages, Chinese and Japanese, along with these three elements, images have to be transmitted by way of *kanji*, the Chinese characters, because different words that have exactly the same sounds as many others can only be distinctly identified by the *kanji* characters. The *kanji* is basically a system of pictorial symbols. More precisely, it is a system being used as verbal symbols but essentially the characters themselves are expositions of symbolized pictures. At this point, I have no intention of going into further details of differences between your language and our languages, but the reason I touched on this matter was to relate an amusing episode which happened during my storytelling class to American children.

At a classroom visit to an elementary school in Manhattan, I gave a booktalk about Japan and told the story of "The Dancing Kettle," a Japanese folktale. The children seemed to be enchanted by my tale. Their eyes twinkled and they laughed at the funny kettle, which was a Japanese badger in disguise. Once in a while, I noticed puzzlement on the children's faces. But they kept listening intently to the end, and I finished the story with "Snip, snout, my breath is out!" There was applause from the teacher and the children. And the children came up one after another and said, "Thank you very much for telling us a story," "I enjoyed your story very much," "I liked your story very much," and so on.

But the words of appreciation of one of the boys were different from the others and unique. He tried to pronounce my name as correctly as possible. He said, "Mr. Wantanaba, you see, I understand almost everything you tell us in Japanese. I thought Japanese language would be much more difficult. Thank you very much for telling us Japanese."

For this Augusta Baker, then supervisor of storytelling of the New York Public Library, named me as one of the year's five outstanding storytellers in the New York Public Library system. For this unfamiliar Japanese sound and rhythm in my English, I was chosen as one of the outstanding storytellers for the Storytelling Festival held at the American Library Association Miami Beach Conference in June 1956.

The third question, "How come? You are a man!" was a very puzzling one to me. So I said, "I beg your pardon." The child repeated the same question, kindly rephrasing it for me: "How come a man like you is working in the children's room?" Then I understood his question and remembered again that I was a man. Even to a child it must have been a unique thing for a man to be a children's librarian. It was indeed so for the New York Public Library at that time because I was the only male children's librarian among more than one hundred qualified children's librarians working throughout the system. Thanks to this, I had to be very popular among female children's librarians. That is the reason why I have been chosen as a lecturer for the May Hill Arbuthnot Honor Lecture. I happen to be a rare species.

I heard that there was another rare species working at the Brooklyn Public Library system and I was dying to meet him though I did not until many years later. His name was Spencer Shaw. He invited me to talk to students in his class at the University of Washington a few years ago. And who do you think there was with him in the same school teaching as a special lecturer? It was none other than John Rowe Townsend, who gave the May Hill Arbuthnot Honor Lecture in the spring of the same year. I had the privilege of visiting with Mr. Townsend and Mr. Shaw for a happy few hours.

I spent a few fruitful years working as a children's librarian in the New York Public Library system at the beginning of my career. The value of the experiences I gained working under such eminent leaders of library services for children as Dr. Frances L. Spain, Augusta Baker, Helen Masten, Maria Cimino, and many other superb children's librarians is beyond my estimation. On St. Nicholas Eve, I met the Fairy Godmother of children's libraries.

At dusk in the great forest of tall buildings, the lions were ready to curl up to sleep on the corner of Fifth Avenue and Forty-second Street in Manhattan. In the Central Children's Room all the lights were turned off and we waited. Only the breathing of the people there was heard. They held small candles in their hands to be lit by the Fairy Godmother. We waited without any move. My palm holding the small candle perspired from excitement.

Then a door in the corner squeaked. The light broke through a narrow opening and as the door opened wider and wider I saw a thin, tall shadow. Then two shadows came into the middle of the circle of waiting people and began to light the candles in the people's hands one by one.

As more candles were lit the more visible the shadows became. The smaller one was Maria Cimino, who was dressed as usual. But the thinner and taller one, lo and behold! Under a red cap, long silver hair went straight down to her shoulders. A bony white face with eyes reflecting the candlelight in her hand looked at each one of us in turn. I gasped and murmured to myself, the Fairy Godmother! She came shaking toward me and with her tremulous candle lit mine. After every candle was lit she told us a story, "Nicholas; A Manhattan Christmas Story." Everybody was enchanted. The Fairy Godmother was, of course, Anne Carroll Moore.

I still do remember very fondly all the children I came across while I worked as a children's librarian at St. George, Port Richmond, Harlem, Fordham, and a few other branches. And the books that I shared the pleasure of reading with these children mean so much to my life. *Harry, The Dirty Dog, My Father's Dragon, Make Way for Ducklings, The Moffats, The Twenty-One Balloons,* and many others gave me everlasting pleasure in working with books and children. These books I brought back to Japan and shared the pleasures once more with our children by translating them into Japanese. Most of them are still being widely read by Japanese children.

When my period of study as an exchange student was over and I had
to leave New York, the children asked, "Mr. Watanabe, are you leaving
us for good?" "I don't want to," I said, "But I have to, for the good of
Japanese children." "Yes," they said. "Please come back!" "I will try."
"Goodbye, Mr. Watanabe." "Goodbye, children." It was exactly twenty
years ago. I want to see them again very, very much.

On my free time while working in New York, I was alone. I felt like
a yellow gingko leaf which was blown into the mouth of a hippo. The
hippo gulps anything which comes into its mouth. The color of the
gingko leaf which was once bright yellow fades into deadly brown in
the saliva of the hippo. Once in a while, I saw a dead crocodile caught
in a girder of the George Washington Bridge. Along the malls of Central Park and in the streets I strolled, a group of cockroaches turned
somersaults and asked me for money and cigarettes. Then, suddenly, I
remembered the cockroach who sneaked into our home when I was a
child.

There was once a photo studio in a small town in Japan. A family
lived in the house, part of which was a studio. November 15 was a busy
day for the town folks and the photographer, because on this day if
they had a child of age three, five, or seven in a family they dressed the
child in a kimono and went to a shrine to express thanks for the child's
healthy growth, and had a picture taken at the photo studio. All over the
country, the shrines were crowded with happy parents and their children.

At midnight, after the day's good business, everyone in the photographer's family was sound asleep. Out in the street a drunken man was
teetering along, pushing this door and that. Had you looked closely at
him you could have seen that he was as sober as he could be. He was a
burglar.

He staggered along toward the photo studio and stopped in front of
the door. He leaned against the door pretending he was intoxicated. Behind his back he turned the knob.

The photographer had forgotten to lock the door. The professional
burglar was very swift after that. He opened the door in a flash,
sneaked in, and shut the door. He pulled out a piece of cloth from his
pocket and covered his face. With a flashlight in his hand he began to explore the house. In the studio there seemed nothing to attract him but
heavy cameras without their costly lenses—lenses were usually kept in a
safe place—and lighting equipment. He tiptoed across the studio into
the family bedrooms. There was a narrow passageway before the bedrooms, then *shoji,* sliding doors, screened the bedrooms.

The burglar tiptoed to the sliding door and knelt down. He very
cautiously slid the door open a bit, then a little bit more. He peeked into
the room. He was surprised out of his wits. In the dimly lit room, from
wall to wall many *futon,* Japanese mattresses, were spread on the *tatami*

floor. And on the mattresses were not a few but what appeared to be a dozen bodies lying asleep. He wished he had not come into this house, but it was too late. When he realized what he had done, the only thing he could do was try to escape. He dashed across the pitch-dark studio and bumped hard against the heavy body of a camera, tripped over the tripod, and fell down. Some children were awakened by the thunderous noise somewhere in the house and started to cry. Then the photographer, having been disturbed in his sleep, shouted, "Don't cry, children! It's only a cockroach!"

I was born and brought up in the family of this poor photographer. I have only seven brothers and four sisters though my father married twice because my mother died when I was five years old. My father had to support his family with anything he was able to obtain cheaper by the dozen. My stepmother, who was really a nice mother to all the children, had to work very hard in bringing up the children and keeping the house clean. I remember one night she fainted after she had done all the washing in the bathroom. She had, of course, no washing machine.

The photographer was a very stern father as he was a pious believer in Buddhism who tried to practice his faith all through his life. He actually practiced Buddhist austerities with the monks in a temple, and, once in a while, took some of us to the temple with him. He built a sizable altar in the house and made all in the household, even his apprentice, observe morning and evening worship services. His children did not enjoy this at all but listened attentively when he told them mystic stories of the incarnation of Buddha. They must have been from the *Jataka* or the *Panchatantra*. He told us not only Buddhistic fables but also other folktales and legends of Japan and sometimes stories of heroic events in other lands.

He told us stories not only in the evenings at home but out in the field, by the beach, and on the dried riverbed when we went for a walk. On summer evenings when the air had cooled off, people in the neighborhood used to bring out their bamboo benches in the street and play *shogi*, Japanese chess. Then my father became very popular among the neighborhood children. It was a thrilling and chilling experience to hear him tell, in the dark, a ghost story written by Lafcadio Hearn.

This kind of scene disappeared a long time ago from the streets in Japan as TV came into the houses. I still wonder how and when my father had learned all these stories while he had received only an elementary education. It was a miracle how my parents had managed to keep the family surviving all through those years. Our house was burnt down in a big fire which swept away the whole town when I was twelve years old. And toward the end of World War II, the whole city was burnt to ashes again. Twice in his life my father had to confront an impossible fate;

a dozen children, no house in which to live, nothing to feed the children, and no work to earn his living.

I am his third son. The third son in any fairy tale sets out on a quest, realizing his ignorance, knowing himself to be a simpleton. Now years have passed. The third son has traveled to many parts of the world, met many people from all walks of life, and has returned home. He is happily married and has three sons of his own.

It is very difficult to observe one's own children intellectually and objectively, even for a person whose profession is in the realm of children. This is particularly true when the parents are young and the children are small. We were not exceptions. When we had the first two sons more than ten years ago we were living a hand-to-mouth existence. My wife was occupied with the physical care of our children and I was busy with my work away from my family. We did not have time to look at our children with calm thoughts about their future in relation to our own society and their future society. But to have a new child in our middle age as we have is just like receiving a gift from God. This child is the greatest pleasure in our family, and he has freshly stimulated my professional interests. I have always marveled at the natural affinity between the childhood of the human race and the childhood of individual human beings. He is now toddling age and a beautiful example of Stone Age man.

Cultural remains left to us from our ancestors, I find, give us hints of what and how a child sees things during the toddling age. They give us clues to the images very small children make in their minds.

My child, like any other child, when he was about nine months old was able to crawl about and to stand and walk a few steps, and his habit of licking and chewing things became more obvious. He licked and chewed anything he could reach: toys, his mother's cosmetic bottles, cups, dishes, spoons, chairs, tables, carpets, bedspreads, pillows, and everything else. Observing his licking and chewing, which no one had taught him to do, I thought, "This child is trying out a way of living the early Homo sapiens used to follow, that is, to try to eat things available in nature." You will never know if a thing is edible at all unless you try it in your mouth. "He is confirming substances around him by his most developed sense, taste, which started functioning long before his eyes were able to see things around him," I thought.

The early Homo sapiens were essentially hunters living off the flesh of the mammoth, woolly rhinoceros, wild horse, bison, and other beasts of forest and plain. The more animals they killed, the longer they survived. They, however, knew by instinct the cycle of life so they practiced rituals to promote fertility of the wild animals and to insure their success in hunting them. They practiced rituals in their underground haunts, in caves too deep and too dark to use as living quarters but providing the emotional environment of mystery and silence necessary to practice such magic. They also needed subjects on which to work their rituals, so they carved and painted images of wild animals on walls, and the world's first art came into being. They believed that to practice certain rites directly against images or around the images of living things gave power over the things themselves. The image of a thing was the thing itself, so they shot the images of wild animals and offered incantations to them.

The most famous of these images may be those found in 1940 in the cavern of Lascaux, France. They reveal not only those animals which man was then hunting for meat, but also ferocious beasts by which he was in turn hunted. With these wild beasts man must have had many dramatic encounters. All the images, whether they are images of an entire beast or of a part of an animal body, are so powerful that we can easily conceive that they must have been images directly imprinted on the memory of Upper Paleolithic man without going through the filters of verbal ideas and meanings. Between the actual beasts and the images of those beasts drawn, man has not used reason for abstracting function nor has he worked out the symbolization function between "a thing which means" and "a thing which is meant." There is only an image directly printed on his memory.

The Stone Age man in my family loves small animals like cats and dogs and he is crazy about cars, trucks, and trains. When he was about ten months old he used to hug teddy bears and other toy animals and talk to them as if they were alive. He used to ride on toy vehicles of any kind and size, even ones as small as a match box. He often would sit on the still pictures of cars and buses in books and magazines as if he were sitting on real cars and buses. There is nothing unusual about behavior of this kind. Any child reacts toward teddy bears and toy cars just as my son does.

Yet there is a very significant resemblance between the pictures drawn by Paleolithic man and the mental images a small child sees. That is, there is no spatial conception in either. Of course, many findings of Paleolithic art reveal a continuous evolution from the most primitive attempts at representation, in which we see little more than the suggestion of figures of animals, to a high degree of realism. Although the evolution of drawing techniques may have taken thousands of years in the Paleolithic Age, it is certain that at the early stages man was unable to represent images in perspective. Nor was he able to compose a picture with a number of different figures. Each object was shown separately with no attempt to show its background and with little regard for other figures.

Children too, in the early stage of development, are unable to measure size, distance, width, depth, length, or any element in space so that they sit on a match box toy car and fall down the steps which outdistance their reach.

The first products of children's drawing are apt to be the results of random impulses and happy accidents. They may draw haphazard lines that by chance approximate circles or other elementary patterns. Unconsciously they are learning at this stage that they can produce visual effects. They little realize what possibilities for development such effects have in store for them.

My description of the developmental stages of children's drawing is not based upon any research at all. I have just made up a parody from an authoritative description of the development of Paleolithic art over thousands of years. Don't they have a shockingly accurate resemblance?

Thousands of years later, people learned to draw a storytelling-type picture. Many figures, human and animal, were combined in dramatic action of a hunt, battle, or dance. They had, by this time, developed spatial conception. They had come to feel the invisible force in the forests and over the plains. They had come to feel the spirits in trees, grasses, insects, animals, and human bodies, and had come to be afraid of supernatural powers in the sun, moon, stars, earth, and sky.

Thus, myths were created out of this imagination. Fantasy came into being. Yet my speculation is that even in the Paleolithic age not all of them were necessarily producing images of natural objects. In certain areas of the world, and Japan is one of them, in spite of extensive excavation for cultural remains, so far there has not been anything found equivalent to the Lascaux mural paintings nor any drawings as old. It is evident that, except for the initial random forms of haphazard lines, forms in abstraction and symbolization are predominant among the images depicted in the archaeological findings in Japan. This may mean that the relations between the artistic styles which express one's imaginations and the conditions of life are governed by the laws of cultural dynamics.

That the vicissitudes of human culture on a hunting basis seem to have influenced the style of Paleolithic art is one thing. The more perilous and dramatic were the encounters with wild animals, the more dynamism and more intensity of emotional feelings and dramatic expression were seen in the art. With the decline of the hunting life, conventionality and abstraction gradually became more predominant in human expression.

I am not an archaeologist, but I say these things because they are very closely related to the essential element of children's literature, which is quality of imagination, and because expressions of imagination and the conditions of life, I believe, are very closely related and are the basis for forming different cultures.

If a man sees every day in his life, besides his own kinfolk, animals and beasts as the natural objects that influence his life most, isn't it only natural that his mind will be filled with the images of these animals and beasts? And when he tries to express what he sees in his mind, wouldn't he use these images? Then his expressions of these images must have realistic appearances or shapes.

But if a man's life is essentially dependent upon catches from the sea or crops from the earth, what does he see? Big waves in the sea, calm water in the lake, currents in the river, or the surface of the earth. The fish are invisible in the water until the man has caught them and the seeds in the soil just give him mystic wonders, so he has to wonder and imagine. What his eyes cannot see, his mind's eye discerns. Then the expression of his images tends to be patterns; the patterns of waves, currents, and of human bodies, insects, or animals. The patterns can't help but be abstract and symbolic.

It may mean that the hunter's imagination tends to be extroverted and the farmer's or fisherman's imagination tends to be introverted. I wonder if it is too wild to suggest that the human culture based on hunting brought out more visionary styles like Upper Paleolithic art in its early stage, and epics, saga, and fantasy after people learned to relate stories, while the human culture based on farming or fishing brought out more sensuous and symbolic styles like Japanese Neolithic culture represented by Jomon pottery, which has only straw-rope patterns, and songs, lyric poetry, and symbolic marchen. Imagination, however, whether it is extroverted or introverted, is a "creative activity" attributed to human nature.

In the Neolithic period, people learned to gather images in their plains of space and to compose or change or integrate them into a new picture relating an idea or feeling. At the same time they tried to sound out what they felt within them. I wonder if it is entirely true as Herbert Read said in his *English Prose Style*, "In the moment of its origination the word is poetry," yet I know from observation of my own children that a small child is more talkative when playing happily, and imitates sounds while paying little attention to what the words really mean. Children cry and shout when they have to express more instinctive needs. Stone Age men also must have shouted and screamed during war or hunting but they must have tried to utter words when they practiced rites or when they were at play.

Japanese myths relate that during the funeral of a god called Ameno Wakahiko, his family and friends tried to call his spirit back to his dead body by mimicking and chirping such bird sounds as heron, magpie, pheasant, and sparrow. We say in Japan that mimicking is the origination of telling. When Amaterasu Omikami, the sun goddess, hid in a cave because of the wild behavior of her mischievous brother, a goddess called Ameno Uzumeno Mikoto sang and danced passionately as if she were possessed by the supernatural. It was the origination of our sacred traditional music and dancing called *kaqura.* The gods and goddesses who gathered around the cave chanted and danced together merrily. Having heard the gaiety and merriment outside, the sun goddess came out from the cave again.

These episodes in Japanese myths signify that mimicking, singing, and dancing are aboriginal languages. Small children mimic and try to dance and sing before they are able to speak. In the age of myths and folktales people must have mimicked to communicate when they met a stranger from a different race. We still do the same when we don't understand each other's language. We mimic, to try to express by the movement of body, which is to mime, dance, and sing to relate a story. At this point what Herbert Read said is true: "In the moment of its origination the word is poetry."

An authoritative written source of Japanese myths recorded in the beginning of the eighth century illustrates very vividly a transition of the language. How it was written illustrates not only the transition from dancing, singing, and oral language to written words but also the transformation of images from one culture to another.

Kojiki, the source of Japanese myths, literally means "a record of the things told from ancient time." It consists of three volumes that tell stories of the gods, of gods and people, and of people. It was compiled by order of Empress Genmyo, who honored the will of her grandfather, the Emperor Tenmu, to record these stories. The Emperor Tenmu had ordered a brilliant young man, who was supposed to be a reciter for the royal family, to learn all the records that had been inherited in a number of royal families. His name was Hiedano Are. He was so brilliant and good in memory that he remembered almost everything he read or heard.

Some years later he was summoned by the Empress Genmyo to recite all the records and stories he remembered in order that they be recorded in manuscripts by a renowned scholar of the time named Ohno Yasumaro. Are recited the stories and Yasumaro wrote them down.

Are recited the stories mimicking, miming, dancing, singing, and telling in the genuinely Japanese traditional manner and speech. Yasumaro wrote them down looking at Are mimic, mime, or dance; listening to him sing or tell; discerning images depicted by them; and thinking of all the meanings behind them. He had to use several different styles, narrative, descriptive, or metaphorical, choosing the most appropriate one for each tone of the recitation. He had to write in Chinese characters transliterating or translating from the Japanese speech and meaning.

As I said earlier, *kanji,* the Chinese characters, are essentially a system of pictorial symbols. They are the pinnacles of symbolization of images. And again the images are expressions of objects or substance seen through the mind's eye. The objects or substance, and the minds that composed *kanji*, were those of China. *Kanji* were born in Chinese culture. Thus, the images of Japanese myths were transformed through the use of Chinese writing and even through other foreign cultures.

The very first sentence of *Kojiki*, which goes like this, "At the very beginning when the world was opened . . . ," according to a Japanese scholar, could not have been either a Chinese or a Japanese metaphor. He claims that this metaphor must have come from the Buddhist scripts that originated in India. Many metaphorical expressions such as "shook as a thunder god," "walk like a tiger," and "crumbled into pieces like fallen tiles" (of course these were written in Chinese characters) were definitely of Chinese origin because there had been no concept of a thunder god in the Japanese culture, and no tigers or tiles existed in Japan.

I believe that this kind of transformation of images has happened numerous times in history when one culture meets another. And as an ancient example in Japan, the written words or letters took on a vital role in transmitting, transforming, integrating, and changing the culture.

The invention of letters enabled us to record, describe, translate, abridge, summarize, embellish, and transmit facts. Images may have been changed or molded into prototypes when orally told stories were recorded by letters and characters. Yet written records, in turn, allow readers to have their own individual interpretations, and meanings and images intended by the written words may be twisted or slanted or completely changed, intentionally or unintentionally, by the translators. Some changes of nuance are inevitable when we translate a message or image described through words from one language to another.

Try this very simple example: "A tree is casting its shadow on the surface of water." You can translate this simple sentence in English into any other language you wish to use. If unfortunately you know only English, translate this combination of words into a picture. You don't have to draw a picture on a piece of paper. Just imagine a scene.

There must be hundreds of different scenes drawn or imagined by you, the readers. Where were you born? Where have you been in your life? What trees have you seen? What waters have you seen? All these questions have implications for the image you have just drawn in your mind. A tree can be a silver spruce by Bear Lake in Colorado, or a cypress in Montenegro by the Adriatic Sea, or a fir tree at a beach of the Sea of Azov, or a palm tree on Bikini Island, or a cherry tree by a stream in Kyoto, or a rubber plant in a small village along the Ganges, or even a cactus along a ditch in the Sahara Desert.

When you decide a meaning from a combination of words like this or even from one word, an image comes into your mind first. Without help from the image or images you project in your mind, it is almost impossible to translate even a simple sentence like this. You might say that a dictionary will help. It does to the extent that we will be able to choose a prototype meaning from a set of generalized meanings. But in many instances it does not mean anything at all. For example, you cannot translate the words *cottage cheese* into Japanese no matter how hard you try, nor can I translate the Japanese word *mochi* into English. According to the most authoritative Japanese–English bilingual dictionary, *mochi* is 'rice cake,' but I am sure that doesn't mean a thing to you. In the Japanese language there isn't such a combination of words as *hot water*. We have only *yu*, which is one word. *Yu* is no longer water just as your *ice* is not water. A very illogical thing happens when you translate Japanese *yuzamashi*, which is *yu* turned cold: it should be translated as 'cold hot water,' because it's not the same water as before you boiled it. I have no intention here of going any further in analyzing etymological differences, but I can say that when we have to use words from dictionaries, we need to infuse them with the time and space of the words. The time and space will imbue a situation with a living condition or with living experiences, and they will give words the reality of life.

Not only expressions of images and meanings of words but also what is symbolized by colors are governed by the laws of cultural dynamics. For example, what does the color white against other colors mean? Before Buddha was born, his mother Mahamaya dreamed of a white elephant who had conceived a child. In many paintings of the Annunciation in the Italian Renaissance, Gabriel was drawn with a white lily in his hand.

In Japan white symbolizes purity, but etymologically the word *white* does not necessarily mean "pure" and its original meaning is obscure. Again the symbolic meaning of white may have come from a different culture, very likely from Korea in the seventh century. In Korea, white symbolizes the sunbeam. It is a sacred color. To Koreans, white is a color for happiness. But in China, it is, on the contrary, the color of unhappiness, and is used for mourning.

White, being sacred, was the most appropriate color concept for the rulers of Japan many centuries ago to symbolize the authority of the imperial regime of the emperor's family, whose ancestral origin was believed to be the sun goddess. In one culture, white may mean purity, but in another culture, it may mean absolutely nothing. In one culture, red may mean happiness, but, in another culture, it may be a taboo.

We are able to put even a criterion of aesthetic standards into a dilemma. For example, let's imagine a shape. In the Western formative arts, symmetry is a criterion of aesthetic beauty. Notwithstanding its broad original meaning, "harmony or balance in the proportions of parts as to the whole," there are many masterpieces of formative arts with calculated harmonious proportion. They are the products of systems of proportions based on complex measurements, products of the thought that the whole universe could be interpreted as a form of measurable harmony. At its extreme, symmetry is a similitude of opposed parts, the exact reproduction on the right side of an axis of that on the left. Many churches, cathedrals, towers, bridges, and even furniture and gardens were made symmetrically.

The marvelous proportion of the south tower of Chartres Cathedral, and the splendor and beauty of the Parthenon on the Acropolis, for example, seem to me to be geometric miracles. But to tell you the truth, to appreciate the beauty and splendor of such miraculously minute accuracy requires emotional strain on my part. For unknown reasons, I was frightened when I looked at the naked structure of ancons and brackets which jutted into the sky from the back side of Chartres Cathedral. On another occasion, in an old Romanesque church in Prague, I felt a mysterious fear when I stood in the doorway and looked at the structure of the interior. I felt as if I were drawn into a negative space which was created by the succession of high domes.

I don't know what Sigmund Freud would say about my emotional strain against symmetry or space formed by domes, but it is true that I can relax and feel comfortable with the asymmetric forms of Japanese art. Jomon Doki, Japanese Neolithic pottery, more recent traditional wares such as those we use in the tea ceremony, flowers arranged in a vase in the Japanese manner are all asymmetrical. When we arrange rocks in a garden we never place them symmetrically. Asymmetrical arrangement is also practiced in placing a bell-tower, a pagoda, a treasure house, etc., against the main building in a temple, but as a whole they are in balance and in harmony.

Although Japanese architecture was greatly influenced in the remote past by Chinese techniques that had been basically symmetrical in formation, Japanese architects infused an asymmetrical sense of beauty and balance into the Chinese influence when they built Japanese shrines and temples. Not only asymmetry in the formative arts but an amoralistic behavior or way of life, and a non-logical way of thought prevalent among the people may be attributed to the naive trust in nature itself on which Japanese civilization is based. This may be the essence of the mysterious charm of Japan for foreigners. I know from my personal encounter how much Ezra Jack Keats was fascinated when he actually saw Japan and met the people there. He had known Japan from *ukiyoe*, the pictures of the floating world, and when he visited Japan, villages and towns were no longer the same ones depicted in the old wood-block prints by Hokusai and other artists. But, I am sure, he was able to discern the mountains in the mist and big waves in the fog that would suddenly become visible when the wind blew. More recently, Michael Ende, author of *Momo,* flew to Japan to enjoy his "time." He enjoyed the most tumultuous of times in Tokyo and the most tranquil times in Kyoto and Nara. I wonder what kind of grey men he has found in Japan if at all.

Now, I come to the topic of literacy. The reason I have been talking vaguely about images, symbols, words, colors, shapes, etc., is that they all have to do with literacy. The word *literacy* in a standard dictionary means (1) the quality or state of being literate, especially having the ability to read and write; or (2) possession of education.

Traditionally, in any culture, literacy has meant, more or less, the ability to read and write verbal symbols. Yet, in the study of communication, we have learned that verbal symbols are only one of many media. Especially in this age of multimedia communication, we are required to be able to read messages through other media besides verbal symbols, or through a combination of several media. We may need verbal literacy for verbal symbols, visual literacy for images, and sensual literacy for sounds, feelings, and emotions. What shall we name it if we were to combine all these three? It may be called cultural literacy. In this age of multimedia and intercultural communication, all of us can be totally illiterate in one way or another.

The Fifteenth Congress of the International Board on Books for Young People was held in Athens toward the end of September 1976. The theme of the congress was "How Can Children's Literature Meet the Needs of Modern Children: Fairy Tales and Poetry Today." For the congress more than 200 specialists in the field of children's books gathered from twenty-four countries. There were a good number of outstanding lectures and reports presented by representatives of different nations. Among these were "Fairy Tales in an Age of Technocracy," by Virginia Haviland of the Library of Congress, and "Poetry for Early Childhood," by Mary Jane Anderson, which included the best poetry presentation in the manner of storytelling that I have heard for years.

And there was one by Dr. Hans A. Halbey, director of the Klingspor Museum in Offenbach, West Germany, and the president of IBBY. Dr. Halbey's topic was "Analyses and Research on Children's Reception of the Picture Book *In the Night Kitchen,* by Maurice Sendak." It was the most impressive and interesting analysis of a picture book I had ever heard, and might remain as one of the most interesting analyses of *In the Night Kitchen.*

Dr. Halbey conducted his research from his "intuitive" first impression of the book, "that there are many symbols and core messages hidden in the book and transmitted by means of words and pictures." He conducted empirical research with the help of his university students on 350 children between five and eight or nine years of age. He collected about seventy prototypes of children's reactions toward the hidden meanings, and added his own interpretations criticising some of the comments of American reviewers. I was excited and intrigued by his findings because of my own reactions to them and the comments by the American reviewers that had become his target.

First, I realized my total illiteracy as to many of the symbols and messages hidden in the words and pictures, such as three bakers, the little boy in his bed, the flying boy, many words in the advertisements, packages, slogans, Mickey's overalls, the moon, the stars, old pieces of furniture, old-fashioned lamps, kitchen tools, the milk, "I'm in the milk and the milk's in me," doughboy, "Mickey Oven," the salt can decorated with the Star of David, the bread dough "all ready to rise in the Night Kitchen," and so on and on. I must have been like an innocent child of two or three when I read the book myself. I had been totally unaware of hidden meanings. I had been able to comprehend only the superficial meaning of the story. What a shame for a specialist on children's books! But could it be helped? I was outside the culture entirely. Now I have been educated a little bit more, so I am not so completely illiterate about the words and pictures of *In the Night Kitchen* as I was before.

But I didn't know that Sendak had used the Little Nemo series as a model, picking up the idea of the little boy in his bed or of the flying boy. Furthermore, I still don't know what the Little Nemo series is. Dr. Halbey reported that many children spontaneously recognized the three bakers as Olly and Stan. Who are they? To Japanese children the three bakers appear to be just three jolly fat men who bake bread and cakes for children. Dr. Halbey said, ". . . many of the symbols cannot be understood by the children in the same way as understood by the author. So it is important to register the understandings as well as the misunderstandings. Misunderstandings seem to protect the children from a too strong personal involvement during the reception. In certain situations children need more or less emotional detachment or freedom from illusion."

But I was shocked to learn that *In the Night Kitchen* had been a subject of controversy and a target of severe criticism because of Mickey's nudity. Dr. Halbey quoted a number of representative phrases and sentences from reviews. For example, "The full frontal nude outside sexual information," or "the sight of the first expo of full frontal nudity for under-sevens"; "The Night Kitchen is a masturbatory fantasy"; it "celebrates childhood sexuality"; appears to be "an orchestration of sexual dream symbols"; "A dream of birth aroused by the sound of parents making love?"; "I believe the book is an autobiographical odyssey through the womb"; "I suspect that Mickey falls out of his clothes simply in order to be fashionable"; and so forth.

When I heard Dr. Halbey quote all of these I was struck dumb in the true sense of those words and then muttered and kept muttering, "What a cultural difference!"

"The full frontal nudity of a child in the family" is the very symbol of complete security at home in Japan. The home is the place where children can be completely naked because there can be nothing there to harm them. Nobody is shocked even if children run about naked in the house after they have taken a bath or gotten up from bed. Please recall the scene in which I described my own father when he told stories surrounded by his own children and the neighborhood children out in the street in the summer evenings. Some small children could have been naked, having just come out of the house after a bath, and my father himself could have been half-naked because of the remaining heat of the day. How would it be possible to enjoy the Japanese public baths in the town or at hot spring spas without being frontally nude?

But the kind of shock I received from the comments quoted by Dr. Halbey was nothing compared with the one that struck me when I learned about the symbolism of the label "Mickey Oven." It symbolizes the most dreadful fate of the European Jewish population during World War II. "Mickey 'underbuttered' in the dough shall be burned in the oven which is labeled as his last destination. . . . In such an interpretation Mickey is taken as a symbol for the whole Jewish population—or we take the scene as a symbol of a possible fate of Sendak's family," according to Dr. Halbey.

Honestly speaking, I was frightened by his interpretation of possible meanings of the symbol and at the same time I felt that no matter how hard I stretched my imagination I could never have reached the same conclusion. Although Dr. Halbey observed the evidence that children in his country understood the core message very well without any knowledge of burning people in an oven, our children in Japan are not able to see any difference between "Mickey Oven" and "Mickey Mouse Oven" or "Charlie Brown Oven" at all, I am sure.

Thanks to his interpretation I am no longer illiterate about the religious meanings of the milk, the salt can, and the bread dough intellectually, but whether or not I should appreciate the messages themselves hidden in these symbols is a different matter because I am not a follower of Christianity or of the Jewish religion. Again, to young readers in Japan, the milk is plain milk, the salt can is a salt can, and the bread dough is bread dough and nothing else. Even if I explained the religious meanings, I wonder if I could impress them at all.

I completely agree with Dr. Halbey when he says, "It doesn't matter when you ask: Do children understand those messages or only a part of them or nothing at all? We have to be aware that there are thousands of impressions . . . and nobody is able to say in advance: this impression will have effect and this one not. . . . Every message is important but the most important and at any time effective are those which are thought and designed on such a high artistic level."

I am grateful to Dr. Halbey for his excellent research not because I have been convinced by his interpretations, but because he has enlightened me about my illiteracy which is largely caused by my lack of study and by the difference of cultural background. He has enlightened me by showing his way of seeing things, which is largely supported by his scholastic study and to some extent by his cultural background.

Another experience of mine happened at Hotel Gloria, one of the most prestigious hotels in Rio de Janeiro. From the twenty-first through the twenty-fifth of October 1974, representatives of twenty-six countries, of IBBY, of UNESCO, and of CERLAL (Centro Regional para de Desrrolo del Livro en America Latina) assembled for the meeting of the Fourteenth Congress of IBBY. The theme of the congress was "The Book as an Instrument for the Education and for the Human Development of Children and of Young People." At this congress a few hundred people attended from local schools, libraries, and other agencies for children.

Each day of the congress one or two national representatives presented a lecture or a report at the plenary session, which was open to the local participants. I was one of these reporters. I presented facts and data about children's books and reading habits in Japan, using some slides to illustrate my talk. I showed slides of typical book stores, which are as numerous as your shoe stores or post offices. I illustrated the poor condition of our school libraries and of public library services for children, and I mentioned that, to counter-balance the poorness of school and public libraries, a traditional social force is working to support our children's reading: family tradition. Parents used to tell stories to their children and nowadays parents read to their children and have their children read by themselves. Families used to buy books and to build their meager collections. This tradition has developed into the "Bunko Library," which means a small private library run by volunteers for the neighborhood children.

But to my surprise my comment on our family tradition irritated local participants very much. Some comments from these participants were as acute as if they were charges against me and, I remember, Bettina Hürlimann, who was sitting next to me, whispered, "They must be thinking of you as a capitalist!" I remembered how poor my parents had been, but it didn't help any.

I was puzzled and frustrated at the time and later became very un-happy and angry when I learned that the coordinator of the session, a local person, wrote down my report as "utterly out of reality." This statement remained in the final report of the congress and has been printed in *Bookbird*. It reads: "The best example, that given by parents who are accustomed to reading to their children and having their children read by themselves, is *far from being a reality*," with a slight modification.[2]

But their irritation and the statement were absolutely well-founded. I had told them the truth, but I was illiterate about their culture and living conditions. During the congress, the same teachers and librarians who had been irritated by my report took me to their schools and guided me through the towns where their students and parents were living. Books I found on the shelves of their school libraries were hardly books at all. They were discarded books from wealthier countries and bound pages of pictures clipped from old magazines. At home many parents don't read even newspapers because they can't read. Children's books by our standards were only for the rich and educated few.

I was very much ashamed of myself. As a pseudo-expert on children's books I had been reading papers on reading problems in many countries. I must have read about the literacy situation in some countries. I realized that I had been reading only "the dead words."

At homes where I peeked in, children and their fathers were beating beautiful rhythms on empty cans. It was their language. During the congress we, the foreign participants, were invited to dance with their traditional Samba School one evening. Many of us danced through the night. We were intoxicated with the beauty of their language. They enlightened my sensual and cultural illiteracy.

I hope the natural affinity between the childhood of humankind and the childhood of individual human beings will remain steady for generations and centuries to come. I hope "the best example, that given by parents who are accustomed to reading to their children and having their children read by themselves," will, in the near future, no longer be "far from being a reality" in any country in the world. But an advanced technology shows the worst example, as well. In Japan, it is almost impossible for any child to be born into an environment where there is no TV set, no matter whether it is a hospital or a home. From the very time when the child is born, the TV set shows moving images and makes all kinds of noises for more than twelve hours a day. TV, in many homes, is taking the place of the mother or the grandmother who used to nurse a baby by singing a lullaby and talking softly. In the same manner, TV is illustrating and telling many things on behalf of the grandparents,

2. "14th Congress of IBBY," *Bookbird*, 1974, no. 4, p.26.

parents, and aunts and uncles who used to tell stories. It is not an exaggeration to say that TV nowadays is taking a vital role in bringing up children in Japan, but this is not to say, however, that TV is contributing much to the growth of our children. On the contrary, it is taking much time away from our children to develop themselves, the precious time they should spend on something constructive such as seeking adventures outside, playing with friends, making things, or reading books and listening to stories.

The lack of communication between child and mother because there is TV in the nursery is producing so-called TV mutes among our young children, who are unable to speak at the proper age. In many homes, children are isolated from parents and elders emotionally, intellectually, and even physically because the TV is there. These children live with the images of new models of cars, airplanes, sports heroes, TV stars, and with heroes and monsters in comics. It is a wonder when and how these children will ever encounter woodcutters, hunters, princes, princesses, and even foxes, toads, billy-goats, and bears, etc. It is a greater wonder when and how these children can conceive of the creation of all things, the origin of evil, and the salvation of the soul.

Our children in Japan are much too busy to read the stories commonly known as fairy tales, legends, and myths, in order to digest the school curriculum, prepare for entrance examinations to upper schools, do the homework during holidays, and watch TV programs and read comics whenever they find time to escape those pressures. Yet books are being sold in millions and millions. It is a paradox!

In the world today, many children share similar experiences, but each child has his or her own life. Children are very sensitive about their homes and their worlds. And in reality it is a mistake to suppose that the same virtues and vices reside in different peoples. That is the reason why "international understanding through children's books" is very important. To understand and appreciate the differences among peoples correctly—the difference in origin, the difference in belief, the difference in history, the difference in manner, the difference in expression, the difference in art, the difference in language, the difference in taste, and the differences in many other things that influence peoples to live differently—is to understand the world.

I will remain as one of thousands and millions of dozens!

Uriel Ofek

Uriel Ofek, a native Israeli, wrote his first book about his experience as a prisoner of war in Jordan during the Israeli War of Independence. He has lectured extensively at home and abroad, has translated children's books, and worked as a writer of scripts for children's films and television plays, but is best known for his many books for children. His novel of the 1973 war in Israel, *Smoke over Golan* (Harper & Row, 1979), was his first book to be published in the United States. Mr. Ofek is also the author of several books about children's literature and the compiler of a children's encyclopedia.

His lecture, "Tom and Laura from Right to Left: American Children's Books Experienced by Young Hebrew Readers," was delivered on April 26, 1978, in Boston, Massachusetts, under the sponsorship of the Boston Public Library and more than twenty other Boston-area institutions.

Tom and Laura
from Right to Left

American Children's Books
Experienced by Young Hebrew Readers

I STAND BEFORE YOU in the hometown of the American Mother Goose and the birthplace of "Mary Had a Little Lamb," after making a trip of five thousand miles in ten hours nonstop, and I am now going to address you. There is no need to say that I am honored and thrilled (or, should I say, nervous?). As I look at you, I see before me a thousand and more faces, belonging to a thousand and more individuals from different states, of different nationalities and faiths. No doubt some of you are Jews, as I am (and to them I'll say in our old national language: "Shalom Aleichem"—Peace be with you!) Yet, two major factors unite all of us: our devotion to the delightful realm of children's books, and the dear memory of May Hill Arbuthnot. Although I came here from the eastern coast of the Mediterranean, the name of Mrs. Arbuthnot is most dear to me. How can it be otherwise? Her monumental *Children and Books* was the first textbook I read when I began to study children's literature in the Hebrew University of Jerusalem twenty years ago. A good friend of mine from St. Louis, Missouri, had sent it to me, since one could not then find even one book about children's literature in Israel. Since then I have read her book over and over again, memorizing her wise words, which seem nowadays to be more pertinent then ever:

We must find stories as realistic and homey as a loaf of bread, and others as fantastic as a mirage. Above all, to balance the speed and confusions of our modern world, we need to find books which build strength and steadfastness in the child, books which give him a feeling for the wonder and goodness of the universe.

My first reaction to the surprising invitation I received from the Association for Library Service to Children, to be the Arbuthnot lecturer this year, was of alarm: What can *I* bring to great America from my tiny Mideastern homeland? But then I saw before me the ancient walls of Jerusalem and remembered that the Bible was written here, in my native land, in Hebrew—my native tongue—and recalled Mrs. Arbuthnot's sage comment that "the Bible still remains a source of strength and wisdom, if children know it well enough to turn back to it and search its richness." For us Israelis, the stories of the Bible are as natural and familiar as bread and water. Recently a teacher in Israel asked her class why Abraham had left Ur and came to dwell in Beer-Sheba. The immediate reply of a pupil was: "Why, because all Jewish newcomers now go to live in our Beer-Sheba . . . ."

I believe there is no need to mention that the roots of American children's literature are settled firmly in the Bible. As an example, let us recall the famous rhymes from the *New England Primer:* "Queen Esther sues / and saves the Jews," or "Uriah's beauteous wife / made David seek his life . . . ." And as we all know also, Lincoln's splendid style grew out of his familiarity with the Bible (no need to mention President Carter's adoration of the Holy Scriptures, which helps our leaders to find a common language with him).

It may surprise you to know that the name "America" is deeply rooted in the beginnings of Hebrew children's literature.

The Discovery of America

The period—the first quarter of the nineteenth century. The region—Central and Eastern Europe, or, to be more definite, the Jewish suburbs in some Russian-Polish towns.

You might know that Hebrew was an unspoken language for over nineteen centuries—from the beginning of the Diaspora (70 A.D.) till the first Jewish pioneers returned to the Land of Israel and revived the language of their forefathers (which is written, by the way, from right to left). During all these centuries, Hebrew literature was mainly religious and Jewish education was almost entirely orthodox. The standard books that children saw at home or at school were therefore the Old Testament, the Talmud, and prayer books. But like other children all over the world, the Hebrew child was always an avid listener to tales told by traveling storytellers, or to legends and fables told to him by gifted teachers and rabbis or by loving grandmothers. Biblical tales and Talmudic legends, with their charm and simplicity, attracted Jewish children; but they had no books to read—because there were no children's books in Hebrew; or, to be more accurate, there were *almost* no books written for the Jewish child.

Then, about 1810, a new and different book was seen in the hands of Jewish youngsters, mostly hidden among the religious textbooks. It was a volume of about 200 pages, entitled: *Metziat Ha'aretz Ha'hadasha*—that is, *The Discovery of the New Land*, and its long subtitle read (in free translation): "Containing all the mighty deeds which had been done in the days when this land was discovered; rewritten in the Holy Language, in pure and clear style, for the instruction and benefit of the young children of Israel, to teach them Hebrew and to let them know the power of God." This book, published by the poet and scholar Moses Mendelssohn-Frankfort of Hamburg, was a free translation of the popular work *Die Entdeckung von Amerika (The Discovery of America)*, written by the famous German educator and author Joachim Heinrich Campe. Thanks to this book, Jewish children and grownups were introduced to the New World for the first time, learned that there is a country named America, and read about the adventures of its explorers. Strangely enough—or perhaps not so strangely—many rabbis and educators looked unfavorably at the growing popularity of this book and tried very hard to convince their pupils that all the stories about the discovery of America were pure fantasy and nothing else: "How is it possible," said the Rabbi of Mohilev in his sermon, "to believe in such a thing, which stands in contradiction to the axiom . . . ?"

But the word "America," however, had a magic charm on thousands of youngsters, who never left their ghettos but longed to do so; hence, three more writers translated *The Discovery of America* into Hebrew. The educator David Samosc published his version in Breslau in 1824. The same year, his colleague of Vilna, Mordecai Aaron Guenzburg, completed his translation; but since there was no Hebrew printing press in his hometown, Guenzburg bought Hebrew type and had the book printed at his own expense in a Christian missionary printing house. Thanks to its absorbing content and clear style, Guenzburg's *Discovery of America* became a best-seller and some progressive teachers used it as a textbook in their classrooms. As to the fourth translator, Abraham Mendl Mohr of Lemberg, his free adaptation was published in 1846, with many additions and remarks of his own, such as this original epilog:

We must thank God, blessed be He, for giving brains to Columbus, so that he dared to cross the ocean and discover America. This deed was a great relief to all other continents, since many millions of people left their homes, emigrated to America, and settled there. And if America did not exist, all these people would remain in Europe and Asia and Africa, living overcrowded, in poverty and hunger, heaven forfend! And all the millions who have emigrated to America are doing very well there, and great business is carried out now between our people and the Americans. And this is the end of the History of the Discovery of America, all three parts.

The three parts of the book are: (1) Columbus, (2) Cortez, and (3) Pizarro; but, strangely enough, in a bibliographical catalog published at the beginning of the century this rare book is entitled *Columbus*, by Cortez Pizarro.

Today it is difficult to imagine the immense influence that this single book had on thousands of young Hebrew readers, especially those locked in the dark Russian-Polish ghettos. I would dare to compare its effect to that which *Uncle Tom's Cabin* had on American readers before the Civil War. This book, in its four different translations and adaptations, turned the word "America" into a magnet; several years after its publication, in the second half of the nineteenth century, the great wave of Jewish immigration from Russia and Poland to the United States began. The immigrants hoped, as the book promised them, to prosper in America. Although not all of them became well-to-do, most of the Jewish immigrants started a new happy life in the New World.

The Discovery of America was written—as mentioned above—by a German writer. Five years after its first publication in Hebrew, the first American book was translated into Hebrew. It was not intended as a juvenile, and it was not a fictional work, but rather a book of instruction. Yet it too had a surprising effect on Jewish youth. The book I am referring to is *The Way to Wealth*, which introduces the last volume of Benjamin Franklin's *Poor Richard's Almanack* (1757).

From Uncle Ben to Uncle Tom

Franklin's name was renowned in Europe in that period; his great reputation was due to his *Way to Wealth*, which taught youth how to earn and use money. It was translated into fifteen European languages and printed over and over again. The prolific writer Mendel Levin of Satanow, whose main goal was to enlighten the Jewish masses, read the German edition of Franklin's book with great admiration and decided to translate it from the German into Hebrew (since he didn't understand English). He rewrote it in a most readable style and entitled it *Heshbon Ha-Nefesh* (i.e., "moral introspection"), "a marvellous device invented by the acclaimed scholar Binyamin Franklin of Philadelphia, North America, to teach morality and through exercises to improve the bestial nature of man."

The appearance of *Heshbon Ha-Nefesh* had a huge influence on the

Jewish community of that time. Thousands of Jewish young people who sought a new, satisfactory way of life were fascinated by this book, which trained them how to acquire better manners, "to plow deep while sluggards sleep—and you will have corn to sell and keep," or how to behave in society; and they adopted the book as we learn from the following, printed in the Hebrew paper *Hamaggid* in 1873 (No. 40, p.364):

Special parties of young people were established in some townlets in Galicia and the Ukraine, whose main goal is to live according to the moral rules printed in *Heshbon Ha-Nefesh*.

So, as we can see now, the influence of American civilization on Hebrew youngsters is an old phenomenon: it began 105 years ago and is still effective.

Twenty years later, in 1896, a first great American novel was translated into Hebrew; it immediately became most popular among our young readers and—believe it or not—is still read eagerly (in modern translations) in Israel. I refer to the most discussed book of its time, the world's second best seller (outranked only by the Bible)—*Uncle Tom's Cabin*, written by the "little lady who started the big war," as Lincoln had named Harriet Beecher Stowe. Although this moving novel is not mentioned in Mrs. Arbuthnot's book (which means she did not regard it as a children's book), I was glad to read in Mrs. Hurlimann's splendid Honor Lecture that in Europe *Uncle Tom's Cabin* was one of the most beloved American books. The first Hebrew edition, entitled *Ohel Tam* (i.e., "Tom's Tent," or "Life among the Lifelong Slaves"), was published in Warsaw in 1896, and since then there has hardly been a Jewish boy or girl who did not shed a tear of identification over its pages. True enough, Tolstoy called it "a great work of literature, flowing from love of God and man"; but the appeal of *Uncle Tom's Cabin* to Jewish youth was much stronger than it was to any other young readers in Europe. There were several reasons for this. First, the institution of slavery was always detested by Jews, for please remember that for thousands of years every Jewish child has recited the words, "We were slaves to Pharaoh in Egypt," at the opening of the Passover feast. Secondly, Uncle Tom's naive yearning for "Jordan banks" and "Canaan's fields" and "New Jerusalem" can be almost entirely compared to the longing of the Jewish youth who lived in repressive exile and prayed, "Next year in Jerusalem."

Thus, the young Hebrew readers found in *Uncle Tom's Cabin* the same values which they themselves cherished so much: the deep affection for the Bible, the Holy Book that Mrs. Stowe had grown up with since her early girlhood. All Jewish children used to spend hours, exactly like Uncle Tom, in (I quote) reading "words of Patriarchs and

Sages, who from early time had spoken courage to them." And linked
with this affection, our readers found in the book the devout attachment to the Almighty, which gave courage and hope to all suffering
people—black slaves and persecuted exiles. Since then, it is no wonder
that *Uncle Tom's Cabin* has been translated into Hebrew four more
times, performed as a children's musical, and is still highly recommended in children's libraries in Israel.

The First of the Mohicans

Till here, I have read to you the long prologue of my lecture. As I
said before, Hebrew was a "dead" language, which existed only in
writings and prayers, until a century ago. Thus all Hebrew juveniles
published till then were read by youngsters who understood the Holy
Language (more or less) but did not speak it. Nevertheless, these
pioneer books provided them with a first impression of America and
its ideals: America had been pictured in their minds as a land of immigration, a faraway region, where noble people struggled against
oppression and for human rights and whose leading writers showed
their readers the way to wealth and to a perfect life of usefulness and
morality. No doubt this bright image of America exists till now in the
eyes of many people in Israel.

These few books were some of the forerunners that predicted the
growth of a normal Hebrew children's literature. The educational and
literary activities of a secret Zionist order in czarist Russia, and the
growing movement for the revival of the Hebrew language, induced
some daring book lovers to turn to publishing activities. The first attempt in this field was made in Warsaw by the secretary of this secret
order, an amateur writer himself named A. L. Ben-Avigdor. In 1896
Ben-Avigdor set up his dynamic publishing house—Tushiya (i.e.,
"Sagacity"). This energetic publisher gathered some skillful young
writers and translators, planning to publish scores of popular children's books. Since his editorial desk was as yet empty of original
manuscripts, Ben-Avigdor decided, rather wisely, to begin his business
with translations. Thus the first book published in Tushiya's youth
section was *The Last of the Mohicans*, a shortened version of James Fenimore Cooper's novel, which marked the beginning of "Indianim," as
we call this lasting genre of popular Indian stories in Hebrew. It is
interesting to note Mrs. Arbuthnot's remark that Indian stories for
young readers began also in America "with such romantically realized
stories as Cooper's *Last of the Mohicans*." In Hebrew they were followed
by European adventure stories, such as *The Headless Horseman* by
British author and adventurer Thomas Mayne Reid; or *Winnetou*, by
the German Karl May, who began writing his seventy adventure
stories in jail. But James Fenimore Cooper's stories were, and still are,
the best and most popular among Israeli young readers, forming in

them a new and exciting image of America: a vanishing paradise of forests and fortresses, rivers and wilderness, inhabited by bold heroes possessing such exciting names as Hawkeye, Pathfinder, or Chingachgook. Cooper's *Leatherstocking Saga*—all five volumes—was translated several times into Hebrew (most recently in 1975), inflamed our imagination, induced us to disguise ourselves on Purim as Indians, and created exciting games played in the fields and woods of Judea. And speaking of translations, I would like to remark that the Hebrew language has an advantage over English, concerning Indians: when *you* say "Indians," one cannot be sure if you refer to "redskins" or to the natives of India. But Hebrew distinguishes between these two peoples. The East Indians are termed *Hoddim,* meaning the natives of Hoddu (the biblical name of India), while the American Indians are called *Indianim.* Only in early translations (which, unfortunately, are sometimes being reprinted without editing), one might find *Hoddim* in Cooper's *The Prairie,* and wonder what, for heaven's sake, are the people of India doing in the Mississippi Valley . . . ?

I would like to mention now one more reason why Cooper is liked by us Israelis: it is on account of his last book, *The Oak Openings.* In this remarkable tale, Cooper introduces us to a wandering priest named Amen, who tells the elders of an Indian tribe that they are descendants of a lost Jewish tribe; hence, they must emigrate to the land of Canaan and reestablish the Kingdom of Israel. Incidentally, *The Oak Openings* was written in 1848—exactly 100 years before the restoration of the State of Israel!

The first Hebrew translator of Cooper, the prolific writer and devoted educator Israel Benjamin Levner, translated another American romance, written by a forgotten Pennsylvania counselor named Homer Greene. This sentimental story, *Blind Brother,* about a young coal miner who gets back his lost eyesight, thanks to the devotion of his loving brother, appealed to many of our readers because of its theme, a theme which suits almost perfectly the Jewish tradition of family love, mutual aid, and the ancient precept of "Be your brother's keeper."

Blind Brother too was published by Ben-Avigdor's Tushiya Publishing House. About the same month—March 1898—Ben-Avigdor published also a shortened translation of *The Prince and the Pauper,* and consequently the Hebrew reader was introduced to Mark Twain for the first time; Mark Twain remains (and no doubt will remain) the favorite American author among young Israeli readers.

Princes, Paupers, and Innocents

Although Mark Twain's stories are so American in style, atmosphere, and background, they have captured our hearts because of their strong sense of freedom and the mixture of delicious humor and quiet sadness. Tom Sawyer (after being translated into Hebrew) was so similar to the prankish-but-good-hearted boys we met in Shalom Aleichem's stories that Mark Twain was nicknamed by some Jewish critics as "the American Shalom Aleichem." Yes, Tom is a real, typical boy, who—just like us—hates being washed or wearing his best clothes, and longs to live an exciting, adventurous life. About forty years ago, three Israeli boys who lived in a village not far from Tel-Aviv (where, just as in Hannibal, Missouri, "everybody was poor, but didn't know it") had read the Hebrew *Harpatkaot Tom Soyer;* and after having read *Tom Sawyer,* they ran away from home to seek adventure on the banks of the Yarkon River and to build "a happy camp of freebooters" there, just like Tom and Joe and Huck. Twenty years later one of those boys—who grew up to become a children's author—wrote a story based on this "Sawyerish" adventure, a story that turned out to be his first best-seller. This person is now standing before you.

So, no doubt I owe a great deal to Mark Twain and his unforgettable books in the making of my literary career; and after growing up it seemed to me almost natural to pay part of my debt to Mark Twain by retranslating some of his books into Hebrew, since the first translations had become too old-fashioned. I must confess that this work of interpreting Huckleberry's language into Israeli lingo was an inspiring experience for me.

Translating Mark Twain's works into Hebrew was always an impelling challenge to some of our gifted writers; and surely you know why. But since our first translators were born in East Europe and didn't understand English, they translated *The Prince and the Pauper, Huckleberry Finn,* and some of Twain's short stories from Russian or German. Such double translations necessarily caused some queer peculiarities, which may not disturb the readers much, but may seem amusing to us; for instance, Sir Hugh was spelled "Sir Gew" (there is no H in the Russian alphabet, and the translator, who was unfamiliar with English names, copied the Russian spelling); King Henry the Eighth became King Heinrich, and the fake Duke of Bridgewater was entitled "Herzog," as if he were a German prince.

But these were only minor oddities. *Huckleberry Finn* presents much greater problems to every translator. "America's most famous novel" (as Professor Ralph Cohen of the University of California calls *Huckleberry Finn*) was first translated into Hebrew when Hebrew became a spoken language again; no need to say that there was not yet a Hebrew slang, nor different forms of speech. Nevertheless, during World War I, a daring young writer named Falk Heilperin sat down to translate Twain's great book into Hebrew; so let us not blame this sedate translator for rewriting Huck's fluent narrative in a pure Biblical style. The result was that instead of his colorful colloquial speech—"I never seen anybody but lied one time or another, without it was Aunt Polly, or the widow, or maybe Mary"—our lively waif says this same sentence as if he lived in the days of King David: "In all the days of my life, never have I met a man whose tongue spoke not falsehood, at one time or another, except it be Aunt Polly, or the widow, or perhaps Maryam."

When I read these early translations today I have double fun: I not only enjoy the story, but also the special flavor of the archaic style, as if I were reading a pseudo-Biblical scroll.

About a year later the first Hebrew translation of *Tom Sawyer* appeared in Odessa, Ukraine. The translator, Israel H. Taviov, was an experienced writer and editor, gifted with a natural sense of humor and a keen linguistic talent. Hence, through his translation Taviov created a Hebrew colloquial style and some slangy idioms, which seemed at first somewhat artificial but were accepted later and are now as natural as a smile and a laugh. Taviov's successful translations of *Tom Sawyer* and of some other works so impressed readers and critics that the leading literary periodical of the time published an enthusiastic article about them, providing it with the headline *Victory!*—that is to say, these translations are a proof that Hebrew has become a normal language just like all other living languages.

It was an impressive victory, but a short one. In the past fifty years the Hebrew language has developed so rapidly that Taviov's brilliant translation has by now become old and hence unreadable. But since Mark Twain was always the favorite American writer in Israel, all his books have been translated into Hebrew over and over again to make these timeless works appealing to each new generation of youngsters. *Tom Sawyer* was translated *seven* different times; *Huckleberry Finn,* six times; *The Prince and the Pauper,* five times; *Tom Sawyer Abroad, Pudd'nhead Wilson,* and *A Connecticut Yankee in King Arthur's Court,* twice or more.

As I mentioned before, some of the recent translations were done by me. I wished to repay the writer the debt I owed him, and I wished to give my daughter and her friends the books I loved so much in my childhood. Most of all I enjoyed working on *Huckleberry Finn;* and, although it was an exhausting job, it was also an unforgettable experience, a gratifying and enriching one. Some of you may ask me now: How did I handle the number of dialects which Mark Twain used in this book? Well, the plain answer is: I didn't handle it. I gave up, after realizing that it was an impossible undertaking. Instead, I thought of Huck as an Israeli boy, saying to myself: How would *he* write the book if his mother tongue were Hebrew? So, I used different dialects and jargons and tried my best to find equivalent expressions that would keep the sparkling humor of the original. For

example, I thought a good deal about what to do with "ol' King Sol-
lermun," as Jim called *our* wise monarch. Solomon's Hebrew name is
Shelomoh, which means "peaceful," but also "his well-being." Finally,
after some trials and erasures, I decided that Jim should call him
"Hamelech Ma-Shlomoh"; that is, King-How-Is-He . . . . I hope *He*
likes it.

After most of Twain's works were published in Hebrew, the Israeli
readers had the opportunity of reading his first book, *Innocents Abroad.*
Although this book is not considered a children's work, it was read
avidly by young and old. Doubtless most of you know why: *Innocents
Abroad* is a debunking account of the author's trip to the Middle East
and contains spicy descriptions of biblical landscapes and of the inhabitants of Jerusalem, Bethlehem, and other old places and some unexpected meetings, like this one for instance:

How touching it was, here in a land of strangers, far away from home, and
friends, and all who cared for me, thus to discover the grave of a blood relation. True, a distant one, but still a relation . . . . I leaned upon a pillar and
burst into tears. I deem it no shame to have wept over the grave of my poor
dead relative. Noble old man—he did not live to see me—he did not live to
see his child. And I - I - alas, did not live to see *him.* Weighed down by sorrow
and disappointment, he died before I was born—six thousand brief summers
before I was born . . . . For right under the roof of this great church—Adam
himself, the father of the human race, lies buried.

The Hebrew edition contains mainly those chapters which tell about
the regions that are now Palestine, or Israel, and is entitled *Massa-
Ta'anugot beEretz haKodesch* ("A joyful journey to the Holy Land"). Oh,
what a joyful journey it was!

Warriors, Pioneers, and Other Heroes

Fifteen years after Sam Clemens' trip to Palestine, another great
American novelist came to tour the Holy Land because of a book he
had written. This time the visitor was General Lew Wallace, author of
Ben Hur. One year after the appearance of this historical novel (1880),
which sold over two million copies, Wallace was appointed American
minister to Turkey. One of the first things he did after arriving in
Constantinople was to visit all the places he had described so vividly in
Ben Hur. Wallace wrote his novel mainly in Santa Fe, when he was
governor of New Mexico and while he was trying very hard to capture
Billy the Kid, the famous outlaw. A large map of the Holy Land hung
on the governor's office wall to help familiarize him with the sites
mentioned in his novel. Now, coming to all those places and seeing
with his own eyes all the places that he had only imagined while writing *Ben Hur,* he sensed a satisfactory surprise: he found that most of
the descriptions in his book were accurate.

I know that in America *Ben Hur* is not considered a children's book;

but all five Hebrew translations since the first (published in 1924) were aimed at the young reader, and the reason is quite obvious. *Ben Hur* is a vivid story, full of drama, based on Jewish history, whose main hero is a brave Jewish nobleman who dedicates his life to the liberation of Judea from Roman occupation. Evidently, all five trans- lators omitted the chapters dealing with Christ, thus emphasizing the part of Ben Hur, Prince of Israel, and his many confrontations with his enemy, the Roman Messala. Incidentally, I wonder if Wallace knew the meaning of his hero's name; Ben Hur (we pronounce it "Ben Hoor") means "a noble son," or "a free and glorious man."

The dramatic story of five other glorious men from ancient Israel is told in another outstanding novel written by an American. I refer to *My Glorious Brothers* by Howard Fast. In this epic novel the youngest brother of the Maccabees tells about the tragic destiny of his elder brothers, who headed the bold revolt against the Greek-Syrian con- querors, until their death in battle. Fast—the son of Jewish parents— like Wallace, did not visit Israel before writing his novel; nevertheless, all its geographic and natural descriptions are amazingly accurate. Al- though *My Glorious Brothers* was not written specifically for young readers, the novel is highly recommended in Israel to boys and girls of twelve years and up because of its heroic theme and high literary qualities. I have no doubt that American youngsters might also enjoy reading this absorbing novel of Fast's, no less than his *Haim Salomon, Son of Liberty*, the life story of the Jew who dedicated his fortune to the service of the American Revolution.

Boys and girls of Israel, who read such books as *Ben Hur, Innocents Abroad, My Glorious Brothers, My Village in Israel* by Tom Gidal, *A Boy of the Lost Crusade* by A. D. Hawes, or *Exodus* by Leon Uris, might get an outlandish impression of modern American literature, particularly about subjects that interest American readers. Most Israelis, young and old, who read the daily papers get the impression that the United States is the big sister of the state of Israel and that the American president and his men spend much of their time on Middle Eastern problems; similarly they might think that many American writers and readers are primarily concerned with books which deal with the his- tory of old and new Israel.

Pardon me; I was exaggerating, of course. A few hundred Ameri- can juveniles were translated, or adapted, into Hebrew in the last thirty years—good and bad books, excellent and poor ones. More American children's books have been translated in Israel than, perhaps, those of any other European language. Hence, our average young reader, who reads two or three books a week, becomes aware that there is no subject, or theme, which cannot be found in books published in the United States. In many books young readers can find problems, events, and characters that are similar to those which surround them; thus they are able to identify with them. Let us take, for example, such a gripping subject as pioneer life. Thousands of Israeli boys and girls remember proudly that their parents and grandparents had left the exile and had come as pioneers to the land of their forefathers, to make the desert bloom. They learn in school and read in books about the toil and trouble of the Jewish pioneers: famine, disease, band attacks, and so on. No wonder that Israeli children would willingly read American stories describing pioneer life, which parallels more or less those of their own country. From time to time they will even find American stories whose plots surprisingly resemble those of the Israeli ones. Laura Wilder's autobiographical classic, *Little House in the Big Woods*, appeals to many Israeli boys and girls, mainly to those who like our Hebrew classic, *Anshei Breshit* ("The Beginners") by Eliezer Smolli. This authentic novel, which appeared in English translation under the unsuccessful title *Frontiersman of Israel*, tells the dramatic story of a pioneer family who lived alone on the edge of a forest in the Galilee, miles from any settlement. Another popular novel on American pioneer life, beloved by our readers, is *The Yearling* by Marjorie Rawlings (entitled in Hebrew *The Fawn*); it may be compared to the moving Hebrew story *Ma'aseh beLoli ha . . .* ("A tale of Loli the . . . ") by the popular author Deborah Omer. A lonely boy living in a small village in the desert adopts an orphan kitten, which grows and turns into a young, frightening tiger. The village wants to get rid of the beast, but the devoted boy refuses to separate from his pet. A third example is the dramatic *Matchlock Gun*, by Walter D. Edmonds, which reminds many Israeli readers of the famous Hebrew story *HaNa'ar Amitz HaLev* ("Brave Lad"), by E. Smolli, about the valiant mission of an eleven-year-old boy who saves his isolated village from marauding bandits. Both are stories of suspense, mounting terror, and heroism and are very similar in plot and quality.

This brings us to the interesting conclusion that two different children's literatures may sometimes contain common elements, especially if the authors have similar backgrounds or know comparable chapters of history. Such books, I believe, can be the wonder-bridge which will bring children from distant countries—or even from close but hostile ones—to become friends.

From Doctor Dolittle to Doctor Seuss

But we all know well that children seek not only books of familiar themes. Give them an exotic tale or a strange and mysterious plot, and they will "swallow" it eagerly. All our boys and girls who love fantasy are fond of *Doctor Dolittle*, all ten amusing volumes of the kind-hearted animal doctor who understands animal language. Besides delightful translations of Lofting's stories, Israeli children are also fortunate to have some rhymed adaptations of *Dolittle* for the very young, in which the doctor's name acquired a Hebrew sound: "Dolitt." To continue with fantasy, our children are highly amused by *The Enormous Egg*, and while chuckling at the funny situations with the twentieth-century dinosaur, they also get some idea of American democracy and daily life. More popular among girls is E. B. White's *Charlotte's Web*, with its tender humor and praise of life. Incidentally, the Hebrew title of this book is *Havat Haksamim*, meaning "The Magic Farm"; and since the word "pig" has an unpleasant sound in Hebrew, the translator diminished the "terrific" Wilbur to a piglet—which sounds more agreeable and is associated also with Winnie the Pooh.

In this category we may include also Thurber's delightful fairy tale *Many Moons*, which was produced in Arabic by the Israeli Broadcasting Service as a successful TV musical; and, of course, the colorful legends of Uncle Remus, which were first translated into Hebrew by our great national poet Haim Nachman Bialik. They appeared in a beautiful volume entitled *Al Haarnevet* ("About the Rabbit") and later broadcast on the radio as a children's series.

Speaking of radio, television, and movies, we all know and remember the vast role that Hollywood played in popularizing children's books. A great number of American juveniles of all kinds were translated into Hebrew and widely read after the appearance of a popular motion picture. The first and best example is, undoubtedly, *Tarzan of the Apes*. I remember myself as a nine-year-old boy running barefoot to the cinema to see Johnny Weissmuller as the adored King of the Jungle. For a couple of years all my friends and I did not miss even one Tarzan movie and, right after that, "swallowed" the dozen Tarzan books, which were poorly translated into Hebrew. We did not know, of course, that *The New York Times* had judged the tales as "Crowded with impossibilities"; but we seemed to agree with the editors of *Liberty* that "all the lure and mystery of the jungle have made Tarzan as well known as Sherlock Holmes . . . ." We played Tarzan games, we climbed to the treetops, we imitated his roaring cry, we longed to be magnificent Tarzans ourselves . . . .

Then came other motion pictures, and new translations followed their footsteps: *The Wizard of Oz*, by Frank Baum, which was translated three times into Hebrew, is still popular in Israel, perhaps because the Wizard's home has a Hebrew name: Utz (the land of Biblical Job). Then came *Little Lord Fauntleroy, Sara Crewe,* and *The Secret Garden* by Mrs. F. H. Burnett, which are read by many Israeli girls to this very day. The Hebrew edition of *Lassie Come Home* was illustrated with photographs from the charming old film, and since then the Hebrew word for a collie has remained "lassie." Then *Toby Tyler* and *My Friend Flicka* and *Pollyanna* were translated, and it is almost unnecessary to

add that the Hebrew edition of *Pollyanna* was illustrated with pictures
from the famous film starring Haley Mills.

Pollyanna brings us almost automatically to Walt Disney. The name
Disney in Israel, as in many other countries, is one of America's most
well-known names. Young and old watch with delight the Disney programs on television and purchase the cheap picture books, comic
books, and printed versions of the Disney productions, all of them in
simple Hebrew translations. But in spite of his great fame, Walt Disney represents in Israel both the charming and the meager qualities
of mass media entertainment. Although the movie theaters of
Jerusalem, Tel Aviv, and Haifa are packed by young and old when a
Disney film is screened there, there are usually strong ambivalent feelings towards his treatment of the great children's classics, chiefly to
those that appeared later in book form. Younger children, of course,
enjoy looking at the big colorful illustrations, with their sweetish atmosphere; but better readers cannot forgive the liberty taken by Disney with works of literary quality, ruining the integrity of the origi-
nals, changing Snow White into a glamor girl, and his oversimplifica-
tion of stories like *Bambi, Pinocchio,* or *Alice in Wonderland.* And what's
more, how can we forgive him the sin of putting out of the child's
mind the names of great children's authors? Ask an average young Israeli reader who wrote *The Jungle Book* or *Peter Pan* or *Mary Poppins*
and the answer will be, "Why, Volt Dissny, of course . . . ."

Fortunately, however, young readers of Hebrew know the names of
many other American book producers, aside from Walt Disney. They
know and admire classic writers whose books are being translated and
read till this very day, like Jack London or Ernest Seton Thompson,
and many youngsters know and like the names of Leo Lionni and
Doctor Seuss.

As to Dr. Seuss (whose name is pronounced in Israel "Zees," which
means "sweet" in Yiddish), his hilarious books are somewhat prob-
lematic in Israel and almost impossible for the translator. How could
you say, for instance, in Hebrew, "Cats in hats" or "Fox in socks"?

Nevertheless, about ten years ago a long article was published in a
popular family magazine printed in Tel Aviv under the title: "Who
Heard of Doctor Seuss?" (by the way: if *Zees* is "sweet" in Yiddish, *Soos*
is a "horse" in Hebrew). The author, Dan Almagor (who had translated *My Fair Lady* into Hebrew), began his article with a story about
his little daughter, who refused to read beginner books (Hebrew ones,
of course) because she found many difficult words in them which she
did not understand. (Unfortunately, she was right: there are many
beginner books in Hebrew that are too difficult for beginners; the
reason lies in the too-speedy development of modern Hebrew.) But
then, Dr. Almagor continues, he went with his daughter to the United

States for a two-year stay. One day he was surprised to see the seven-year-old girl enjoying enormously a beginner-book (in English, of course), and laughing delightedly. He bent over her to see the title; it read, *One Fish, Two Fish, Red Fish, Blue Fish,* written and illustrated by a certain Doctor Seuss.

After introducing Dr. Seuss to Israeli fathers and mothers, the writer stated enviously that American children were fortunate to have such an entertaining doctor, who has created such amusing books for them, which they can read without difficulty. Dr. Almagor concluded his long article with a question: "When will *our* children be fortunate enough to have a Hebrew Dr. Seuss of their own? Or, at least, where is the talented translator who will succeed in rewriting Dr. Seuss' verse into an equivalent Hebrew version?"

I am not sure it was as a result of Almagor's article, but a few months later the first Dr. Seuss book appeared in Hebrew. It was *Yertle the Turtle,* or as it was entitled in Hebrew: *HaMelekh Tzav-Tsav* (King Turtle-Turtle). But although the translator was one of our leading scholars and poets, Professor Leah Goldberg (yes, she too was a doctor), her translation was rather mediocre. But let us not blame *her* for this failure; my friend, a children's book editor of a large publishing house, showed me just a few weeks ago five different translations of Seuss' book which she rejected, for it is almost impossible to achieve a satisfactory translation of Dr. Seuss, or of Ogden Nash, or of Laura Richards.

"Hands Across the Border"

For some reason or other our translators were more fortunate in dealing with British verse, like Stevenson's *A Child's Garden of Verses* or Milne's *Now We Are Six.* I myself had great fun in translating Tolkien's *Adventures of Tom Bombadil,* although I am aware that my product is inferior to the brilliant original. During my unforgettable stay at the Toronto Public Libraries (especially at the Osborne Collection of Early Children's Books), I discovered the fascinating treasure of children's folk rhymes and verse from many countries and have published them in a volume which has enjoyed a surprising distribution. Consequently, the children of Israel became familiar with Mother Goose, Mary and her little lamb, and many other figures from the international treasury of children's folklore. Thus I believe that good poetry can be a central link which should bring together children from different countries. Incidentally, the role of poetry in the life of a modern child was, as you certainly know, a major topic of discussion in the fifteenth Congress of the International Board on Books for Young People.

But the typical child wants to find his or her own realistic world in books, and this, as we know, is found mainly in fiction. Most boys and girls, no matter what their nationality, seek identification in books; when they read a translated story, they subconsciously compare their own problems with those they find in the book. In Pearl Buck's sensible little story *Beech Tree*, children find a satisfactory answer to the troublesome questions of getting old, and life after death. Most Israeli girls love the old-fashioned translation of *Little Women*, feel like one of the March sisters, identify with their first sense of romance, with their dreams of maturity. An Israeli boy might identify with problems he meets in the moving story *Antelope Singer* by Ruth Underhill (which is, I'm afraid, not very popular in this country), which shows the significance of true friendship between different boys. Such problems—life and death, being grown-up, getting old, true friendship—are common to children all over the world; but do believe me, they have a deeper meaning to the boys and girls of Israel. Therefore our children are grateful to every author who helps them in finding a solution to these problems.

There are, of course, many more American stories that are popular with our young readers. Allow me to mention only two more: the old, attractive adventure story *Merrylips*, by Beulah Dix, about the energetic girl who wanted to be a boy; and the laudable *Island of the Blue Dolphins*, by Scott O'Dell, a gripping tale of courage, self-reliance, and acceptance of fate.

On the other hand, not all American stories translated into Hebrew are liked by our young readers. The wayward reading taste of boys and girls is a mystery that no Sherlock Holmes can solve. Thus, for some reason or other, they reject the fabulous *Twenty-One Balloons*, in spite of the beautiful translation and print. Beverly Cleary's gay *Ramona the Pest* did not enjoy its deserved popularity, maybe because of the feeble translation. Also American juveniles about children of other lands, like *Little Pear* of China or the *Little Flute Player of India*, have not captured the hearts of our young readers. Nevertheless, more and more fiction—old and modern—is being translated continually. It is hard to find any specific system in the choice of titles for translation, and the publishers' selection is quite casual, depending on the editors' taste, vague information, or an agent's recommendation. One day, just before my departure, I discovered in a bookstore window the old classic *Story of a Bad Boy*, by Thomas Bailey Aldrich, and the modern classic *Mr. Popper's Penguins*, both in recent Hebrew translations. Also the amusing *Henry Reed, Inc.* has just been translated, and no doubt Henry's gay journal will be popular among Israeli young readers, just as it is in this country. While reading and laughing, our children will acquire a humorous picture of daily life in New Jersey, with its summer enterprises. While preparing this lengthy paper, I had great fun translating the adventurous fantasy of Norton Juster, *The Phantom Tollbooth*, especially the numerous word-jokes scattered between the marketplace of Dictionopolis and the Mountains of Ignorance. I am eager to find out, when, I return home, our readers' reactions to this witty allegory.

As you can infer from this report, most Hebrew readers have quite a good knowledge of American children's books and their authors. Not all writers do, of course. They have not yet made an acquaintance with the works of such authors as Eleanor Estes, Joseph Krumgold, Lois Lenski, or Howard Pyle (I do hope they will be able to do so soon). On the other hand, they have never heard also—luckily for them!—the names of *Nancy Drew, The Hardy Boys,* or *The Bobbsey Twins,* maybe because they are content with similar Hebrew trash. (But most of them are very well acquainted with Popeye, not only from television but also from translated comics magazines, where the spinach lover talks in an awful biblical jargon.)

The young readers of Israel have always been familiar with America's rich children's literature; they appreciate it, they absorb it, and they learn from it about this great friendly democracy, its people, nature, and history. But let me ask you now: How much do American children know about the youth literature of my country? Almost nothing, I am afraid (except ancient Bible stories). Many younger children of the United States might have heard the name of Uri Shulevitz; but do they know that the roots of this talented author-illustrator originated in an Israeli kibbutz? Other American Jewish writers associated with Israel are the sisters Judith and Shulamit Ish-Kishor, authors of *Drusila* and *Adventure in Israel;* Meir Levin, who now lives not far from my house on the Mediterranean seashore; and Isaac Bashevis Singer, whose fabulous tales are being translated into Hebrew from the original Yiddish. From time to time American children are able to read fictional stories about modern Israel, published originally in the United States, like *Dance Around the Fire* by Molly Cone, about a girl who is the unwitting accomplice to an Arab terrorist act; or *Abu* by Joseph Trigoboff, about an Israeli soldier befriending a nine-year-old Arab street urchin. Unfortunately, most of these stories are superficial or too melodramatic. Only seldom does it happen that a good Israeli juvenile is translated into a foreign language and published abroad. After careful investigation I have listed no more than seven Hebrew children's titles that have been published in the United States in the last ten years. Among them are *The Fifth Wheel,* a delightful story by Moshe Shamir about life in a kibbutz; *The Gideonites,* a well-written historical novel about the Zionist underground, and *Rebirth,* a gripping story about the founder of modern spoken Hebrew as told from the point of view of his son, both by Deborah Omer; *Azeet, the Paratrooper Dog,* by Motta Gur, who is now Chief of Staff of the Israeli Defense Forces; and *The Dog That Flew,* a representative anthology of eleven short stories written by favorite writers. But how many of these books are found in the thousands of libraries all over America, or read by your boys and girls? I am afraid to hear the answer.

True, Israel is a very small country, no larger than Massachusetts; its population equals that of Greater Boston, and the Hebrew language, written from right to left, is so difficult and complicated. But I hope you'll agree that these reasons are unjustifiable. Mrs. Arbuthnot urged us (in chapter 16 of *Children and Books*) to recall the latest slogans—"Hands across the Border" and "One World." Thus let us remember that good books translated from foreign languages convince young readers that other places and cultures—although different from their own—are of equal worth; they reveal the values of human ways of life outside the reader's own limits. American children, as well as Israelis, are blessed with good translations from Swedish, Italian, Dutch, or Japanese languages. Good for them! It is one of the advantages of removing the barriers in our "One World" and being aware that a good book is a good book, regardless of where and in what language it was written. I do hope that these words of mine will help in introducing the American child to more worthy books written originally in Hebrew, or Turkish, or any other little-spoken language. The books and their writers deserve it; the children of America deserve it no less.

When one writes a novel about grown people (thus said Mark Twain) he knows exactly where to stop: with a marriage perhaps; but when he writes of juveniles, he must stop where he best can. Allow me to add to these witty words, that when one delivers a lecture, he must stop after saying half of what he intended to say. So, let me conclude now with words said once by our national poet, Haim Nachman Bialik, when a children's book editor complained that he, the poet, put difficult words in his children's verse: "Hard words are like hard nuts," Bialik told him. "Let the children bite into them and their teeth will strengthen."

A Selected List of American Children's Books in Hebrew Translation

Alcott, Louisa May. *Little Men.*
  G'varim K'tanim. Keter, 1977.
Baum, Lyman Frank. *The Wonderful Wizard of Oz.*
  HaKosem m'Eretz Utz. Dora, 1974.
Buck, Pearl S. *The Big Wave.*
  HaGal haGadol. Hadar, 1958.
Butterworth, Oliver. *The Enormous Egg.*
  Ta'alumat haBeitza haAnakit. Hadar, 1964.
Cleary, Beverly. *Ramona the Pest.*

Du Bois, William Pene. *The Twenty One Ballons.*
  Esrim veEhad Kadurim Porhim. Massada, 1966.
Johnson, Crockett. *Harold and the Purple Crayon.*
  Aharon vehalpparon haSagol. Am Oved, 1975.
Juster, Norton. *The Phantom Tollbooth.*
  Migdal haPoreakh baAvir. Zmora, Bitan, Moda, 1978.

Rimmona haPirkhakhit. Jezreel, 1974.
Cleaver, Vera and Bill. *Where the Lilies Bloom.*
  Kama Yafe Poreakh haLilach. Bronfman, 1971.
  Kol Kedumim. Keter, 1975.
O'Dell, Scott. *Island of the Blue Dolphins.*
  Ee haDolfinim haKehulim. Am Oved, 1967.
O'Hara, Mary. *My Friend Flicka.*
  Yedidati Flicka. Zmora, Bitan, Modan, 1978.
Otis, James. *Toby Tyler.*
  Toby Tailer baKirkas. Sreberk, 1964.
Rawlings, Marjorie Kinnan. *The Yearling.*
  HaOfer. Bronfman, 1948.
Robertson, Keith. *Henry Reed, Inc.*
  Henry Reed veShut. Zmora, Bitan, Modan, 1978.
Singer, Isaac Bashevis. *When Shlemiel Went to Warsaw.*
  Shlomiel Ish Chelm. Am Oved, 1977.
Sobol, Donald J. *Encyclopedia Brown, Boy Detective.*
  Dani Yad'ani haNa'ar ha'Balash. Friedman, 1978.
Stowe, Harriet Beecher. *Uncle Tom's Cabin.*
  Ohel haDod Tom. Sreberk, 1965.
Thurber, James. *Many Moons.*
  HaNesikha vehaYareach. Ofer, 1976.
White, E. B. *Charlotte's Web.*
  Havat haK'samim. Zmora, Bitan, Modan, 1977.

Knight, Eric. *Lassie Come Home.*
  Lassi Hozeret haBaita. Achiasaf, 1974.
Lofting, Hugh. *The Story of Doctor Dolittle.*
  Alilot Dolitl haRofe. Massada, 1975.
London, Jack. *The Call of the Wild.*
Wilder, Laura Ingalls. *Little House in the Big Woods.*
  Bait Katan baYa'ar haGadol. Zmora, Bitan, Modan. 1977.

Addresses of Publishers

Achiasaf Publishing House, Ltd., 13 Joseph Nassi St., Tel Aviv. Am Oved Publishers, Ltd., 22 Mazeh St., Tel Aviv.
Bronfman Publishers, 2 Chlenov St., Tel Aviv.
Dora Publishers, c/o Carmi, 13 Tiomkin St., Tel Aviv.
Friedman Publishing House, 27 Gruzenberg St., Tel Aviv.
Hadar Publishing House, 15 Fichman St., Tel Aviv.
Jezreel Publishing House, Ltd., 76 Dizengoff St., Tel Aviv.
Keter Publishing House, Givat Shaul, POB 7145, Jerusalem.
Massada Publishing Company, Ltd., 21 Jabotinsky Road, Ramat Gan.
Ofer Publishers, 7 Shvil Akko, Tel Aviv.
Sreberk Publishers, 16 Balfour St., Tel Aviv.
Zmora, Bitan, Modan Publishers, 88 Ussishkin St., Tel Aviv.

Sheila Egoff

Sheila Egoff is a professor at the School of
Librarianship, University of British Columbia, in
Vancouver, British Columbia. She has served as a
Canadian juror on the international jury that selects
the Hans Christian Andersen Award, and is a fellow
of the British Library Association. She is co-editor,
with G. T. Stubbs and L. F. Ashley, of a book of
readings on children's literature, *Only Connect*
(Oxford University Press, 1969), and author of a
guide to English-language children's books
published in Canada, *The Republic of Childhood*
(Oxford University Press, 1967, 1975).

Sheila Egoff's lecture, "Beyond the Garden Wall:
Some Observations on Current Trends in
Children's Literature," was presented May 5, 1979,
in Columbia, South Carolina, at the College of
Librarianship, University of South Carolina.

Beyond the Garden Wall

Some Observations on Current Trends in
Children's Literature

MY TITLE COMES TO YOU BY CONSENSUS. When I gave my students and faculty colleagues a list of alternative titles that might convey the theme of current trends in children's literature, they opted, with near unanimity, for "Beyond the Garden Wall."

Why the popularity of this image, especially since none of the voters (including myself) had ever so much as seen a garden wall until we were aged enough to join an American Express tour group in search of Victorian London? The answer of course, is, that we had all been steeped in the classic children's literature and knew how well the garden wall symbolized it. And we also knew that the very essence of our own time is the passion for the new and the shocking—"beyondness" in many senses. "Beyond the Garden Wall," then—how very appropriate it seems, even if the commendation is self-administered.

How did the garden grow? In effect, it began in Victorian times when books for children came no longer to be seen as mere instructional manuals or vehicles for sermonizing. The Victorian era brought together genuine literary talents and a whole new concept of childhood—and the result was the "Golden Age of Children's Literature." For the first time a separate state called "childhood" was envisioned. The child was basically good and innocent and childhood was to be valued for its own sake. "Heaven," Wordsworth claimed, "lies about us in our infancy." George MacDonald's books for children, in many ways, voice this Victorian, middle-class view of childhood. Children were to be cherished for their innocence, clearsightedness, and perception. Paradoxically (and children's literature is full of paradoxes), they were also to be trained in the manners and virtues of the day, fulfilling the maxim "as the twig is bent, so grows the tree." In MacDonald's *The Princess and the Goblin* (1872) he introduces two concepts that were to be an integral part of children's literature up until the end of the 1950s. Gillian Avery has described them as "the doctrine of perception" and "the doctrine of good breeding." The former doctrine posits the natural goodness of children and their unique understanding of the true essence of things. But this involves an innate trust on the part of children in God and his surrogates on earth. The second doctrine, "good breeding," emphasizes the essential role of manners. Behaviour rather than birth made little boys into gentlemen and little girls into princesses. For the children themselves, though, these qualities of character were not achieved without a struggle.

In spite of their common view of childhood as a state of innocence, Victorian writers were by no means saccharine; they could be as tough and uncompromising as Kingsley who, it should be remembered, thought of a children's book as a perfectly appropriate vehicle for diatribes against Catholics, uncleanliness, and schoolmasters (in ascending order of denigration!). But Victorian writers were basically animated by idealism and optimism. Their chief achievement was a change in emphasis from narrowly religious and doctrinaire adherence to "rules of conduct" to a view which spoke in childlike terms of broad moral standards and universal values. And in addition, they took delight in entertainment, creating marvellous plots with uniquely interesting characters—both innovations in children's literature. With this enlargement of outlook, they sent their books on a journey across time and space. The great Victorian classics can still stir the hearts and minds of children who have scarcely heard of England and for whom the nineteenth century is utterly remote.

Building the wall even higher, the Edwardians intensified the sense of difference and distance between childhood and adulthood. Nowhere is this more charmingly expressed than in Kenneth Grahame's account of his own childhood, *The Golden Age*. The children there see themselves as the fortunate ones; the adults are "the Olympians," powerful but misguided. When adults have the power to do otherwise, how can they possibly wish to spend a lovely Sunday going to church and drinking tea on the lawn instead of climbing a tree and tickling trout? Childhood is the ideal state. This can also be deduced from other books of the period such as *The Wind in the Willows* (the animals are really children), the Nesbit books, and, most of all, Barrie's *Peter Pan*. It is not, however, that the children in these books want to evade the growth to responsibility; it is rather that childhood had its own special character and flavour which could not be given up without a sense of loss.

In the period just before and then between the two world wars, and perhaps because of adult feelings of ethical responsibility for them, writers created childlike superheroes and heroines. You may be unaware that *The Boy Allies* won World War I singlehandedly. Heroines, such as *Elsie Dinsmore, Pollyanna, Anne of Green Gables*, and *A Girl of the Limberlost*, moved on a different front but they too were conquerors. They subjugated all around them with their "sweetness and light" and solved everybody's problems. Always, though, their youth and innocence kept them from harm.

And still behind the wall. In the post–World War II years children's writers took many new directions and mustered a remarkable roster of diverse talents. In spite of the considerable variation in the works of the best writers from the 1940s to the end of the 1950s, they agreed so strongly on basic outlooks and values as to suggest that there was still a "public view" or consensus on the nature of children and their literature. At the heart of this view was the feeling of childhood as an existence in tandem with adult society. The young protagonists were engaged in an almost unconscious preparation for adulthood, in the sense that the children's activities called for the development of self-reliance, generosity, friendship, imagination, integrity—qualities that were deemed vital for maturity. Nevertheless the boundaries between the two worlds were to be carefully maintained: children who aped the dress and manners of adults were guilty of presumption and affectation. In seeking, prematurely, to leave childhood behind, they seemed to denigrate and betray their fellows and therefore to lose their respect. Thus we see, in C. S. Lewis' *The Last Battle*, severe condemnation for Susan, once a queen in Narnia, who has lost her balance by becoming interested in "nothing but nylons and lipstick and invitations. She was always a jolly sight too keen on being grown-up."

There was no sex and no violence in books of this period—if such episodes occurred they were of a remote and archetypal kind. The writers used their talents to infuse their books with a marvellous warmth of feeling—most vividly, that of the children for one another and for the few adults who shared their play and concerns; more remotely, in children's attachment to their parents, who moved on the periphery of their adventures but nonetheless were there and always ready to offer support. The trust that parents placed in their children was sometimes startling. Arthur Ransome's *Swallows and Amazons* (1930) describes a father who, on being asked for his permission to let his children go off alone on a sailing and camping expedition, promptly telegraphed them: "Better drowned than duffers; if not duffers, won't drown." Ransome, however, had not strained our credulity. Mr. Walker was a sea captain and his children had been well trained. They could do more than "mess about with boats."

Finally, we thought we knew what children were in those decades of the 1930s, 1940s, and 1950s. They were not just little adults, and they were not just children; they were on their way to adulthood and we treated their minds as we did their bodies. Not too much too soon. No excess. A steady progression. We also thought we knew what children's literature was. It was, first of all, literature—that is, how the writer said it was as important as what the writer said. We saw no difference, really, between the best written for adults and the best written for children. *"Best"* was the operative word rather than *child* or *adult*. Didacticism was therefore shunned. It was both irrelevant (in departing from the main goal of literary merit) and insulting (in suggesting that the audience needed instruction more than enjoyment). Literature meant enrichment, both in the sense of giving pleasure and in the sense of broadening experience and developing taste—and we did not mind using the word *taste*. This did not mean that literature was necessarily to be equated with profundity. Literature could be light and even frivolous; the essential point was that, whatever its type, quality had to be present.

By the end of the 1950s children's books had reached a very high plateau. With such writers as Tolkien, C. S. Lewis, Philippa Pearce, Scott O'Dell, E. B. White, Robert McCloskey, Lucy Boston, Eleanor Estes, Elizabeth Enright, Laura Ingalls Wilder, and the early works by such writers as William Mayne and Rosemary Sutcliff, the period could be called the Second Golden Age of Children's Literature. These authors (and many others) were practitioners of fine writing in the traditional style. And it could be expected that readers of such books would have no difficulty in making the transition from children's literature to adult literature and that of the finest sort.

You see, then, why I think the garden wall is such a treasured and traditional metaphor of this earlier children's literature and why it is so very apt. Actually it is a multiple metaphor (I hope not a mixed one!). The wall represents seclusion, protection, confinement; the garden—order, serenity, aesthetic delight—no weeds, no intrusion from the wild and the naturalistic. But the metaphor is not as narrow as it may at first suggest. If the garden wall represents the family, or innocence or safety or imaginative play, it also, and above all, represents time. Time was the chief shock-absorber that society and writers gave to its children. Time to let children grow (intellectually and emotionally), time to explore their own interests and problems away from adults; and when the wall was to be finally breached it was to be through the children's own efforts and at their own pace. In Philippa Pearce's *Tom's Midnight Garden* the children's imaginative games and wanderings through the rich, intricate landscape of the garden are held in check by garden walls. But the walls are also there for climbing, to give an extensive view of the world outside, and they open out to the freedom and danger of skating on the river of ice. Just so, the sheltered security of childhood gives way to the open space of adulthood and maturity.

Looking back at all this with the wisdom of hindsight, we can see now that the social outlook displayed in these books was (taken in toto) perhaps *too* safe, too bland, so very limited. Certainly there was a repetitive quality to them no matter how interesting the plot, characters, and setting. Aside from a few intimations of change in the more introspective writers, such as Lucy Boston, Philippa Pearce, and Rosemary Sutcliff, the writers of the 1940s and 1950s did not deal with the unusual child, the alienated child, the troubled child, the outsider. There were few fresh insights into childhood and certainly no exploration of uncertainties or the dark corners of the child mind. In speaking of the Ransome children, one critic said, "They were so bloody healthy and well-adjusted"! In short, the writers gave a picture of what society hoped for from its children rather than of what those children—many of them at least—really were.

Was there then a tarnish on the Golden Age? It certainly seemed so as the serene and certain '50s turned into the restless and anxious '60s and—you were waiting for this, weren't you?—the walls came tumbling down! If the '60s are not easily explainable, they are certainly memorable. It was a period of social convulsion, when, among other important happenings, the young denied the wisdom of their elders, defied established authority, and discovered the word *relevance*. The changes came thick and fast—indeed rapid change itself came to be regarded as both inevitable and desirable. In particular, the young (and here the word is used for people up to about age twenty-five) eagerly and aggressively took on the problems which had hitherto been left to their elders. It really was like breaching a confining wall—a new viewpoint that represented a definite change in society and, arguably, a salutary one.

There are two axioms that apply to this kind of social situation. The first is that any change in attitude and mores is likely to affect children more dramatically than any other segment of society. The second is that changes which affect children will be very rapidly reflected in the books written for them. Put the two axioms together and you will understand why the 1960s may be characterized as the age of turmoil in children's literature shown, particularly, in books emanating from the United States.

The most obvious manifestation of this turmoil—or was it really cause rather than effect?—was that the long-standing surety of what a child was at last faltered and failed. Children no longer appeared to be special or different but were back in the adult world again to an extent not known since the Middle Ages. There were many reasons for this and they all seemed to come to fruition at once. It is of some significance, I think, that the adolescents had been steadily assuming more and more of the attributes, perquisites, and problems of their elders. Like adults, teenagers now had money, cars, jobs and also drugs, liquor, sex, and the assorted difficulties arising therefrom. Even if one takes the simple theory that the youngest child in the family gets more freedom than the oldest had in similar circumstances, I think it can be assumed that much of this newish adolescent freedom "rubbed off" on children. And many of the children now had their own share of weighty responsibilities. Do you remember the term "latch-key children"? It was coined during World War II to describe those children who had to let themselves into empty houses or apartments because there would be no parent at home to greet them after school. Well, by the 1960s, with the increasing incidence of one-parent families and working mothers, the number of such latch-key children increased to the point where the term itself disappeared. The social phenomenon was too common to warrant a special name.

Another assault on the wall came out of that odd mixture of benevolence and belligerence—the demand for "openness" in our dealings with each other. No more evasions—everybody—yes children, too—had a right to know. Indeed children's rights became a battle cry. The American Library Association joined in with a resolution that age was no longer to constitute grounds for special treatment. Children were to be liberated from the restrictions of childhood.

Quite often, these libertarians found useful ammunition from the fields of physiology and psychology. It was thus claimed, probably plausibly enough, that children matured earlier, in a physical sense, than they used to. Freud's theories on the early sexuality of children became argument for greater frankness, and modern child psychology revealed that children had fears and anxieties and suppressions and repressions as had their older counterparts. And was this harsh finding a matter for regret? Not at all. In that vaunted spirit of "telling it like it was," the children's books no longer soothed a nightmare with a night light in the nursery, but faced them head-on by providing gruesome illustrations depicting a child's vision of monsters.

All this was to suggest, then, that children were no longer deemed to be innately innocent. Indeed the very opposite view was often advanced, holding that children could be savage, even evil. Think how popular and influential William Golding's *Lord of the Flies* was. Not just because it was well written but it was thought to be a revelation of the way things really were with children. The underlying position of adults seemed to be that childhood itself was no longer especially valuable and, as a result, it became fleeting and ephemeral, if not entirely eroded. Children might still be seen as the hope of the world but this did not exempt them from an early exposure to society's harsh problems.

Before I go on to describe, discuss, and deplore the "problem book," let me do a little stage setting in terms of economics. A noteworthy characteristic of the 1960s was the large increase in the number of publications for children. Between 1957 and 1977 about 100,000 children's books were issued in Britain and the U.S.A., and omitting as I do the large number of informational books, and concentrating only on those that have surfaced, the numbers are great indeed.

One result of this spate of publishing (Frances Clarke Sayers in 1956, you may remember, complained about the "muchness" of children's literature) was a centrifugal effect. Sheer numbers made for diversity and reduced commonality. No longer, as before, were a great many children reading the same few titles. Traditional values weakened as books sought their market by appeals to various special interest groups.

A second market effect—also tending to push children's writing into new directions—was the growing influence of the United States. With the American market now so much larger than any other in the English-speaking world, publishers were moved to select books which reflected American attitudes and attributes. In the 1960s the U.S. came to exercise a dominant influence on writing for children. The new trends were set here, the issues were fought here. The United States exported and eventually "converted" the world into accepting them as their own.

That export was—you see, I made it back again—the "problem book" and like Coca-Cola, that other American product of worldwide influence, it has won more acceptance than acclaim. The "problem book" at least is very aptly named.

This vastly changed view of childhood seemed to arrive with wrenching suddenness in the 1960s. (I suspect now that the wrench was what made it seem so sudden, but no matter.) And with equal force and speed the new mood and the new mores were reflected in the children's books themselves. The most notable, debatable, obvious manifestation of this trend was in the establishment of that new genre—the problem book. But I stress this point here and will "prove" it later on—every genre of children's writing in some degree was affected by it.

It was very strongly subject-oriented with the interest primarily residing in the topic rather than in the telling. The topics—all adult-oriented—sound like chapter titles from a textbook on social pathology: divorce, drugs, disappearing parents, desertion, and death (makes a nicely alliterative litany, doesn't it?). And towering above all such minor matters, the two superstar problems—sex and alienation.

The popularity of the problem novel is so widespread as to warrant an attempt to account for its appeal. One explanation—or perhaps claim is the more accurate word—is that the problem novel has therapeutic value. Many children suffer from the very difficulties depicted in these novels and presumably it is good for these children to know that they are not alone in their suffering—"This is a book about a child just like me."

Conversely, for those children who do not identify with the protagonists in a real-life way, there is the appeal of the exotic. Just as adult, upperclass suburbanites find *The Godfather* absorbing, so well brought up girls may find a kind of romance and excitement in the "hard-boiled" naturalism of the problem novels. It comes as no surprise to learn that girls far outnumber boys as an audience for them.

I myself prefer a third theory and the fact that it is of my own devising is only coincidental, of course. It seems to me that the problem novel wins its audience by flattery. Children want to feel grown-up and problem novels offer to youngsters—in simple language that they can perfectly well follow—the implication that they are ready to deal with issues and themes that are indisputably "adult." After all, the movie makers have long known that the way to attract a juvenile audience is to label their wares "for mature viewers."

Lastly and most obviously, there are the appeals of the "p's"— prurience and peer pressure. How welcome it must be to find between the covers of a book both words and subjects that have been considered taboo and may still be so in an individual child's home or school environment. While they may give the child a delicious *frisson*, they also spell respectability. Peer pressure also undeniably plays a part in popularity. Not to have read Judy Blume seems as socially unacceptable as not being familiar with the latest "in" television show.

This long list of appeals suggests that the problem novel has pretty substantial assets to its credit and indeed it is true that the genre has vastly extended the scope of children's literature, both in content and tone. Writers are free, as never before, to attempt themes of almost any kind. But along with the heady new freedom also have come some interdictions. The pressure to find subjects of "social importance" leads to the loss of that which formerly seemed the very essence of children's literature. More important, the sad fact is that the problem novel is almost inherently inimical to the traditional literary values of imagination and style. The problem book, in fact, is basically journalistic in approach rather than literary. Like many a newspaper, it depends on the shock value of the subject to catch and hold the reader, rather than on any skill in narration. Like "yellow journalism," too, the problem books offer the appeal of "easy reading"—nothing here to require effort. It is no accident at all that although many problem novels are intended for young adults, they have moved down very quickly into the reading of children—even very young children. Lastly, the problem book's criterion of success is exactly that of journalism: will it sell? And by this straightforward test the problem books have become a success indeed—so numerous and so alike that today they seem turned out by a copying machine.

Well, there is of course nothing at all new about commercialism as a factor in writing for children, nor for that matter the production of books by formula. Horatio Alger, dime novels, and the Hardy Boys all fit neatly into the above two categories. But where these older publications stood rather apart from children's literature and hardly affected it—in much the same relationship, I suggest, that pulp fiction had to the adult novel—the problem book has had a very significant effect on contemporary children's literature. I by no means intend to suggest that the very greatest writers, such as Ivan Southall or Rosemary Sutcliff or Lucy Boston, follow trends—if they are in the new wave, and I think they are, it is simply because they have always been ahead of their time. More to the point is the fact that several writers who had previously done all their work in other genres have now tried their hand at the problem book—Scott O'Dell, Ursula Le Guin and, most recently, K. M. Paterson with *The Great Gilly Hopkins*. When substantial, established writers of this sort are led to venture into a wholly new type of writing, it is safe to say that that new type of writing—the problem novel—is exercising a strong influence.

That influence is most visible in what one might call the "casting" of contemporary children's literature. The previous generations tended to think of themes and characters in terms of very broad range and wide appeal. Oh yes, there was some subdivision by age and sex—one could think of boys' books and girls' books, or books for younger children and books for older children. Essentially, however, it was not a particular species of child but rather childhood itself that occupied center stage. The characters that one remembers from the older writing—Alice, Lord Fauntleroy, Huck Finn, Babar, Pinocchio, Johnny Tremain—represented no particular typology but rather spoke for *all* of childhood.

Contemporary literature, particularly as influenced by the problem book, tends to work in a much narrower focus, to typecast its characters. The child—a particular type of child in each case—now has pushed childhood off center stage. Rather than being universalized, the characters are now "representative"—that is, each one incarnates a class or category of problem. So we now have novels about the Alienated Child, the Minority Child, the Abused Child, the Retarded Child, the Rejected Child. These central figures, however powerfully depicted, are all nameless for me because it is the category and not the individual person that I remember. Indeed, in my mind's eye these categories always appear as though printed in red ink and capitalized—because they so much resemble subject headings in a catalogue!

Was that jibe unfair? I hope not, but sometimes I do feel a little ashamed of myself for derogating books which are obviously so well intentioned. Heaven knows, the problems they deal with are real enough and large enough, and I suppose that I ought to commend the authors for their earnestness.

But dear me, need the earnestness be so deadly and omnipresent? Thanks largely, I feel, to the misplaced influence of the problem novel, much of recent writing for children seems to bear out John Rowe Townsend's worries about "didacticism in modern dress."

I must not exaggerate. Present-day writers do not offer their "audiences" anything like the overt sermons and precepts that used to occupy half the pages of children's books. But the basic point of view is not all different. Like their predecessors of the seventeenth and eighteenth centuries, today's writers want to *teach* children, to show them what to do about their problems and crises. This new didacticism takes two forms. The first is not readily definable. It comes from the writers' assumptions that they have indeed solved everything, that the protagonists have faced their problems and conquered them. When the protagonists are between the ages of seven and fourteen, generally, I find this a pretty dubious expectation. The second type is simply a matter of modernizing some old wording. It is no longer acceptable for writers (or parents and teachers for that matter) to tell a child to be "good"; on the other hand, the contemporary mode states that it is perfectly all right to harangue children to be nonracist, nonsexist, and antiwar! Just the same, it is well to remember that children are not as responsive to fashion as are we adults. In the past children threw away the books that baldly told them what to do and I suspect that children of the present will be not much different in their reactions to didacticism.

Didacticism need not, of course, be synonymous with dullness— Dickens is sure proof of that contention. But the do-gooder *does* tend to be pretty much of a sobersides and I suppose that this is why one of the most marked characteristics of modern children's literature is its sheer solemnity. It sounds pretty silly, doesn't it, to talk about "angst" pervading books for ten-year-olds but, believe me, it is *there* and often in full-blown form.

It is perfectly true that much of earlier children's literature was serious, chiefly because its writers took childhood seriously. Still, for the reader there was always the comfort of knowing that things would turn out fine eventually, because the child protagonists were what I like to call "safe survivors." Their dangers lent excitement rather than anxiety. Conversely, modern young protagonists are "dangerous survivors." They walk a tightrope of disaster and in many instances indeed fall off to become victims. Goodbye the security of the assured happy ending.

Rather more important, there was also a great deal of humour in the older books—a welcome feature which modern books almost completely lack. I suppose that the very themes of current writing preclude the light touch. The classic definition of comedy is that it proceeds through confusion to order and pattern and integration with society. In a society steeped in disintegration and fragmentation we should not be surprised that the comic spirit has gone underground or has become "black" or ironic as in the works of John Gardner or Roald Dahl. It takes a Leon Garfield to remind us that the comic is part of life even amid portentous events. And Jane Gardam, in a book such as *Bilgewater*, can still show a young protagonist who accepts and enjoys her father's eccentricities. But such writers are rare. The only truly light-hearted contemporary books, such as John D. Fitzgerald's The Great Brain series, seem deliberately to recall the mood and manner of an earlier era—a Tom Sawyer revisited, so to speak. In that sense, they succeed in being good humourous writing indeed but at the expense of having lost their contemporaneity. Thus even the finest and most perceptive of the realistic novels—K. M. Paterson's *Bridge to Terabithia* and Jill Paton Walsh's *Fireweed*—have a bittersweet tone, as their characters move from childhood to adolescence or adolescence to adulthood. Indeed most of them are novelistic forms of Gerard Manley Hopkins' elegiac poem "Spring and Fall," which begins:

> Margaret are you grieving
> Over Goldengrove unleaving?

and ends

> It is the blight man was born for,
> It is Margaret you mourn for.

Both *Goldengrove* and *Unleaving* are, appropriately enough, titles of two of Walsh's books.

Genres other than the problem novel and realistic fiction also contribute their share to the general heaviness of current children's literature. Writers of historical fiction, for example, have eschewed adventure in favor of the representation of the past as it might actually have felt to a youngster living in that era. The emphasis is on the reality of history rather than its romance and the adjective that usually applies to this reality is "grim." The historicity of their representation is unquestionably accurate and it is certainly a considerable relief to have historical novels centered on something other than the traditional subject matter of wars of conquests and voyages of discovery. So one may welcome the variety and freshness shown in the current historical novelists' choices of theme—religious and economic crises as seen in the works of Hester Burton, slavery in Paula Fox's *The Slave Dancer*, the Suffragette movement in Marjorie Darke's *A Question of Courage*, the clash of cultures so often depicted by Rosemary Sutcliff. And yet, distinctive and original as is the writing of each of these excellent historical novelists, there is among them a commonality of mood and approach. Their books portray not heroes or heroines, but small people caught in events almost beyond their understanding and certainly beyond their control. The protagonists do not win brave victories, and their triumphs, if achieved at all, are only to have *learned* how to come to terms with themselves and their times. In short, the setting and incidents are historical but the psychology is very much contemporary.

And so it continues with astonishing consistency—whatever genre of modern children's writing one examines, the dominant tonal colouring is dark. Here is science fiction, for example, still fulfilling its traditional role of making us more perceptive about our present world by visualizing the possibility of a very different order of things. But where the older science fiction offered us utopias, the present-day writers more often present us with portents of disaster. Their imaginative powers are often great, great enough to make their new worlds plausible—which very plausibility, of course, only makes their creations all the more terrifying.

Let me repeat this last sentence, because, curiously enough, it applies just as well to contemporary picture books as it does to science fiction. Yes, I mean it—picture books! Indeed, it is in the modern picture book that one can see all the threads of modern children's literature pulled together—a true microcosm. Picture books have perforce a kind of directness and frankness that exceeds that of any other kind of children's book. There is no text to hide behind, none of the vaguenesses that words are so good at. What is meant is shown, not implied, and shown in the absolutely basic terms very young children can recognize. Thus I consider it highly significant that the "artistic" (i.e., noncommercial) picture books of our day have almost completely divested themselves of anthropomorphized animals and machines and the sentimentality these represented. There is no counterpart to *Curious George*, to *Petunia, Little Toot*, and *Hercules the Fire Engine*. Such an approach seems to be deemed too coy and childish by the often bold and experimental creators of the modern picture book. We have in their place an emphasis on the young child's day-to-day living, represented by John Burningham's "Little Books" and many more that involve the young child's pain and distress. In Alex Deveaux's *Na-Ni*, a small child passes the day wishing for her mother's welfare cheque; the small boy in Paul Zindel's *I Love My Mother* goes on so much about it that you know he really desperately misses his father. Particularly in the multiplicity of books about the single family, a genuine note of sadness lingers. And where the contemporary picture book does not play on the emotions of the young reader, it seems designed to titillate the sensibilities of adults. In the many fantasy picture books, especially, there can be seen a new artistic sophistication and thematic complexity which, whatever its avowed audience, can probably be fully appreciated only by adults. It is very likely this aspect, above all, that has made the picture book almost a cult today.

I come now to the last of the major genres—fantasy. Perhaps as a reaction to all the grubby realism in modern children's literature, the newer fantasy has taken on an awesome, almost religious tone. It is not, praise be, solemn, but it most certainly is highly serious. Gone is the light magic of a Mary Poppins sliding *up* the banister or five children with a psammead that can grant wishes. Still, fantasy retains its most basic traditional quality and even extends it. I refer to fantasy's link with the mythic past and the way it sets itself to deal with the very greatest issues of existence—life, death, time, space, good and evil. Fantasists regard most realists as naively aping life rather than actually portraying its essence. Narrow realists work in small, portraying obvious problems, offering guide solutions; the major fantasists try to see life in broad rather than as "cabin'd cribb'd and confined." The cry of the fantasist is "there is another kind of real," one that is truer to the human spirit, and they set out on a pilgrim's progress to find it. Perhaps the greatest achievement of such fine fantasists as Susan Cooper, Alan Garner, William Mayne, Ursula Le Guin, Joy Chant, Mollie Hunter, Penelope Lively, Penelope Farmer, Natalie Babbitt, and Robert Westall is to make us see our universe as a whole when so many realists are determined to fragment us. Penelope Farmer, in an article on myth, suggests that science is really now only catching up with myth—the great reality on which most modern fantasy is based. She notes that modern physicists are proclaiming that the universe is a paradox, that matter, energy, space, time are all one and interchangeable—as the myths, poets, and mystics have always proclaimed them to be. Modern fantasists have joined this community and are deeply involved in bringing together the essence of this knowledge, along with their own personal visions.

I have now completed my all-too-rapid review of the individual genres and it is not by chance that fantasy came at the very end. Why? Because I want to close this examination of contemporary children's literature by considering the two very largest questions: What does it all amount to? Just how good is it, anyhow? And having hitherto carped aplenty at this or that feature, I would like at least to *begin* this overall evaluation on a positive note. Looking back at the whole corpus of contemporary children's literature, looking back most immediately at the extraordinary flourishing of fantasy, I can with good conscience say: much of modern children's literature is very good indeed, perhaps better than anything that has gone before. At its best, it is courageous in theme and innovative in style. It is strong, poetic, and rich in imagery. It is unadorned, spare, and taut. As in fine modern poetry, its writers have learned to say much in little room.

In proof of the foregoing assertions, let me offer you two sample passages, one from a British book, the other from an American. The first is a few lines from the opening of Leon Garfield's *The Drummer Boy:*

As far as the eye can see, scarlet men are marching. The hillside is in bloom with them. Regiment upon regiment are mounting as if to capture the sun . . . . Now comes a breeze that flutters the advancing pennants and briskens the glinting lines. They are like a tide—a sea of scarlet waves, flecked with silver, brass, white and blue. A rich and splendid company; and none more so than the drummer boy . . . .

Perhaps he struts a little, but no one minds. The drummer boy is their golden lad and he's caught the rhythm of their hearts.

And, from the ending of Scott O'Dell's *Sing Down the Moon:*

I took my son from his carrying board and held him up so that he could see the lamb. He wanted to touch it, but with both hands he was grasping a toy which his father had given him, a willow spear tipped with stone. Tall Boy had made up a song about the Long Knives and how the spear would kill many of them. Every night he sang this song to his son.

I took the spear and dropped it in the grass and stepped upon it, hearing it snap beneath my foot . . . .

Rain had begun to fall. It made a hissing sound in the tall grass as we started toward the cave high up in the western cliff. Tall Boy had finished the steps and handholds and now stood under the cave's stone lip, waving at us.

I waved back at him and hurried across the meadow. I raised my face to the falling rain. It was Navaho rain.

Were you people moved by these samples from very good contemporary children's literature? I expect so, I hope so. Yet I am also afraid so. Because, you see, I keep thinking that there is something wrong when books written for children speak so easily, so directly to adults. The sad fact is that contemporary children's literature, whether for its virtues or its faults, seems to be moving perilously close in tone, in theme and language to the adult world.

I see three consequences as flowing from the adult character of modern children's books. The first result is bearable enough: the unprecedented resurgence of the commercial series such as the Hardy Boys and Nancy Drew. This renewed popularity came before the TV series and does not, I believe, really derive from them. My guess is that children who seek escape and entertainment cannot find much of it in the serious children's books of today and go elsewhere for it. Well, no matter—something of this sort of cleavage between quality reading and mere pastime has always occurred and no doubt always will. We just have a sharper distinction nowadays.

The second consequence is more substantial. There is a remarkable lack of current books for what I call the "middle-aged" child, that is, from about nine to eleven. The picture books are wholly selected *by* adults and, as I have said, they look like they were produced *for* them. The older readers have their fantasy, historical fiction, and problem novels, all calculated to appeal to the adult within the adolescent. But my "middle-aged" child, all child still, who writes for him and her?

Which brings me to my third consequence and almost to my peroration. In Matthew we are asked, "What profiteth a man if he shall gain the whole world and lose his own soul?" I am very much afraid that in contemporary children's literature, when it gained the whole world of adult freedom and power and vast expansion of subject matter, it lost some of its soul—its identity as a separate and distinctive branch of writing. In our children's literature and indeed in contemporary society itself, we have taken down the walls that surrounded children. In the process of this extending of horizons, we have also run the risk of removing the circumstances that sheltered and nourished and developed those special characteristics of *children's* literature: warmth, wonder, gaiety, sentiment, simplicity—in a word, the *childlike*.

The walls will probably not come back and perhaps they shouldn't. But writers will continue to cultivate their gardens. I hope that in so doing, they will share with me the view that childhood *does* have its own identity and deserves to retain it.